"In this timely book, Roxana Cavalcanti explores the impact of public security policies on two different poor neighborhoods of Recife in the northeastern state of Pernambuco in Brazil. Based on painstaking research in a city the author knows well, the book captures the voices of residents of these communities, and especially those of young people, and analyzes the limitations of mainstream managerial approaches to crime and violence. The book's arguments in favor of more democratic and transparent approaches to public security are nuanced, well-reasoned, and a refreshing alternative to contemporary calls for more violent policing in Brazil. This book deserves a broad readership".

Anthony Pereira, Director, Brazil Institute, King's College London

"Global police studies has been enriched by this careful study of Brazilian policing which provides a worrying indicator of the trend towards transnational insecurity. This book sheds much needed light onto the politics of policing in the Global South".

James Sheptycki, McLaughlin College, York University, Toronto, Canada

"Cavalcanti's book is a splendid addition to a growing literature drawing attention to policing's often 'darker' *southern* aspects, where the legacies of post-colonialism or military dictatorship still cast their shadows. As the book compellingly demonstrates, in such contexts, policing often faces far greater threats and challenges, while police reform is itself so much harder to secure".

Peter Squires, Emeritus Professor of Criminology and Public Policy, University of Brighton

"A first class empirical study of policing and securitisation policies in Brazil. Cavalcanti establishes the themes of 'southern' criminology and social science in the distinct trajectories of the global south from colonialism and military dictatorship to neoliberal security, by contrast to the 'northern' experience of neoliberalism as the weakening of the welfare state. She shows how the southern experience, reflected in Brazil, makes for an altogether harsher, more militarised and violent neoliberalism. High levels of violence and social polarisation combine with traditions of militarised policing to render popular northern crime control models such as situational crime prevention prone to exacerbate rather than ameliorate the marginalisation of poor communities. This book should also be read as a caution against complacent assumptions regarding possible futures for the global north".

John Lea, Visiting Professor of Criminology, Goldsmiths, University of London

"This book brilliantly presents an analysis of the rise of violence in Brazil in the last decades and empirically evaluates the changing discourses and practices in crime control policies in marginalized areas of large urban cities. A must read for criminologists worldwide interested in both the rise of crime and criminalization in the Southern Hemisphere".

Mauricio Dieter, Professor of Criminology and Criminal Law, University of São Paulo

A Southern Criminology of Violence, Youth and Policing

A Southern Criminology of Violence, Youth and Policing examines public experiences of insecurity and the social impacts of security programmes that aim to address violence in Brazil. This book contributes to the emerging field of southern criminology by engaging with the perils faced by people living in "favelas" in Brazil and critically investigating the discourse of state actors. It combines original ethnographic data with critical analysis to expand understandings of violence and control in urban and post-colonial contexts.

This study challenges dominant practices and notions of security and control. Its objective is to decolonise knowledge and shed light on issues relating to policing, coercion and the great socioeconomic, historical and spatial inequalities that shape the lives of millions of people in the Global South. The findings of this book expose the exacerbation of social problems by the expansion of the penal and crime industry, unsettling the applicability and universalism of mainstream managerial criminology.

The evidence reveals that new modes of securitisation have not addressed long-standing issues of sexism, racism, classism and brutalisation in the police. Moreover, through the increasing use of methods of control and incarceration, security programmes have failed to prevent diverse forms of violence and challenge the expansion of organised crime. Instead they have exacerbated the inequalities that affect the most marginalised populations.

Written in a clear and direct style, this book will appeal to students and scholars in criminology, sociology, cultural studies, social theory and those interested in learning about the social injustices that exist in the Global South.

Roxana Pessoa Cavalcanti is a lecturer in criminology at the University of Brighton. She conducts critical research about violence, policing and insecurity. Her previous work has focused on theorising social inequalities relating to class, gender and ethnicity in the context of Brazil, the politics of control, critical theory, justice and human rights.

Routledge Studies in Crime and Justice in Asia and the Global South

Edited by Wing Hong Chui, City University of Hong Kong
Russell Hogg, Queensland University of Technology
John Scott, Queensland University of Technology

Crime and justice studies, as with much social science, has concentrated mainly on problems in the metropolitan centres of the Global North, while Asia and the Global South have remained largely invisible in criminological thinking. This research series aims to redress this imbalance by showcasing exciting new ways of thinking and doing crime and justice research from the global periphery.

Bringing together scholarly work from a range of disciplines, from criminology, law and sociology to psychology, cultural geography and comparative social sciences, this series offers grounded empirical research and fresh theoretical approaches and covers a range of pressing topics, including international corruption, drug use, environmental issues, sex work, organized crime, innovative models of justice, and punishment and penology.

Criminal Legalities in the Global South
Cultural Dynamics, Political Tensions, and Institutional Practices
Edited by Pablo Ciocchini and George Baylon Radics

Organized Crime and Corruption Across Borders
Exploring the Belt and Road Initiative
Edited by T. Wing Lo, Dina Siegel, and Sharon I. Kwok

Mapping Security in the Pacific
A Focus on Context, Gender and Organisational Culture
Sara N. Amin and Danielle Watson and Christian Girard

A Southern Criminology of Violence, Youth and Policing
Governing Insecurity in Urban Brazil
Roxana Pessoa Cavalcanti

For more information about this series, please visit: www.routledge.com/criminology/series/RSCJAGS

A Southern Criminology of Violence, Youth and Policing

Governing Insecurity in Urban Brazil

Roxana Pessoa Cavalcanti

Routledge
Taylor & Francis Group
LONDON AND NEW YORK

First published 2020
by Routledge
2 Park Square, Milton Park, Abingdon, Oxon OX14 4RN

and by Routledge
52 Vanderbilt Avenue, New York, NY 10017

Routledge is an imprint of the Taylor & Francis Group, an informa business

British Library Cataloguing-in-Publication Data
A catalogue record for this book is available from the British Library

Library of Congress Cataloging-in-Publication Data
Names: Cavalcanti, Roxana Pessoa, author.
Title: A southern criminology of violence, youth and policing : governing insecurity in urban Brazil / Roxana Pessoa Cavalcanti.
Description: Milton Park, Abingdon, Oxon ; New York, NY : Routledge, 2020. |
Series: Routledge studies in crime and justice in Asia and the global south |
Includes bibliographical references and index. |
Identifiers: LCCN 2019054103 | ISBN 9781138584709 (hardback) | ISBN 9780429505805 (ebook)
Subjects: LCSH: Policing–Brazil. | Urban violence–Brazil. | Urban youth–Brazil.
Classification: LCC HV8182 .C38 2020 | DDC 363.20981–dc23
LC record available at https://lccn.loc.gov/2019054103

ISBN: 978-1-138-58470-9 (hbk)
ISBN: 978-1-032-26458-5 (pbk)
ISBN: 978-0-429-50580-5 (ebk)

Typeset in Bembo
by Integra Software Services Pvt. Ltd.

Contents

Figures and Tables

Figures

Table

Acknowledgements

My motivation to write this book emerged from the experience of living in Brazil for over 18 years, a place where I have family ties and conduct research on continuing field trips. I am grateful to all the friends and family members in Brazil who supported me during my fieldwork trips and with whom I have discussed the ideas here.

I have gained much from talking to my research participants and am indebted to my two research collaborators from Recife: Luther and Lourdes. Considerable thanks are also due to Tom Sutton and Jess Phillips at Routledge for their editorial support, and to the anonymous referees for their suggestions, which helped refine the final product. Anthony Pereira and Jeff Garmany have also read this work closely, providing much encouragement. Their comments greatly improved the academic rigour of this work. A number of colleagues and friends have made this work better than it would otherwise have been by providing comments and suggestions, debating or reading sections of it: Eddie Falvey, David McLaughling, Katrin Weller, Mike Wolff, Murillo Marschner, Viviane Cubas, Grace Souza, Christopher Barton, Rob Coates and Kim Beecheno all contributed in their own ways. I learned a great deal from talking about this work to Alba Zaluar, Flavio Sapori, Renato Alves, Bruno Paes Manso, Gabriel Feltran, Jose Vincente Tavares dos Santos, José Luiz Ratton, Fiona Macaulay, Graham Denyer-Willis, Alvaro Comin, Desmond Arias, Peter Squires, Carlie Goldsmith, John Lea, Amanda Holt, Penny Green, Rosalind Gill, Lynda Measor and Humeira Iqtidar. I take full responsibility for this text and any inaccuracies it might contain.

I am enormously grateful to my partner and children for accompanying me during my fieldwork trips in Brazil and during my fellowship at the Library of Congress in the US, and for providing the emotional support I needed to persevere with this research. My family members have been dedicated suppliers of love and welcome distractions, helping me stay grounded and continue hoping for a world with more social justice. I am also grateful for the research support and collegiality I encountered at the University of Brighton, special thanks to Deanna Dadusc, Raphael

Schlembach and Robin Dunford. Last but not least, I am thankful to the Economic and Social Research Council (ESRC), and the Arts and Humanities Research Council (AHRC) for funding my research. I hope this book is a step towards developing criminological theory and texts that are no longer blind to the context and knowledge emerging from the Global South.

Prologue

In July 1997, the police went on strike in Recife, the capital city of Pernambuco in the northeast of Brazil. Although illegal, police strikes are not uncommon in Brazil. Armed men circulated the city, chiefly in low-income neighbourhoods, making no effort to conceal their weapons. A series of armed robberies and executions occurred, resulting in no investigations, with no identified suspects. One of such cases occurred in a low-income neighbourhood located in the edges of the city where residents were routinely victimised. Adauto – a short hard-working elderly indigenous man, father of ten, who owned a local bakery – had decided to take a rifle with him to work during the police strikes. He had been robbed of his earnings multiple times, so despite his relatives warning him against the risks he was talking, he was determined to "protect" his family and his employees' wages by trying to scare armed robbers away with his rifle. This tactic had apparently worked a couple of times in the past. It was the end of the month and his employees would be getting paid in cash that evening, so when two armed men pointed guns at him requesting he hand over the cash, Adauto did not hesitate to pick up his rifle. He was shot at point-blank range in the forehead. His wife, who was in the same room at the time, watched the incident in shock. The neighbours helped them get to hospital but the shot had been fatal.

Five years later, in a middle-class neighbourhood in Recife, Adauto's grandson was leaving school with his best friend Joaquim when an armed teenager approached them demanding their phones, wallets and watches. Adauto's grandson handed everything he had as calmly as he could. But Joaquim decided to run and was shot on the back. The incident happened in the afternoon, in a busy avenue, so Adauto's grandson tried to stop a car to help them get to hospital. Eventually, a man stopped his car, asked his family to get out and took Joaquim and Adauto's grandson to hospital. Adauto's grandson held his bleeding best friend on route to hospital, where he arrived dead. Perhaps neither of these cases would be so remarkable for me, personally, had I not been Adauto's granddaughter, and had I not been the sister of the 15-year-old boy who took Joaquim to hospital. These memories in addition to the knowledge of bereavement and life changes my family, grandmother and my brother endured, provide motivation for understanding violence in Brazil and thinking about justice.

This book, however, is not about my family. Yet, my positionality and lived experiences are important for understanding my vested interest in Brazil, and the impetus for conducting the research for this book. Here, I adopt the feminist conceptualisation of the personal as political by situating circumstances that are often portrayed as individual and private in the context of structural and public issues. This book is about insecurity in Brazil today and about what happens to marginalised and subaltern people when a failing colonial criminal justice system is used to attempt to control violence.

Chapter 1

Over, under and through the walls

On 27 January 2016, I obtained permission to attend yet another security meeting at the Secretariat for Planning and Management of the State of Pernambuco (aka SEPLAG – *Secretaria de Planejamento e Gestão*) in the northeast of Brazil. Initially, through personal and academic networks, and later though snowballing methods, I gained access to some of the meetings of the local security apparatus. My status as a Brazilian student living abroad and conducting research at a London university seemed to indicate that I posed little threat in terms of local politics. Academic networks, my own background – as local (*nordestina)* turned British – and my understanding of local cultural norms allowed me to access those meetings. Moreover, the gatekeepers associated with me were trusted and well liked in SEPLAG, introducing me as someone who wanted to understand the "success" of a local homicide reduction programme entitled *Pact for Life* (*Pacto pela vida* in Portuguese, or PPV), all of which facilitated my entry into the security apparatus as a researcher.

At PPV meetings I could observe first-hand the complexity of counting the dead. A *delegado* (chief of civil police) approached the head of statistics sitting next to me to informally request the change of classification for a case. Bones had been found in his jurisdiction and classified as a homicide, affecting his targets. The *delegado* argued that often these deaths occurred in neighbouring states, but these dead bodies were buried in his jurisdiction. He also contended that the death may have been manslaughter (*homicidio culposo*) instead of homicide (*homicidio doloso*), in which case, the *delegado* reminded the statistician that the death would not affect his targets. This concern with targets, classifications and counting are part of a new securitising agenda in Brazil, the product of new forms of governance – new approaches to urban social control. The dialogues among government officials, planners, statisticians and high-ranking members of the military and civil police during closed public security government meetings reveal the ways in which crime data is used and misused for personal and political ends. There is no question that statistics released by the public security apparatus are "adjusted, manipulated, subcategorized, or poorly represented to convey rosier images of public security" (Denyer Willis 2015, 51).

Only 4 days prior to the security apparatus meeting in question, a large-scale prison escape had shaken any remaining public confidence in the security system. In Recife, the capital city of the state of Pernambuco, prisoners used explosives to blast a hole in one of the walls of the *Complexo do Curado* prison, leading to the escape of forty prisoners on 23 January 2016. One of the largest prisons in Latin America, the *Complexo do Curado* housed at the time approximately 7,000 inmates (four times its capacity). A few days before the explosion, on 20 January 2016, over 50 prisoners had escaped from another prison in the state of Pernambuco. The police recaptured many escapees and killed others, raising concerns about the routine disrespect for human rights in overcrowded prisons and in Brazilian society more widely. The prison breaks increased public fear, feelings of insecurity and doubts about the sustainability of the existing public security system. During the government meeting on 27 January 2016, one of the *delegados* present expressed his concern with the level of prisoner organisation and the failures of the system:

> We have tightened security inside and outside the prison. We discovered sixteen tunnels connecting the prison to the outside and we closed those. The problem used to be people throwing parcels over the walls, so as we increased surveillance around the walls, prisoners started to build tunnels. Now, as we found the tunnels, they started to blow the walls up.

As a solution, he argued that the way to solve the situation would be to build more prisons, as long as they were smaller and more manageable: "we need smaller prisons but it is going to take years to build enough prisons for all the inmates we already have". From a critical criminological perspective, this seemed to be a catch 22 situation: whatever the police tried to do, the police-criminals pursuit would be unending. Incarcerating suspects and increasing surveillance did not seem sustainable or efficient methods for creating or maintaining public safety, especially when deeper structural, institutional and societal problems are inadequately addressed.

Anecdotes about homicide data, prison escapes and the manipulation of quantitative data illustrate and epitomise some of the limits of managerialism in crime control, the flaws of attempts at "modernizing" policing and incarceration in Brazil's context. They are bare illustrations of the salient symptoms of multiple failures to generate and implement meaningful and transformative public policies. Such accounts shed light on powerful state actors' perceptions of threats associated with, and proposed solutions for, high-crime areas, prison escapes and popular insecurity. Contradictions inherent in such perceptions, dialogues and discourses can be compared with perceptions of low-income communities perceived as peripheral, informal and dangerous. Such communities are often described as favelas; they are feared spaces, seen as no-go areas that need to be avoided by middle and upper class citizens.

In what follows, first-hand ethnographic data from these communities is explored, revealing the diverse ways of perceiving such places, as humane, populated by people living in hardship and yet culturally rich, financially impoverished but deeply interconnected in multiple ways, through politics and work, to the rest of the city. This chapter provides a brief overview of the book's content and situates the work in the developing field of southern criminology (Carrington, Hogg, and Sozzo 2016).

Favelas: life on the edge?

At nearly 2:00 p.m., in July 2013 I got off a bus, which could barely squeeze through the narrow roads and alleys leading to the community. As I walked into the unpaved roads of the community I noticed cheerful people sitting outdoors on plastic chairs chatting. There were occasional stretches of pavement to walk on, open sewage running down the street, uncollected piles of rubbish scattered around and obnoxious smells hung in the air. There was no breeze and heat reflected off brick and concrete walls. Some of the decaying small brick houses that formed the community and the apartment blocks had been built in the 1970s near the prison, but the community had a longer history, dating back to the early part of the 20th century. Despite the appearance of deterioration, I learned that rents were surprisingly high so the research funding I had naively set aside for accommodation would hardly cover the monthly cost (R$350, approximately £116 at the time) of renting a single room in a home in the community of Tourinho.[1]

Outward appearances told me little about the people who live in these poor communities. Many of the people encountered during the fieldwork were active members of social movements, active in local politics, innovative people capable of reinventing themselves and being creative and organised. In a meeting with Lourdes in the small building from which she ran a non-governmental organisation (NGO) in Tourinho providing leisure and cultural activities, sports and arts training to young people in the peripheries of the city, she explained there is a high demand for housing in the area as many of the prisoners' family members want to live near the prison, as well as traffickers who kept business ties with inmates, pushing the price of rents upwards. Lourdes was quick to deflect attention away from negative connotations about the community and was keen to present positive and innovative images of its people. She explained her work in the community:

> The group [NGO] started in the porch of my house. Some of the guys used to tag walls with spray paint during the night … we didn't have the financial means but we decided to get together and put what little we had together to form a group that would do something for the community … using drawing, tagging, graffiti. We have been together 10 years […] and have won prizes due to our community work taking kids off the street.

Lourdes became one of the co-researchers on this project and enabled access to a larger sample of residents and young participants; she also became a key informant. Deeply aware of the social inequalities in the city, she was well read and talked freely about feminism, the afro-movement, hip-hop and art. She epitomises the context of hardship and cultural richness, experiencing financial impoverishment but maintaining deep political and economic interconnections to the rest of the city.

Outsiders view favelas as undesirable spaces. They are working-class barrios where workers such as labourers, service-sector employees and domestic workers live. They are spaces replete with community associations, organisers and leaders, places in which family, hard work and social mobility are highly valued. Still, they have been constructed in the global gaze as violent spaces, known for high levels of violence and cinematographic representations ingrained in public consciousness through films such as *City of God*. Indeed, *favelas* are often socially and spatially marginalised in the city, in the sense that they are segregated spaces, sometimes being separated from wealthier communities by walls, distance, disparities in access to services or other socio-economic disadvantages.

Brazilian favelas and informal communities can be traced back to colonial times, sometimes formed by escapee slaves or, after the abolition of slavery at the end of the 19th century, when a large population of former slaves, peasants and indigenous people were left destitute and with no land rights (Zaluar and Alvito 2006; Garmany and Pereira 2019). Although often perceived as "problems", favelas have endured because they serve key roles to the city and capitalist development. Brazilian political scientist Lúcio Kowarick developed the concept of *espoliação urbana* or urban spoliation (Kowarick 1979) to explain how urban informality is not an abnormal characteristic of capitalist development. Instead, he argued, urban informality is produced by capitalist development because it enables a workforce to live and socially reproduce with little cost for private capital or the State. Favelas provide not only a reserve army of labour, but also housing for subaltern and marginalised working people, so that income and wealth remain unequally distributed and concentrated, and urban growth can continue despite the "spoliation" or dilapidation of the urban landscape dotted by informal communities. Kowarick's work and concept expands our understanding of urban growth and development around the world.

Just as in other parts of the world, informal settlements built on state, private or public land have become established with the explicit or implicit connivance of government and politicians trying to expand their support base through often clientelist offers of financial support or infrastructure (Arias 2006; Lasslett 2018). This has not enabled residents to secure housing titles or avoided threats of forced evictions. Yet, residents are entangled in the city, and in politics. They work outside their communities, often in minimum wage jobs, which do not permit access to private housing. Residents vote, protest, make music, dance and claim the right to the city by self-building their own communities.

In contrast to other large Brazilian metropolises, where poor communities are concentrated in peripheral areas, in Recife a large number of slums are scattered across the city. Its *periferias* do nonetheless tend to have higher concentrations of poverty. The region was a hub for the sugar cane industry in the 16th century, but although sugar cane remains the most important crop in the area, its economic importance has declined. There are large industrial plants in the city's suburbs, but most of the economy relies on the service sector. It is estimated that 60% of the population works in the private service sector (Koster 2009).

The first case study community, Tourinho (Figure 1.1), comprises two adjacent neighbourhoods located in the peripheries of the metropolitan region of Recife, with over 40,000 inhabitants. In the 19th century, the territory belonged to an *engenho* (sugar mill) and early in the 20th century the population began to settle in the area. Today the community is constituted of a combination of small gated terraced houses, some two- and three-storey buildings, some irregular settlements and some small local businesses. Most residents have metal bars around their houses' windows and doors, gates and sometimes guard dogs. The average monthly household income in 2013 was R$1,296 (the equivalent of £298) to supply for at least three people – a far cry from rental prices or the minimum required for a dignified living.

Figure 1.1 Tourinho, Pernambuco 2013.

According to State definitions most households in the communities are "abnormal agglomerates", or in other words, "abnormal housing", slums or irregular settlements. Half of the population is ethnically mixed (54%), 35% white, 9% black and a minority self-classify as indigenous (Prefeitura do Recife 2013). The second case study community, Vitoria (Figure 1.2), is similarly diverse in terms of ethnicity, situated in the north part of Recife, adjacent to a middle-class neighbourhood and constituted of several smaller low-income communities. The average monthly household income in 2013 was R$ 1,166 (the equivalent of £268). Socioeconomic conditions in both studied communities were similar. The Human Development Index (HDI) in Tourinho was 0.751 and in Vitoria, it was 0.731 in 2000, respectively equivalent to the HDI of Kazakhstan and Ecuador (Bitoun 2005). As a point of comparison between countries, the HDI includes data about income, life expectancy and education. In the upper-class neighbourhood of Boa Viagem in Recife, the HDI was 0.964 in 2000; this was equivalent to Norway's HDI. Such demographic data illustrate the extent of social inequalities within the city.

Figure 1.2 Main Street in Vitoria, 2013.

Violence

A significant literature has begun to emerge identifying the issue of youth violence in poor urban communities around the world (Hagedorn 2007; Hagedorn, Davis, and Ebrary 2008; Feltran 2011). Sometimes this violence is associated with "gangs" (Jones and Rodgers 2009; Fernandes 2013), or with other forms of organised crime – especially drug dealing and trafficking (Bourgois 2003; Arias 2006; Denyer Willis 2015). Sometimes it takes the form of political or community resistance (Scheper-Hughes 2004; Davies 2006). Sometimes violence is perpetrated by young people, but often it is perpetrated against them, by police and security agencies (Chevigny 1995; Huggins 1997; Arias 2006; Zaluar 2010).

Poor urban communities in Brazil have been gravely affected by rising cases of murder and the use of firearms in homicides since the 1980s. The country has the highest homicide rate among the 12 most populous countries in the world (Waiselfisz 2013). According to official data from Brazil's Ministry of Health (Sistema de Informações sobre Mortalidade, or SIM/MS), 65,602 homicides were recorded in 2017, the equivalent of 31.6 deaths per 100,000 inhabitants – the highest level of mortality ever recorded in the country (Cerqueira et al. 2019). According to this data, violence against young people, women, members of the LGBTI community and poor black people has been on the rise.

There is a markedly unequal distribution of deaths in the country, with the north and northeast regions seeing much higher increases. In the northeast, the homicide rate per 100,000 inhabitants went from 19.4 in 2000 to 33.5 in 2009 (Souza, Ribeiro, and Valadares 2012, 52). The southeast region of the country (e.g. Rio de Janeiro, São Paulo) was the only region to register a drop in the homicide rates in the 2000s (ibid). While there is a geographical aspect to this phenomenon, there are also gender, "racial" and class dimensions to it. The likelihood of death for a young, black male aged 15–25 in 2008 was 127.6% greater than for a white male in the same age bracket (Waiselfisz 2011, 60). In the 30 years between 1980 and 2010, the rate of youth homicide (15–29 years old) with a firearm in Brazil quintupled, reaching 42.5/100,000 in 2010 as compared with 9.1/100,000 in 1980 (Waiselfisz 2013). By 2017, most of the deaths of young men (aged 15–19 years old) continued to be attributed to homicide (59.1%) (Cerqueira et al. 2019).

Pinheiro (2006, XVIII) suggests that our failure to listen to young people has led to a failure to respond to their needs. Thus examining how urban violence and insecurity affect young people's daily life in Recife's poor communities is paramount to attending to issues of social justice. How do residents of these communities employ practices and discourses to comprehend, explain and live in a context of high violence and insecurity? What roles do the State and its policies play in the fluctuation – continuation, expansion or reduction – of violence in the most socially excluded communities? Criminology has been criticised for leaving out the theorisation of the State, despite its crucial importance for understanding control over the exercise of force. As Neocleous (2000) puts it:

> The history of the police is the history of state power, and the overlapping consensus that this power is rooted in the control of the exercise of force – a consensus stretching from Hobbes to Webber – should suggest that the police as one of the institutions which has been granted the right to exercise this force, needs to be understood in the wider context of the State. As a consequence, any theory of police must involve a theory of state power; conversely, any theory of state power must necessarily consist of a theory of police.
>
> (Neocleous 2000, xi)

The State is a blurry and contested category. It can be constructed as an abstract imagined category as well as a real entity that manifests itself in multiple spheres of social life (Gupta 2006). It is not intended here to equate the State with the government. Governments shift and change in periodical intervals (at least in democracies), and govern populations in delineated territories and nation states. This difference helps delineate some of the boundaries that separate members of the government from other state actors, such as the police. The police are state actors but are not the government or the State itself. Brenner et al. (2003) deploy the metaphor of a container to define the State, with a geographical focus, as a territory or spatial entity differentiated from other States by the borders that they patrol, which divide domestic politics from international relations. While this definition emphasises the importance of spatiality to state theory, it leaves out the significance of a key function of the State, as defined by Max Weber. For Weber (1946), the State is an entity that "claims the monopoly of the legitimate use of physical force within a territory" (78).

Both frameworks have relevance with different foci, one on the territorial aspects and the other on the attempt to legitimately monopolise the use of force (whether successfully or not). But rather than discussing its contested definitions, this book focuses on how the State affects populations. In line with Neocleous' (2000) critique of criminology, this book considers the role of the State by asking how state actors, security policies and practices affect people in poor communities.

Stereotypical views of favelas and peripheries portray their residents as uncivil and violent, requiring state repression or a hard-line approach on the part of the authorities. In popular stereotypes, violence is often simplistically explained as an outcome of poverty or individual "evil" (Caldeira 2000). However, ethnographic studies have begun to reveal profound heterogeneity in the causes and political meanings of violence in these regions (Feltran 2011). This book explores the heterogeneity in the dynamics of security practices and the relations of violence within which people in poor communities and *periferias* are often involved.

Security

Studies conducted in Rio de Janeiro and São Paulo have indicated that policing and security, especially private security, are often provided in rich and upper-class parts of the city, while in low-income communities policing tends to be sporadic and reactive rather than preventive, with police responses limited to periods of crises (Soares 2000; Cubas 2002; Arias 2006). Security policies have continuously changed in different parts of Brazil, often this depends on the ethos of the state (as opposed to the federal) government in place; and results in diversified outcomes.

In the state of Rio de Janeiro, a programme known as pacifying police units (*Unidades de Polícia Pacificadora* or UPPs) emerged amid contested and transnationally circulating policing and governance practices (Machado da Silva 2010; Amar 2013; Torresan and Cunha 2013; Menezes 2014; Wolff 2014). The UPPs have marked differences to security programmes elsewhere in Brazil and their effects are contested. As an intervention they are centred on the notion of "policing by proximity", which means foot patrols, the attempt to develop positive or non-adversarial relationships between the police and the community being policed, and the permanent occupation of favelas by the police. The police as an occupying force are part of an unstable articulation of militarised forms of governance that are part and parcel of changing and contradictory repressive and emancipatory tactics within the Global South.

The state of Minas Gerais in the 2000s also saw the rise of a new security intervention, an innovative programme known as *Fica Vivo* (Stay alive). Brazilian researchers have defined *Fica Vivo* as a programme that combined methods of social crime prevention with criminal justice and policing interventions (Andrade and Peixoto 2007; Silveira et al. 2010; Beato Filho 2013), drawing on the famous American violence reduction programme "Operation Ceasefire". Unlike the security programmes in other parts of Brazil, the *Fica Vivo* intervention offered central roles to methods of social crime prevention, such as conflict resolution, youth sports activities and workshops.

The effects of these violence reduction programmes are hard to measure. Lethal violence and fear fluctuate according to place. In some communities residents feel more marginalised and criminalised by these programmes, while in others they have welcomed interventions. Sometimes the impact of security interventions relates to speculation and rumours about reduction in local income and the negative effect on local economies or to new insecurities with "changing patterns of crime and conflict" (Menezes 2014, 675). These are not homogenous or omnipresent outcomes. This book does not evaluate homicide reduction programmes across Brazil. The point made here is that there is much heterogeneity in different communities, in security policies and in their social effects, which needs to be studied and contextualised. This is a task that a number of researchers have undertaken, as illustrated above.

Various organisations and institutions, such as the State, non-governmental organisations (NGOs) and churches, have at times assumed an active role with the aim of reducing violence, occasionally working together in partnership. In some communities, drug traffickers control local organisations, such as residents associations and local NGOs, thus directly impacting political life in the area. In some cases, communities have become complicit with the drug trade through coercion; in others trafficking has become a welcome source of financial support. In others, militias formed by ex-policemen have influenced the governance of the area, sometimes with the double-edged effect of reducing local theft while increasing mortality rates (through killings of petty criminals) and practising extortion for the supply of services (e.g. charging residents for security). Thus violence, security policies and interventions have taken distinctive forms and have had diverse effects in different parts of Brazil.

Large sporting events, such as the football World Cup of 2014 and the Olympic Games in Rio de Janeiro in 2016 led many Brazilian states to take a more proactive role in the governance of security in low-income communities. Some researchers have begun to examine the effects of new security programs in Rio de Janeiro (Monteiro 2013; Torresan and Cunha 2013), in Salvador (Gledhill 2013, 2015) and even in "Southern" comparisons between Brazil and Egypt (Amar 2013). These changes and new modes of security have generated new concerns and revived some old ones, such as the provision of services to slum or informal communities (e.g. sanitation, access to health and education), which in some cases has accompanied the security agenda; the issue of land title, housing and gentrification of "securitised" communities; and the impact of increased policing on the country's already large prison population. But given that Brazil is a continental-sized country, it has different histories, cultures and socio-economic contexts within each of its regions. This study grasps some of the heterogeneity of the situation in Brazil, and the differences that exist between different communities and regions. It focuses on case studies in the northeast of the country, on which fewer Brazilian and international academics have focused.

Numerous paradoxes permeate Brazilian society. The return to democracy in 1985 progressed in parallel with debt crises, the restructuring of production and the winding down of industrialisation in cities such as Rio de Janeiro and São Paulo (Perlman 2010; Feltran 2011). In the 2000s Brazil experienced a reduction of labour informality (Comin, Barbosa, and Carvalhaes 2012) and poverty (Neri 2009; Barros et al. 2010). These improvements fuelled by new state interventions and policies – including increased spending on education, health, conditional cash transfers and increases in the minimum wage – were particularly noticeable in the north and northeast of the country. Paradoxically, there was a reduction in the number of victims of homicide in the southeast of Brazil and an increase in homicides in the northeastern region of the country (Pita 2012). This suggests a need to look beyond the hypothesis of "State abandonment" (Wacquant 1996, 2003, 2008) often applied to the poorest communities in the region. The State is often part of the problem (Arias 2006; Gledhill 2013, 2015). Instead of examining "state abandonment" per se, it is preferable to look at the State's sporadic interventions and analyse how they take place, their dynamics, the barriers that are faced, and ultimately, how they are interpreted and experienced by those at the receiving end.

One of the state government's mottoes, where Recife is located, was *Pernambuco está em obras* (my translation: "Pernambuco is under construction"), meaning there was much economic growth and development taking place in the 2000s. What are the impacts of these recent political and socio-economic changes? What can be learned about violence and its context, causes, lessons, alternatives, facilitators, consequences and cycles? Few international and ethnographic studies have focused on Recife, one of Brazil's largest cities. This study examines what Brazil can contribute to our thinking about violence and security beyond the Global North.

While homicide rates were going up in most of Brazil, especially in the states of the north and northeast, the state of Pernambuco experienced declining homicide rates from the second half of the 2000s (Ratton, Galvão, and Fernandez 2014; Waiselfisz 2014). In the media and even in some academic circles, this decline was attributed to the programme of public security and police reform called the "Pact for Life" (*Pacto pela Vida* – PPV), created and implemented during the administration of state governor Eduardo Campos (2007–2014), who was re-elected and subsequently became a candidate in the presidential elections in 2014. A large part of Campos' campaign was based on his apparent success in "saving lives" or reducing homicide rates through the PPV.

By and large, the PPV was based on influential mainstream ideologies and theories of crime control developed in the Anglo-Saxon world, such as situational crime prevention, deterrence through incarceration and police performance technologies such as the controversial New York COMPSTAT. The details of the PPV as a programme of securitisation, and the narratives of professionals involved with or exposed to its implementation, are examined in more detail in Chapters 2 and 5, alongside a theoretical critique of the theories on which it is based. For now, it suffices to say that this book poses challenges to the ways in which dominant or mainstream criminological theories developed in the Global North have been emulated and adapted by crime-fighting institutions in the Global South.[2] I explore the impacts or effects of the adaptation of security agendas in the lives of people who are most exposed to their methods, namely, people living in low-income communities and the marginalised spaces of large cities in the Global South. In doing so, this work explores the hidden perspectives of the northeastern marginalised, who have been largely neglected by the Brazilian literature on public security and by the international criminological literature.

The Southern Criminology approach

The work of Connell (2007) and de Sousa Santos (2014) have provoked much debate in the social sciences (Rosa 2014; Moosavi 2018) and inspired the emergence of a new paradigm, project, approach, critique, academic movement and enterprise known as Southern Criminology (Carrington, Hogg, and Sozzo 2016; Carrington et al. 2019). Criminology and the social sciences more generally are known to be anglo-centric, eurocentric and westerncentric enterprises, which have produced dominant forms of scientific knowledge based on the experiences of advanced capitalist societies in the Global North, especially Western Europe and the US. The Southern Criminology paradigm seeks to address these biases and inequalities in knowledge production.

Orthodox northern social sciences address social problems relating to the changes that these societies have undergone while developing a yardstick normative narrative for the development of other societies (Carrington et al. 2019, 3). Under this universal narrative, global economic inequalities, exploitation and the history of empire are forgotten. The subordinate position and experiences of the colonised world are not incorporated as relevant for the theories and concepts developed. As Connell (2007) suggests, social sciences have presented themselves as timeless, universal and placeless. At times, data could be extracted, just as raw materials, from the periphery, othered societies, countries outside the Global North for the application of northern theories but ideas, concepts and theoretical insights from the South would not gain traction in the social sciences. As Moosavi (2019, 258) puts it, "there is widespread belief in the social sciences, founded on an orientalist attitude, that academic scholarship beyond the West is low-quality, irrelevant or even non-existent". Southern Criminology problematises and challenges these imbalances in criminological knowledge production with the intention of decolonising criminology. Decolonising criminology is part of a wider movement to decolonise knowledge, which calls for better-quality representation of non-European intellectuals and historical consciousness of the contexts in which knowledge has been produced. With this in mind, this book deliberately engages with the work of southern theorists, whose work is often marginalised due to dominant orientalist[3] attitudes, imbalances in the structures of academic institutions, including inequities in the publishing trade, and on occasion because of language barriers.

As a discipline, criminology is still dominated by the insights of white men from the US and UK, whose work is most cited and taught because of social and historic factors that privilege their accounts (Bosworth and Hoyle 2011; Moosavi 2019). Take as an example the incredible global influence and traction gained by the conservative, atheoretical and non-empirically grounded Broken Windows Theory. Multiple criminological studies have been produced in the Global South but their insights are often ignored. This book introduces some of the best interdisciplinary academic work on security, violence and crime in

Brazil, some of which is only available in Portuguese. As such, it seeks to break down the barriers of language, culture and discipline that can place southern theorists in academic ghettos. Moreover, through an engagement with original empirical research conducted over years in Brazil, the book cultivates criminological research that is no longer blind to the realities, context and theories emerging from the Global South.

It is important to acknowledge the constructive and "friendly" critiques of Southern Criminology (Moosavi 2018; Travers 2019) and southern theories (Rosa 2014). Such insights have questioned how easy it is to actually achieve the goals of this new paradigm and whether the southern criminological venture is entirely new. In fact, postcolonial critiques of criminology have been developing since the 1980s (Agozino 2004). But the "southern" movement in criminology has only gained traction since the publication of Carrington, Hogg, and Sozzo (2016). Critics of the movement towards southern theory have questioned the extent to which hierarchies within academia in the Global South permit or reproduce the same problems that are inherent in North-South relations. For instance, despite the existence of critical studies in the sociology of crime and justice in the Global South, southern academics have often been influenced by European theories. In Brazil, academics often accept subordinate theoretical spaces by applying northern theories to the south and reproducing knowledge-production hierarchies. Latin American academics that study in Europe bring back European frameworks of analysis to the periphery while southern theorists themselves frequently disregard "internal processes of colonization of the social sciences by Euro-American narratives" (Rosa 2014, 3). Much of the work that exists in the social sciences is produced by colonial elites interested in aligning themselves with the proposals of Giddens, Bourdieu and Beck (Rosa 2014, 12), adopting grand universal theories from the North due to the colonised nature of universities. This is not to argue against southern theorising, but rather to point to some of its limitations and the challenges that it needs to address.

The contribution made here to Southern Criminology is at least threefold. First, I examine lived experiences in understudied and feared communities in the northeast of Brazil where rates of homicide are comparably higher than in countries at war. Second, I critically engage with the voices of both powerful and powerless groups in the region, drawing on the work of progressive thinkers across the world. Third, I problematise ideas that emerge in the Global North, providing a critique of dominant socio-political and criminological discourses about crime control that fail to escape the fallacies of the war on drugs. In these three ways, the book contributes to the development of Southern Criminology and to the development of critical transnational and comparative criminologies. This approach enables an investigation of the social effects of the North-South domination of knowledge production. It embraces Southern Criminology's concern with exploring how global criminological knowledge is produced and shared; as well as the voices that dominate academic and political discourses about crime, punishment and control.

In sum, this book examines public experiences of insecurity and the social impacts of security programmes that aim to address violence in Brazil. It explores how the everyday pervasiveness of violence is sanctioned by the state and connected to particular cultural, contextual and institutional aspects of Brazil. Through accounts of lived experiences and interviews with Brazilian police, state actors and people living in Brazilian favelas, this work introduces knowledge that is grounded in the context of the Global South and which challenges the dominance of mainstream criminological theories. The study shows that through the increasing use of repressive policing and hyper-incarceration as methods of crime control, security programmes have failed to inhibit diverse forms of violent and organised crime and exacerbated existing inequalities affecting the most marginalised populations. Ultimately, the book captures systemic tensions between theory, policy and practice, security and insecurity, and between the contradictory narratives of powerful and powerless groups.

Outline of chapters

As levels of violence continuously grow in Brazil, having reached epidemic levels, this book provides a timely account of the fallacies of securitisation, policy and practice. It sheds light on the context in which the emergence of far-right political leaders like President Jair Bolsonaro (2019–) was made possible. As "solutions" for violence and crime, Bolsonaro has argued for reducing restrictions on gun possession and a range of authoritarian crime fighting practices such as the legalisation of capital punishment, torture and killings of crime suspects and the further expansion of mass incarceration. This book challenges these discourses while providing an ethnographical account, which seeks to develop knowledge that contributes to our larger understanding of violence, policing and social justice in an increasingly unequal world.

Chapter 2 details the methodology of the study, as well as the case studies selected and begins to unpack the concept of security and the forms and ways in which criminological theory travels. Chapter 3 explores some of the interdisciplinary work that has emerged in and about Brazil. It outlines the context and issues of violence and policing in Brazil. Then it starts the examination of how new security logics and technologies emerged and became justified. Chapter 4 focuses on the particularities of policing in Brazil. Drawing on original data, it explores the contradictions in narratives of and the issues faced by Brazilian military and civil police, as well as the effects of new modes of security and control on their work. Chapters 5 and 6 expose the ways in which security policies emulated from mainstream criminologies of crime control from the Global North produce large-scale perverse effects in the context of the Global South.

The empirical data analysed here focus on the effects of new security interventions and the interactions between residents of low-income communities and institutions of the Brazilian public security system, especially the police and the prison. Original data were gathered through interviews, observations and focus groups with diverse groups in the under-studied northeast of Brazil. Participants included young people and community activists living in Brazilian low-income communities and informal neighbourhoods known as *favelas*. Other participants comprised of high- and low-ranking members of the military and civil police and staff at the public security secretariat. Secondary sources such as official data about levels of incarceration and homicide were also employed. Chapter 7 explores the challenges of changing policy and practice in Brazil. It explores critiques emerging from civil society activists and the problem of militarisation, or more to the point, the difficulty of de-militarising security in Brazil. Finally, the conclusion evaluates the lessons learned from the Brazilian case. I consider the role of inequalities in knowledge production and make suggestions for further research.

Notes

1 For ethical reasons I use pseudonyms for the names of the communities and people involved in the research.

2 I adopt the dichotomy Global North/Global South as a metaphor to the contested and debatable categories that depend on the context of use. While the metaphor relates to some extent to geographical areas, the countries included in each category are not necessarily located in the south or north hemisphere. For instance, with the exception of Japan, Asian countries tend to be included in the "global South" category. GDP and per capita income are not necessarily the defining and dividing specification of categories either here, since the Asian tigers (Singapore, Taiwan and South Korea) are economically rich. The metaphor focuses more on development and on a post-colonial critique of the European and North American (the Global North) dominance in knowledge production in the social sciences. Thus "global South" relates to what is subaltern, marginalised, invisible or other. As Carrington, Hogg, and Sozzo (2016, 6) put it, deploying the north/south metaphor needs not to ignore or neglect that "there are enclaves of the south within the north and unresolved North/South tensions *within* many societies".

3 Here I use the terms "orientalism" and "occidentalism", in the same way Cain (2000) defines them, that is, respectively, romanticisation of the "other" and the presumption of sameness in culture, practices and institutions.

References

Agozino, B. 2004. "Imperialism, Crime and Criminology: Towards the Decolonisation of Criminology." *Crime, Law and Social Change* 41 (4): 343–358.

Amar, P. 2013. *The Security Archipelago: Human-Security States, Sexuality Politics, and the End of Neoliberalism*. Durham, NC: Duke University Press.

Andrade, M. V., and B. T. Peixoto. 2007. *Avaliação econômica de programas de prevenção e controle da criminalidade no Brasil*. Belo Horizonte: UFMG/Cedeplar.

Arias, E. D. 2006. *Drugs & Democracy in Rio de Janeiro: Trafficking, Social Networks, & Public Security*. Chapel Hill: University of North Carolina Press.

Barros, R., M. d. Carvalho, S. Franco, and R. Mendonça. 2010. "Markets, the State, and the Dynamics of Inequality in Brazil." In *Declining Inequality in Latin America: A Decade of Progress?* edited by L. López-Calva and N. Lustig, 134–174. New York and Washington, DC: UNDP and Brookings University Press.

Beato Filho, C. C. 2013. *Estudio de caso: Programa Fica Vivo en Brasil*. CAPSI Iniciativa Centroamericana del Sector Privado. Accessed 22 June 2016. www.capsinitiative.net/wp-content/uploads/2014/07/Caso-Fica-Vivo-Version-final-Claudio-Beato-Espanol.pdf.

Bitoun, J. 2005. "O que revelam os índices de desenvolvimento humano." *Desenvolvimento Humano no Recife: Atlas Municipal* PNUD, Programa das Nações Unidas para o Desenvolvimento. Accessed 15 August 2015. http://dhnet.org.br/dados/idh/idh/bitoun_idh_que_revelam.pdf.

Bosworth, M., and C. Hoyle. 2011. "What Is Criminology? An Introduction." In *What Is Criminology?* edited by M. Bosworth and C. Hoyle, 1–12. Oxford: Oxford University Press.

Bourgois, P. I. 2003. *In Search of Respect: Selling Crack in El Barrio*. 2nd ed. Cambridge: Cambridge University Press.

Brenner, N., B. Jessop, M. Jones, and G. MacLeod. 2003. "Introduction." In *State/Space: A Reader*, edited by N. Brenner, B. Jessop, M. Jones, and G. MacLeod, ix, 355 p. Malden, MA, and Oxford: Blackwell Publishing.

Cain, M. 2000. "Orientalism, Occidentalism and the Sociology of Crime." *British Journal of Criminology* 40: 239–260.

Caldeira, T. P. d. R. 2000. *City of Walls: Crime, Segregation, and Citizenship in São Paulo*. Berkeley: University of California Press.

Carrington, K., B. Dixon, D. Fonseca, D. R. Goyes, J. Liu, and D. Zysman. 2019. "Criminologies of the Global South: Critical Reflections." *Critical Criminology*. doi:10.1007/s10612-019-09450-y.

Carrington, K., R. Hogg, and M. Sozzo. 2016. "Southern Criminology." *British Journal of Criminology* 56 (1): 1–20.

Cerqueira, D., S. Bueno, R. S. de Lima, C. Neme, H. Ferreira, P. Palmieri Alves, D. Marques et al. 2019. *Atlas da Violencia*. Brasília, Rio de Janeiro, and São Paulo. www.ipea.gov.br/portal/images/stories/PDFs/relatorio_institucional/190605_atlas_da_violencia_2019.pdf.

Chevigny, P. 1995. *Edge of the Knife: Police Violence in the Americas*. New York: New Press.

Comin, A. A., R. J. Barbosa, and F. O. Carvalhaes. 2012. *Manufacturing Jobs: Economic Cycles, Job Creation and Structural Change*. ESRC Pathfinder Programme on Collaborative Analysis of Microdata Resources, Warwick Institute for Employment Research (IER). Accessed 20 July 2013. https://www2.warwick.ac.uk/fac/soc/ier/research/glmf/heeer/manufacturing_jobs_in_brazil_-_comin_js_pdf.pdf.

Connell, R. 2007. *Southern Theory: The Global Dynamics of Knowledge in Social Science*. Cambridge: Polity.

Cubas, V. 2002. "A expansão das Empresas de Segurança Privada em São Paulo." Masters in Sociology, University of São Paulo, São Paulo.

Davies, M. 2006. *Planet of Slums: Urban Involution and the Informal Working Class*. London and New York: Verso.

Denyer Willis, G. 2015. *The Killing Consensus: Police, Organized Crime, and the Regulation of Life and Death in Urban Brazil*. Berkeley: University of California Press.

Feltran, G. d. S. 2011. *Fronteiras de Tensão: Política e Violência nas Periferias de São Paulo*. São Paulo: Unesp.

Fernandes, F. L. 2013. "Youth Gang Members in Rio de Janeiro: The Face of a 'Lost Generation' in an Age of Fear and Mistrust." *Bulletin of Latin American Research* 32 (2): 210–223. doi:10.1111/blar.12030.

Garmany, J., and A. W. Pereira. 2019. *Understanding Contemporary Brazil*. Abingdon and New York: Routledge.

Gledhill, J. 2013. "The Production of Insecurity in Brazil and Mexico." SLAS 2013 Annual Conference, University of Manchester, April 11–12.

Gledhill, J. 2015. *The New War on the Poor: The Production of Insecurity in Latin America*. London: Zed Books.

Gupta, A. 2006. "Blurred Boundaries: The Discourse of Corruption, the Culture of Politics, and the Imagined State." In *The Anthropology of the State: A Reader*, edited by A. Gupta and A. Sharma, 211–242. London: Blackwell.

Hagedorn, J. 2007. *Gangs in the Global City: Alternatives to Traditional Criminology*. Urbana: University of Illinois Press.

Hagedorn, J., M. Davis, and I. Ebrary. 2008. *A World of Gangs: Armed Young Men and Gangsta Culture*. Minneapolis: University of Minnesota Press.

Huggins, M. K. 1997. "From Bureaucratic Consolidation to Structural Devolution: Police Death Squads in Brazil." *Policing and Society* 7 (4): 207–234.

Jones, G. A., and D. Rodgers. 2009. *Youth Violence in Latin America* [Electronic Resource]. Basingstoke: Palgrave Macmillan.

Koster, M. 2009. "In Fear of Abandonment: Slum Life, Community Leaders and Politics in Recife, Brazil." PhD, Wageningen University, Netherlands.

Kowarick, L. 1979. *A espoliação urbana*. Rio de Janeiro: Paz e Terra.

Lasslett, K. 2018. *Uncovering the Crimes of Urbanisation: Researching Corruption, Violence and Urban Conflict*. 1st ed. Abingdon and New York: Routledge.

Machado da Silva, L. A. 2010. *Afinal, qual é a das UPPs?* UFRJ. www.observatoriodasmetropoles.ufrj.br.

Menezes, P. V. 2014. "Os rumores da 'pacificação': A chegada da UPP e as mudanças nos problemas públicos no Santa Marta e na Cidade de Deus." *Dilemas: Revista de Estudos de Conflito e Controle Social* 7 (4): 665–684.

Monteiro, R. 2013. "Changes and Uncertainties in Public Security at Rio de Janeiro." SLAS 2013 Annual Conference, University of Manchester, April. 11–12.

Moosavi, L. 2018. "A Friendly Critique of 'Asian Criminology' and 'Southern Criminology'." *The British Journal of Criminology* 59 (2): 257–275. doi:10.1093/bjc/azy045.

Moosavi, L. 2019. "Decolonising Criminology: Syed Hussein Alatas on Crimes of the Powerful." *Critical Criminology* 27 (2): 229–242. doi:10.1007/s10612-018-9396-9.

Neocleous, M. 2000. *The Fabrication of Social Order: A Critical Theory of Police Power*. Sterling, VA: Pluto Press.

Neri, M. 2009. "Income Policies, Income Distribution, and the Distribution of Opportunities in Brazil." In *Brazil as an Economic Superpower?* edited by L. Brainard and L. Martínez-Diaz, 221–269. Washington, DC: Brookings Institution Press.

Perlman, J. E. 2010. *Favela: Four Decades of Living on the Edge in Rio de Janeiro*. Oxford and New York: Oxford University Press.

Pinheiro, P. S. 2006. *World Report on Violence against Children*. Geneva. United Nations Secretary-General's Study on Violence against Children. Accessed 9 January 2020. https://resourcecentre.savethechildren.net/node/2999/pdf/2999.pdf.

Pita, A. 2012. "A cada mil adolescentes do País, três morrem antes de completar 19 anos: Taxa, fruto de pesquisa da UFRJ, teve um crescimento de 14% em relação a 2009 e é a maior desde o começo do levantamento, há cinco anos." *O Estado de São Paulo*, December 13. www.estadao.com.br/noticias/cidades,a-cada-mil-adolescentes-do-pais-tres-morrem-antes-de-completar-19-anos,973161,0.htm.

Prefeitura do Recife. 2013. "A cidade." Accessed 13 January 2015. www2.recife.pe.gov.br/a-cidade/perfil-dos-bairros/rpa-3.

Ratton, J. L., C. Galvão, and M. Fernandez. 2014. "Pact for Life and the Reduction of Homicides in the State of Pernambuco." *Stability: International Journal of Security & Development* 3 (1): 1–15.

Rosa, M. 2014. "Theories of the South: Limits and Perspectives of an Emergent Movement in Social Sciences." *Current Sociology* 62: 851–867.

Santos, B. d. S. 2014. *Epistemologies of the South: Justice against Epistemicide*. London and New York: Routledge.

Scheper-Hughes, N. 2004. "Dangerous and Endangered Youth: Social Structures and Determinants of Violence." In *Youth Violence: Scientific Approaches to Prevention*, edited by J. Devine, J. Gilligan, K. A. Miczek, R. Shaikh, and D. Pfaff, 13–46. New York: New York Academy of Sciences.

Silveira, A. M., R. M. Assunção, B. A. F. d. Silva, and C. C. Beato Filho. 2010. "Impact of the Staying Alive Program on the Reduction of Homicides in a Community in Belo Horizonte." *Rev Saúde Pública* 44 (3): 1–6.

Soares, L. E. 2000. *Meu casaco de general: 500 dias no front da segurança pública do Rio de Janeiro*. São Paulo: Companhia das Letras.

Souza, E. R. d., A. P. Ribeiro, and F. C. Valadares. 2012. *Informações sobre os homicídios no Brasil: uma ferramenta para a consolidação da democracia e da cidadania*. www.usp.br/imprensa/wp-content/uploads/5%C2%BA-Relat%C3%B3rio-Nacional-sobre-os-Direitos-Humanos-no-Brasil-2001-2010.pdf.

Torresan, A., and N. V. d. Cunha. 2013. "Pacifying the Poor: The Effects of Rio de Janeiro's Public Security Policy." SLAS 2013 Annual Conference, University of Manchester, April 11–12.

Travers, M. 2019. "The Idea of a Southern Criminology." *International Journal of Comparative and Applied Criminal Justice* 43 (1): 1–12. doi:10.1080/01924036.2017.1394337.

Wacquant, L. c. J. D. 1996. "The Rise of Advanced Marginality: Notes on Its Nature and Implications." *Acta Sociologica* 39 (2): 121–139.

Wacquant, L. c. J. D. 2003. "Toward a Dictatorship over the Poor? Notes on the Penalization of Poverty in Brazil." *Punishment & Society-International Journal of Penology* 5 (2): 197–205. doi:10.1177/146247450352004.

Wacquant, L. c. J. D. 2008. *Urban Outcasts: A Comparative Sociology of Advanced Marginality*. Cambridge and Malden, MA: Polity.

Waiselfisz, J. J. 2011. *Mapa da Violência: Os Jovens do Brasil*. Accessed 1 October 2012. https://www.mapadaviolencia.org.br/pdf2011/MapaViolencia2011.pdf.

Waiselfisz, J. J. 2013. *Mortes Matadas por Armas de Fogo: Mapa da Violencia*. http://mapadaviolencia.org.br/.

Waiselfisz, J. J. 2014. *Mapa da Violencia 2014: Os jovens do Brasil*. www.mapadaviolencia.org.br/pdf2014/Mapa2014_JovensBrasil_Preliminar.pdf.

Weber, M. 1946. "Politics as a Vocation." In *From Max Weber: Essays in Sociology*, edited by Hans H. Gerth and Charles W. Mills. New York: Oxford University Press.

Wolff, M. J. 2014. "Criminal Authorities and the State: Gangs, Organized Crime, and Police in Brazil." PhD, University of New Mexico, USA.

Zaluar, A. 2010. "Youth, Drug Traffic and Hypermasculinity in Rio de Janeiro." *Vibrant – Virtual Brazilian Anthropology* 7 (2): 7–27.

Zaluar, A., and M. Alvito. 2006. *Um século de Favela*. 5th ed. Rio de Janeiro: Fundação Getulio Vargas.

Chapter 2

Unpacking security, context and research design

Half of the world's people under the age of 25 live in developing regions, such as Latin America, the region with the highest levels of youth homicide in the world (Pinheiro 2006). Since the 1980s Brazil has seen a significant growth in urban violence, which placed the nation in the ranking of countries with the world's highest homicide rates (Zaluar 1998; Adorno and Salla 2007). This growth of lethal violence and the fear it provokes have been some of the most alarming changes for Brazilian society. Homicide has become the leading cause of death in Brazil for young people and indeed the country ranks as the sixth most dangerous in the world for the young (Waiselfisz 2011). In 2004, Brazil's rate of 27 homicides per 100,000 inhabitants placed it in fourth position out of 84 countries; and the homicide rate among adolescents and young people was much higher, at 57.1 homicides per 100,000 (UNESCO 2013). Murder accounts for approximately one in every three deaths of young people in Brazil (Rangel and Bourgois 2005). Even more concerning, is the disproportionate percentage of black and mixed ethnicity young people who are murdered. In 2002, the state of Pernambuco had the second highest homicide rate of black youth (aged 15–24) in the country: 71.4% of victims of homicide were black and young (Waiselfisz 2004). In this context, the process of securitisation, inherent in attempts to allegedly control violence has had significant impacts on marginalised communities and poor young people.

This chapter examines the debates about violence that influenced the developers of new security interventions. It deconstructs the concept of security, arguing that it is value laden, relational, rooted in unequal race, class and gender relations, and influenced by theories that gain currency. The chapter offers a reflective section on the movement of criminological theory and a reflective section on the methods used, including the challenges that they pose. It also explores the socio-economic background of the study's cases in the city of Recife to highlight the importance of understanding regional differences and contemporary unequal social relations, in an exploration of the failure of northern mainstream criminological theory to address challenges in the Global South. It argues that the genesis of the new security agendas is partly influenced by the context of high levels of armed violence, private and real estate interests and partly by debates at times implicitly, at times explicitly, influenced by criminological theories of the Global North.

Methodology

An indispensable prerequisite for achieving the decolonisation of criminology and the advancement of Southern Criminology is the production of knowledge that is grounded in the voices and context in which marginalised and previously enslaved people live. With this in mind, this study was accomplished through a four-year ethnographic project (2012–2016) and recurrent engagement with gatekeepers, key informants, contacts, friends and family in Brazil over the last 17 years. Such exchanges led me to select two case-study communities which met the research criteria. That is, both communities were large urban and well-established informal settlements, which were the subjects of new security interventions. The communities chosen as case studies were selected using a variety of contacts in civil society organisations and local grass-roots social movements, professional academic contacts in Brazilian universities and personal acquaintances with local residents. Using the snow-balling method I was able to expand this network of contacts to reach government officials, members of the security secretariat, politicians, police ombudsmen, civil and military police of high and low ranks across the city with the aim of documenting their discourses and contrasting their views with the views from below, the perceptions of those who live in poor urban communities.

My status as a bilingual Brazilian and British citizen, fluent in both English and Portuguese, attuned to local cultural norms, facilitated my ability to build rapport with those who participated in the research. Being affiliated with British universities enabled dual-benefits: a respected level of status among powerful elites and state actors and simultaneously the ability to sabotage eurocentrism from within. My own personal history, which I have already alluded to, being a *nordestina* (someone who was born and raised in the northeast of Brazil) with family in peripheral communities and direct experience of life and loss at the margins, brought me closer to the participants in the case study communities, sparking endless conversations during extensive fieldwork trips in Brazil. I tried to systematise the analysis of these conversations while collecting data through a combination of methods, including semi-structured and unstructured interviews, focus groups, fieldwork observations and analysis of government documents. My analysis critically engages with official sources and also incorporates examination of newspaper coverage and other forms of media.

I also attended and observed meetings between state officials and police at the Secretariat for Planning and Management of the State of Pernambuco (*Secretaria de Planejamento e Gestão*, or SEPLAG). I recruited and trained two co-researchers from the local communities who took part in focus groups and conducted some of the interviews with local residents in the communities.

Both co-researches were well-connected activists holding high status in the communities due to their voluntary work organising community events and celebrations, providing education, arts and sports workshops for young people in hardship. This enabled us to access the views of a larger group of residents who were willing and keen to be interviewed. In total, 185 interviews were conducted.

Although the case studies were conducted in one particular region – the northeast of Brazil – much about their context will be familiar to researchers and activists working in other large cities in the Global South. There are, however, local differences, cultural and regional contexts, which limit the generalisability of the findings of this study. It was never my aim to make universal generalisations, since epistemologically this study adopts a qualitative, interpretivist, constructivist and explicitly value-laden approach. This is a project focused on exposing injustice and developing cognitive justice (de Sousa Santos 2014) in criminological research.

The case studies

The ethnographic research carried out in two low-income communities focused on examining locals' views and lived experiences of insecurity and securitisation. At this stage it is important to explore the context in which these communities exist. Low-income communities, "occupations", favelas or informal settlements have existed for over a century in Brazil, at least since the end of slavery (Zaluar and Alvito 2006), remaining one of the main forms of housing for a large proportion of Brazil's population. Historically, residents in these settlements self-build their houses and organise their own communities on squatted or public land with little or no governmental support in the form of housing or services such as water and sewage provision, rubbish collection and public transport. Since the re-democratisation of Brazil in the 1980s, many residents of informal settlements, low-income communities and favelas have gained the right to housing titles. Yet, many have continued to face eviction threats, especially where land has become desirable in the wake of mega-events or in the eyes of real estate developers. At the federal and state level, housing programmes have been limited, with interventions in the 1990s and 2000s, such as the programmes *Favela-Bairro* and *Minha Casa Minha Vida*, making a small dent in addressing the housing gap (McCann 2008, 67–68).

The communities studied face extraordinary structural challenges, including the effects of Brazil's colonial history, income inequality and a disjunctive democracy, where democratic elections exist but the realisation of civil rights of citizenship remains inoperative (Holston and Caldeira 1998). The political, social and cultural transformations necessary to consolidate a democratic rule of law and establish the civil component of citizenship – including the principles of liberty and justice – remain hindered. Democratic elections occur alongside systematic violence against citizens, routine violations of citizens' rights and the criminalisation of poverty.

Social and institutional relations and state-civil society interactions are impinged by multiple inequalities. Brazil is one of the most polarised countries in the world in terms of income. Half of the country's total income is concentrated in the pockets of the richest 10% of the population (Perlman 2010, 48–49). So even though the country experienced mild declines in income inequality in the 2000s, inequality remains high. The north and northeast of Brazil are the poorest and least developed parts of the country, with higher concentrations of poverty. Yet, most Brazilian studies and Brazilian theories are developed in wealthier cities, such as Rio de Janeiro and São Paulo. These cities have contrasting contexts in comparison with the majority of Brazil; they are the exception rather than the norm. Recife has one of the country's highest concentrations of violence when measured by homicide rates (57.1/100,000 inhabitants in 2011, Waiselfisz 2014, 63). The city is one of the northeast's largest economic hubs and ranks among the ten largest Brazilian capitals, with a metropolitan population estimated at about 3,750,000 inhabitants (IBGE 2010). Focusing on Recife expands understandings of violence and security in the Global South beyond the contexts of Rio de Janeiro and São Paulo.

Low-income communities have become attractive locales for the drug trade, providing spaces for large shipments to be broken down into smaller packages before either being sold locally or trafficked to other parts of the globe. Their narrow alleys and multiple hiding spaces, alongside a high proportion of unemployed and out-of-school young people make an ideal setting for the establishment of underground economies (Arias 2006; Perlman 2010). Thirty years ago, the main fear in the lives of people living in informal communities was fear of displacement and eviction. Now, they mostly fear for their lives, "never knowing when they may be caught in the crossfire of drug gang violence or shot indiscriminately during a police raid" (see Perlman 2010, X).

High levels of violence, the associated marginalisation of stigmatised territories and greater fear of violent death are three of the most dramatic changes in Latin America post-democratisation. Violence and extortion have become more widespread and unpredictable. Gangs and organised brotherhoods have become more established in the country, and firearms have become more easily accessible. As a consequence, residents of the most affected communities have found it harder to deploy strategies to avoid violence. They describe a loss of trust in the community, which resembles the features of Currie's (1997) theory of post-industrial violence in market societies. They also face discrimination, stigma and reduced job opportunities outside the community. All of these factors perpetuate the cycle of violence by encouraging more young people to seek protection and financial gains in gangs and in the criminal economy.

Despite the challenges that poor communities face, and in spite of widespread deficit or pathological constructions depicting them as disorganised peripheral "breeding grounds for violence", these are highly organised and heterogeneous spaces. As illustrated in the first chapter, they are racially mixed spaces with around half of all residents identifying themselves as mixed, 35% as white and 10% as black. This is not to say that these demographics are matched in the rest of the city, but they do indicate that favelas and poor communities are not racial ghettos. Neither are they strictly "peripheral". Although there is a higher concentration of low-income communities in peripheral urban areas, poor communities and favelas are geographically spread across the city. Moreover, these communities are not the jobless ghettos that they may appear to be. Their residents are not "marginal" to the city or the economy; they perform key roles, for example through work, childcare provision, participation in politics and grass-roots social movements. But they feel more marginalised than ever. Residents have had to come up with creative responses to adversity, including through political bargaining via community associations, a variety of informal, sometimes illegal services and precarious work.

It was in this highly diverse, unequal and challenging context that debates about what needs to be done to curb violence emerged. Such debates concerned with how best to control crime – whether through long-term structural changes (such as poverty reduction) or short-term measures (such as controlling firearms) – influenced a new security programme developed in the state of Pernambuco.

Securitising Brazil

Securitisation refers to the reformation and reconstruction of political discourses and ideas around social justice and participation into technocratic operations of control, management and targeting of "dangerous" populations. As Amar (2013, 27) notes, "when security logics come to serve as the articulating hub for governance and socio-political discourse, this process is called securitisation". Focusing on the notion of security as lenses or an object of analysis can extend criminological debates beyond narrow or state-defined notions of crime. Crime as the object of analysis leaves out the harms and acts that are wilfully or unintentionally undetected, not criminalised and that transcend the remits of national boundaries. A Southern Criminology proposes to go beyond the confines of nation states, embracing a transnational and inclusive approach focusing on issues of global justice and security. As an idea, the term security has already entered criminological debate. The term is rhetorically powerful (Zedner 2009), versatile (Buzan 2007) and used to pursue diverse agendas by different social actors.

Any account of the development of notions of security – or violence, crime and control for that matter – must be grounded in the underlying structural and historic context in which such concepts and ideas are embedded. This is because the ontology of crime and danger is fluid, contested and mutates at different times in history. So do the meanings, uses and misuses of the notions of security and what constitutes violence. For instance, the concept of security during Brazil's last military dictatorship (1964–1985) was linked to a notion of national security, which was concerned with fighting external threats, political subversives and communist ideologies (Szabó de Carvalho and Corrêa 2007). As the dictatorship regime came to an end, these concerns shifted to focus on internal enemies, perceived as the young black poor males from favelas involved with narcotics. So as the security discourse shifted during Brazil's transition to democracy – from a narrative of national security to citizen security (Szabó de Carvalho and Corrêa 2007); from tackling communism to tackling narcotics (Huggins 1998); from targeting political "subversives" (often students, unions, political opponents, activists and middle-class academics) to targeting those perceived as marginal (the urban dispossessed, young offenders, drug-related and petty criminals) – new security interventions and new modes of control emerged. In the 2000s, especially in the run up to mega events such as the World Cup and Olympics in Brazil, efforts to securitise large cities became evident in programmes such as Fica Vivo in Minas Gerais, pacifying police units (or UPPs) in Rio and Pact for Life in Pernambuco.

The global geopolitical interests of corporations, multinationals and US governments had in the past been disguised in secretive or covert police assistance, security and aid operations during the Cold War (Huggins 1998). Now, corporate influence and penetration have become openly acknowledged in security policy convergence and in the adoption of ideas and methods emerging from global homicide reduction programmes. The control industry and apparatus began to discursively move away from notions of eliminating or disappearing the "other" towards incarcerating the offender, the marginalised, dispossessed or socially undesirable. New securitisation agendas accompanied the fast growth of the use of the penal system. But in Brazil, high records of police killings continued despite difficulties in accurately classifying and counting these crimes. For the most part, and in most of Brazil, crime control and securitisation continue to be heavily based on the use of policing, even if in some programmes, such as the pacifying police units in Rio de Janeiro came in alliance with new humanitarian interventions and service provision such as health centres and electricity (Amar 2013). For most of Brazil, social crime prevention and the radical adoption of decriminalising measures remain deficient. Nonetheless, modes of securitisation during the 2000s, especially during the governance of left political parties, signified a new approach of seemingly incomprehensible alliances between military and humanitarian efforts, stakeholders and ethos. This is illustrated in the combination of capitalism with redistributive justice, in the parallel efforts to launch truth commissions into disappearances and torture during the military dictatorship (1964–1985) while maintaining a military police and political coalitions between radical social movements, conservative evangelical groups, human rights groups, private-security agencies and property developers.

Public security

Brazilian academics have made efforts to research and understand the area of study that has come to be loosely labelled "public security" (Lima and Ratton 2011). As a research topic, public security has not yet become as consolidated as other themes such as delinquency, violence, policing and the criminal justice system. The term *public security* emphasises the protection of people, property and democratic political institutions from internal or external threats (Bailey and Dammert 2006). As such, it differs from the term *national security*, often used in the Cold War period, which focused on the protection of a State and its territorial integrity from other state actors and political opponents. The notion of public security thus relies on the process of state building and establishment of state monopoly of violence. The police as the most visible, albeit not the only, state presence in Brazilian poor communities is often seen as key to promoting public security. As an institution in charge of protection, control and the use of force, policing generates direct impact on the prison population, on who goes to prison and who is targeted or not by their work, and thus delineates boundaries between perceived criminals and non-criminals, reinforcing marginalising relations between "us" and "them".

While there is a discourse in Brazil that the problem of violence cannot be resolved without profound reforms in the penal system or a change to the socio-economic structure, academics such as Soares (2008) and Sapori (2007) argue that changing policies and the governance of public security institutions can reduce crime. The focus is thus on tangible measures of crime reduction as opposed to addressing the deeper inequalities or the multitude of (often contested) causes of crime in Brazil. The latter could take far longer to produce results and would require shifts in various long-term social policies, such as those in the field of education and development. This is not to say that these researchers fail to understand or promote a more equal society, but rather that they perceive the need to take specific measures to promote public safety, beyond and in addition to long-term policies to address structural inequalities. For Adorno and Salla, public security policies need to adapt to rapid societal change and turbulence:

> Crime has increased and become more violent; organised criminality has spread through society reaching economic activities far beyond traditional crimes against property, increasing the homicide rates, above all among adolescents and young adults, and disorganising forms of social life and standards of inter- and intra-class sociability. Nevertheless, public safety policies continue to be formulated and implanted according to conventional, aged models, which are incapable of accompanying the quality of the social and institutional changes underway within society.
>
> (Adorno and Salla 2007, 10)

Adorno and Salla suggest that while crime has become more widespread and innovative, making use of new technologies (e.g. telecommunications, transport, modern firearms), the application of law and order continues to consist largely of old, militarised police models of chasing known criminals. Researchers have observed that increasing spending on public security has not necessarily led to reductions in the level of violent mortality (Caldeira 2000; Turollo and Guimarães 2013). As Pereira (2008, 205) neatly puts it:

> If resources are being poured into a system in which collusion between state agents and organised crime is common, in which corruption and illegal violence by state agents is widespread, in which basic sharing of information and cooperation between different agencies is often impossible, in which partisan political loyalties are more important than technical skill and diligence in police promotions and the implementation of state policy, and in which private security interests cream off public intelligence and personnel for profit – then much of these resources will be wasted

In Recife, since the government of Eduardo Campos (2007–2014), public security policies and the securitisation agenda has been grouped together under the project "Pact for Life" (*Pacto pela Vida* or PPV). Over one hundred projects were proposed as part of *Pacto pela Vida*, including: police reforms; the creation of specialised police stations for certain groups (e.g. the elderly, women, LGBT, children and young people); disarmament projects; social and educational projects. Their alleged aim was to reduce mortality in the state of Pernambuco. The next section examines PPV's inherent theoretical influences, highlighting some of the electoral profiteering associated with it.

The adaptation of criminological theories from the Global North

In Brazil, the construction of security interventions often focuses on fluctuations of levels of homicide. But homicide figures do not provide a complete understanding of crime and violence. In fact, as Wacquant reminds us, "public policies result from a mix of leadership intention, bureaucratic groping, organisational slippage, practical trial-and-error and electoral profiteering" (Wacquant 2012, 252). Nonetheless, homicide rates help to construct and portray an important picture of the need for and potential effect of public security policies. Putting aside all the issues of quantification,[1] a significant decline in lethal crime occurred in Pernambuco in tandem with the implementation of PPV. The state of Pernambuco accounted for a large proportion of Brazil's and the world's homicides. In 2005, approximately 10% of the world's homicides – 47,578 deaths – happened in Brazil (DATASUS 2015). In 2007, approximately 10% of Brazil's homicides happened in Pernambuco: a total of 4,592 deaths in one year (ibid). PPV was created with the aim of reducing these extraordinarily high levels of homicide in the state of Pernambuco. It was launched in 2007, when violent mortality was at its highest in this state.

Government data show a gradual decrease in homicide rates in this state between 2008 and 2013. The average homicide rate in the state of Pernambuco between the years 2000 and 2005 was 54.13/100,000 (DATA-SUS 2015) then it dropped to 46.67/100,000 between the years 2006 and 2011 (ibid). To provide a context for comparison, Pernambuco's average homicide rate was over five times higher than the world average homicide rate in the year 2000, which was 8.8/100,000 (Bailey and Dammert 2006). For high-income countries the average homicide rate was 2.9; for low- and middle-income countries it was 10.1 (ibid).

PPV has become a high-profile intervention for the reduction of homicides. It received international awards from the Inter-American Development Bank in 2014 and from the United Nations in 2013 (GEPE 2013; Ribeiro 2014) as well as extensive media coverage in Brazil. Its creators and supporters have travelled to other states in Brazil and other countries in Latin America to share their expertise. It has been promoted as a model by Brazil's federal public security secretariat (SENASP) and some Brazilian states have developed programmes inspired by it, for instance Pará, Bahia and Alagoas (Macedo 2012). The intervention was one of the main marketing points in the political campaign of the state governor of Pernambuco Eduardo Campos (2007–2014), who was also a candidate in the 2014 presidential elections. As argued by Wolff (2014) highly publicised reductions in violent crime associated with PPV facilitated Campos' re-election for a second term in office and launched his political career at the national level.[2]

Despite the historical, political, social and discursive significance of PPV, very few studies have examined its impact. Ratton – an academic who was involved with the development of PPV, while employed as advisor to Eduardo Campos, and who therefore is not a fully independent evaluator – has published a small-scale study ($N = 25$) focusing on the views of actors involved in the policy's development at the government and civil society level (see Ratton, Galvão, and Fernandez 2014). He portrays a very positive image of the policy that he was involved in designing, claiming PPV is a "success"[3] (ibid, 26). Nóbrega (2012) and Wolff (2014) have dedicated very small sections in their studies to PPV and have not gone into much depth in their analysis of the program. Macedo (2012) conducted the most extensive study of PPV so far, focusing on the governance of the programme. She attended PPV-related official meetings and interviewed policymakers and actors involved with the project. However, none of these studies examined the underlying theories that inform PPV's ideologies or compared the discourses of state actors and civil society actors in recipient communities in any depth. Neither did they examine the wider effects of this securitisation programme. This book presents an independent analysis of PPV drawing on the experiences of marginalised people in Recife, especially (albeit not exclusively) the young. It analyses the effects (intended and unintended) of this programme, enabling a deeper discussion of the hegemonic discourse of success.

In 2013, I met with sociologists involved with the design of PPV, who explained that the rationale for the programme emerged from successful homicide reduction programmes implemented elsewhere, such as Bogotá, Minas Gerais and New York. PPV's design has clear similarities with US homicide reduction programmes, including similarities with notorious American police performance management programme known as COMPSTAT (Macedo 2012). For instance, both the New York programme and PPV territorialised police work by enforcing responsibility for policing particular geographical areas. In the PPV case, the state of Pernambuco was divided into 26 areas known as AIS (*Áreas Integradas de Segurança or* Integrated Areas of Security). Other similarities are the emphasis placed on police performance targets, monitoring levels of homicide and demanding reductions. This does not mean a clear and simple reproduction of US models but rather the emulation of some aspects of these security programmes.

The proliferation of such managerialist approaches and support for the modernisation of security systems is illustrated in an edited Brazilian book by Veloso and Ferreira (2008), which was based on a seminar in Rio de Janeiro in 2007 about what violence reduction programmes work around the world. The experts and policy makers who contributed to Veloso's book put forward the idea that cities such as Bogotá, Medellín, Minas Gerais, New York and São Paulo have experienced reductions in homicide because of the implementation of new security policies based on managerial police reforms (p. 18, p. 20). The authors clearly state their admiration and support for police performance management programmes such as COMPSTAT from New York (pp. 26–28). COMPSTAT, a police governance system, which focuses on the use of computers and statistics to track crime and deploy resources, has been widely influential among proponents of managerialism in Brazil. Advocates of this model of governance perceive managerial reforms in the security system not only as a tool to reduce violence, but also as a technique to make police accountable to the most disadvantaged sectors of society (Soares 2008, 12–15). Whether the latter is possible through those means – managerial police reforms – is yet unclear in practice, as this book demonstrates.

PPV, as a securitisation programme, is founded on the idea that crime can be managed, and even prevented by focusing on reducing opportunities for crime through deterrence, policing and incarceration. This approach is influenced by situational crime prevention (SCP) theories (Ratton et al. 2011), which emerged initially in the work of criminologists in the Global North (Felson 2002; Clarke and Felson 2004). The situational crime prevention approach is centred on state interventions such as increased surveillance through CCTV cameras and increased policing and control of those marginalised populations perceived as criminal. As such, it ignores important definitional limitations of crime: the adopted definitions do not focus on the crimes perpetrated by the State and the powerful (such as police abuse of force or deaths caused at work). The criminal is perceived as a rational actor who has calculated the risks against the gains of committing criminal actions. According to the SCP model, increasing the risks of capture through surveillance and more control would prevent crime. Emotive (bravado, anger, impulsivity and immaturity) and uncalculated aspects of crime explored in other studies (Katz 1988; Lyng 1990; Hayward 2007; Drybread 2014) are neglected. The theoretical foundations of SCP have been widely criticised elsewhere on a number of grounds (see Raymen 2015 for an extensive review). As Raymen puts it, the majority of these critiques pull to pieces the idea of the wholly rational criminal actor, questioning the foundations of classical criminology on which these notions are centered (p. 1). SCP approaches offer "false promises of their ability to control much crime and deviance" (ibid).

The interventions that are justified under the situational crime prevention framework have perverse social control effects. These include the reproduction of inequalities in the criminal justice system, as seen in the overrepresentation of poor people in prisons, the deterioration or continuation of poor police-community relations and the displacement of certain crimes to areas that are unsupervised, to the further disadvantage of the most marginalised groups. Situational studies can portray a blame-the-victim view, failing to acknowledge the significance of unequal security provision. When justice, deterrence, policing or security are administered, the overwhelming use of the prison as a form of punishment tends to exacerbate inequalities and social exclusion through the application of the law against the poorest, most marginalised and stigmatised groups in society (Wacquant 2009; Cavadino, Dignan, and Mair 2013).

Conclusion

This chapter introduced and unpacked the foundational, contested and adaptable concept of security, which is indispensable to understand forms of control and the uses and misuses of policies and practices of control. This chapter's second contribution has been to provide a glimpse into the structural context of low-income communities in Brazil. In these communities, marginality and poverty have come to signify "criminality", even if very few people in poor communities become criminals – they are often criminalised. Rather, poor communities are central to Brazilian society, economy and culture. These communities are, however, marginalised in that they are often neglected by the State, having the worst access to housing and public services including security. Third, the chapter began to explore the challenges and barriers to reducing violence and securitising Brazil. It has been argued here that these challenges provide fertile ground for political profiteering and emulation of Global North theories of control.

Notes

1 Violent crime trends tend to rely on homicide rates as a guideline for measuring violence in Latin American because governments lack standard vocabulary and data-collection methods about different types of crime. Cadavers are easily countable in comparison to other types of violent crime, such as non-lethal violence and torture, which are often hidden and unreported in Brazil.

2 Campos was a candidate in the presidential elections of 2014 but he died in an airplane accident during the campaign.

3 Ratton maintains the claim that PPV was a "success", but recently publicly criticised the programme, arguing that its successful aspects had been derailed and pointing to the many failures of the programme: its lack of attention to the prisons and youth offender institutions, the absence of conflict resolution programmes (24 September 2016, *Jornal do Comércio*, available online: http://jconline.ne10.uol.com.br/canal/politica/pernambuco/noticia/2016/09/24/pacto-pela-vida-morreu-diz-mentor-do-programa-254101.php).

References

Adorno, S., and F. Salla. 2007. "Criminalidade organizada nas prisões e os ataques do PCC." *Estudos Avançados* 21 (61): 7–29.

Amar, P. 2013. *The Security Archipelago; Human-Security States, Sexuality Politics, and the End of Neoliberalism*. Durham, NC: Duke University Press.

Arias, E. D. 2006. *Drugs & Democracy in Rio de Janeiro: Trafficking, Social Networks, & Public Security*. Chapel Hill: University of North Carolina Press.

Bailey, J., and L. Dammert. 2006. "Public Security and Police Reform in the Americas." In *Public Security and Police Reform in the Americas*, edited by J. Bailey and L. Dammert, 1–23. Pittsburgh, PA: University of Pittsburgh Press.

Buzan, B. 2007. *People, States and Fear: An Agenda for International Security Studies in the Post-Cold War Era*. ECPR classics 2nd ed. Colchester: ECPR Press.

Caldeira, T. P. d. R. 2000. *City of Walls: Crime, Segregation, and Citizenship in São Paulo*. Berkeley: University of California Press.

Cavadino, M., J. Dignan, and G. Mair. 2013. *The Penal System: An Introduction*. 5th ed. London: SAGE.

Clarke, R. V. G., and M. Felson. 2004. *Routine Activity and Rational Choice*. New Brunswick, NJ: Transaction Publishers.

Currie, E. 1997. "Market, Crime and Community: Toward a Mid-Range Theory of Post-Industrial Violence." *Theoretical Criminology* 1 (2): 147–172. doi:10.1177/1362480697001002001.

DATASUS. 2015. *Indicadores da Mortalidade*. Accessed 13 April 2015. http://tabnet.datasus.gov.br/cgi/tabcgi.exe?idb2011/c09.def.

de Sousa Santos, Boaventura. 2014. *Epistemologies of the South: Justice against Epistemicide*. London and New York: Routledge.

Drybread, K. 2014. "Murder and the Making of Man-Subjects in a Brazilian Juvenile Prison." *American Anthropologist* 116 (4): 752–764. doi:10.1111/aman.12147.

Felson, M. 2002. *Crime and Everyday Life*. 3rd ed. Thousand Oaks, CA: Sage Publications.

GEPE, G. d. E. d. P. 2013. "Governo de Pernambuco recebe prêmio da ONU pelo êxito do Pacto Pela Vida."

Hayward, K. 2007. "Situational Crime Prevention and Its Discontents: Rational Choice Theory versus the 'Culture of Now'." *Social Policy & Administration* 41 (3): 232–250. doi:10.1111/j.1467-9515.2007.00550.x.

Holston, J., and T. P. r. Caldeira. 1998. "Democracy, Law, and Violence: Disjunctions of Brazilian Citizenship." In *Fault Lines of Democracy in Post-Transition Latin America*, edited by F. Aguero and J. Stark, 263–296. Coral Gables, FL: North South Centre Press, University of Miami.

Huggins, M. K. 1998. *Political Policing: The United States and Latin America*. Durham, NC: Duke University Press.

IBGE. 2010. *Censo Demográfico: Aglomerados Subnormais*. Accessed 4 August 2015. https://biblioteca.ibge.gov.br/pt/biblioteca-catalogo?view=detalhes&id=7552.

Katz, J. 1988. *Seductions of Crime: Moral and Sensual Attractions in Doing Evil*. New York: Basic Books.

Lima, R. S. d., and J. L. Ratton. 2011. *As ciências sociais e os pioneiros nos estudos sobre crime, violência e direitos humanos no Brasil*. São Paulo: Fórum Brasileiro de Segurança Pública; Urbania; ANPOCS.

Lyng, S. 1990. "Edgework: A Social-Psychological Analysis of Voluntary Risk-Taking." *American Journal of Sociology* 95 (4): 851–886.

Macedo, A. d. O. 2012. "'Policia, quando quer, faz!' Analise da Estrutura de Governanca do 'Pacto pela Vida' de Pernambuco." Masters, Universidade de Brasilia.

McCann, B. 2008. *The Throes of Democracy: Brazil since 1989*. Halifax, NS and London: Fernwood; Zed Books.

Nóbrega, José Maria Jr. 2012. *Homicídios no Nordeste: Dinamica. Relações causais e desmistificação da violência homicida*. Campina Grande: EDUFCG.

Pereira, A. 2008. "Public Security, Private Interests, and Police Reform in Brazil." In *Democratic Brazil Revisited*, edited by Peter R. Kingstone and Timothy J. Power. Pittsburgh, PA: University of Pittsburgh Press.

Perlman, J. E. 2010. *Favela: Four Decades of Living on the Edge in Rio de Janeiro*. Oxford and New York: Oxford University Press.

Pinheiro, P. S. 2006. *World Report on Violence against Children*. Geneva. United Nations Secretary-General's Study on Violence Against Children. Accessed 9 January 2020. https://resourcecentre.savethechildren.net/node/2999/pdf/2999.pdf.

Rangel, A. B., and J. Bourgois. 2005. *Armas de Fogo: Proteção ou Risco? Guia Pratico – 100 Perguntas e Respostas*. Rio de Janeiro: Viva Rio/ISER.

Ratton, J. L., C. Galvão, R. Andrade, and N. Pavão. 2011. "Configurações de Homicídios em Recife: um estudo de caso." *Segurança, Justiça e Cidadania, Ano* 3 (6): 73–89.

Ratton, J. L., C. Galvão, and M. Fernandez. 2014. "Pact for Life and the Reduction of Homicides in the State of Pernambuco." *Stability: International Journal of Security & Development* 3 (1): 1–15.

Raymen, T. 2015. "Designing-In Crime by Designing-Out the Social? Situational Crime Prevention and the Intensification of Harmful Subjectivities." *British Journal of Criminology*. doi:10.1093/bjc/azv069.

Ribeiro, L. M. L. 2014. *Modelo de Gestão por Resultados do programa Pacto pela Vida, Pernambuco, Brasil*. GobernArte: Categoria Governo Seguro. http://publications.iadb.org/bitstream/handle/11319/6564/GobernArte, Categoria governo seguro (Version en Portugues).pdf?sequence=4.

Sapori, F. L. 2007. *Segurança Pública no Brasil: Desafios e Perspectivas*. Rio de Janeiro: FGV.

Soares, L. E. 2008. "Pausa para reflexão como um convite à ação." In *É Possível: Gestão sa Segurança Pública e Redução da Violência*, edited by F. Veloso and S. G. Ferreira, 9–15. Rio de Janeiro: Contra Capa/Instituto de Estudos de Política Econômica (IEPE).

Szabó de Carvalho, I., and R. M. C. Corrêa. 2007. "Brazilian Perspectives on Human Security." *Policy: Issues & Actors* 20 (8): 1–19.

Turollo, Reynaldo, and Thiago Guimarães. 2013. "Homicídios Crescem em Estados que mais aumentaram gasto com segurança." *Folha de S. Paulo*. Accessed 12 November 2013. www1.folha.uol.com.br/cotidiano/2013/11/1370172-homicidios-crescem-mesmo-em-estados-que-mais-aumentaram-gasto-com-seguranca-publica.shtml.

UNESCO. 2013. *Peace and Human Security in Brazil*. Accessed 1 November 2013. www.unesco.org/new/en/brasilia/social-and-human-sciences/peace-and-human-security/.

Veloso, F., and S. G. Ferreira. 2008. "Introdução." In *É Possível: Gestão sa Segurança Pública e Redução da Violência*, edited by F. Veloso and S. G. Ferreira, 17–21. Rio de Janeiro: Contra Capa/Instituto de Estudos de política Econômica (IEPE).

Wacquant, L. c. 2012. "The Wedding of Workfare and Prisonfare in the 21st Century: Responses to Critica and Commentators." In *Criminalisation and Advanced Marginality: Critically Exploring the Work of Loïc Wacquant*, edited by P. Squires and J. Lea, 243–258. Bristol: The Policy Press.

Wacquant, L. c. J. D. 2009. *Prisons of Poverty*. Vol. 23. Minneapolis and London: University of Minnesota Press.

Waiselfisz, J. J. 2004. *Mapa da Violencia IV: Os Jovens do Brasil*. Brasília. www.mapadaviolencia.org.br/publicacoes/MapaViolencia_IV.pdf.

Waiselfisz, J. J. 2011. *Mapa da Violência: Os Jovens do Brasil*. Accessed 1 October 2012. https://www.mapadaviolencia.org.br/pdf2011/MapaViolencia2011.pdf.

Waiselfisz, J. J. 2014. *Mapa da Violencia 2014: Os jovens do Brasil*. www.mapadaviolencia.org.br/pdf2014/Mapa2014_JovensBrasil_Preliminar.pdf.

Wolff, M. J. 2014. "Criminal Authorities and the State: Gangs, Organized Crime, and Police in Brazil." PhD, University of New Mexico, USA.

Zaluar, A. 1998. "Para não dizer que não falei de samba: os enigmas da violênciano Brasil." In *História da vida privada no Brasil: contrastes da intimidade contemporânea*, edited by L. M. Schwarcz, Vol. 4, 245–318. São Paulo: Companhia das Letras.

Zaluar, A., and M. Alvito. 2006. *Um século de Favela*. 5th ed. Rio de Janeiro: Fundação Getulio Vargas.

Zedner, L. 2009. *Security*. London and New York: Routledge.

Chapter 3

Southern criminologies of violence and control

Poor urban communities experience marginalisation as a state of exclusion, human tragedy and limited opportunities for a fulfilling life. The lives of the poor have been increasingly devalued in the context of drug and arms traffic since their mortality rates are far higher in comparison with the rest of the city. This new violence is "the ultimate manifestation of the marginalisation of the poor, the reality of marginality" (Perlman 2010, 162). Yet while the term marginalisation conveys some of the living realities of many Brazilians, it fails to allow for an analysis of agency and heterogeneity. People living in such conditions often refute the label "marginal" or "marginalised".

In the 1960s, development theories had deployed the concept of marginality in academic and public policy discourse to depict the poor as immoral, deficient, responsible for their own poverty and unable to become integrated into the formal labour and housing markets (Perlman 2010). In the 1970s, this victim-blaming ideology was deployed to justify the removal and evictions of favela communities. The term "marginal" continues to signify "criminal" in everyday language in Brazil. This pathological view of poor communities, that is, the notion that they are socially disorganised breeding grounds of crime, violence, prostitution and family breakdown has been widely contested (Perlman 1976, 2010; Feltran 2011).

The notion of "marginality" returned to academic discourse in the 1990s, starting with an article by Wacquant (1996). Wacquant developed the concept of "advanced marginality" to describe how global capitalism has provoked the warehousing of the poor in prisons and territorial segregation of groups of the population who are viewed as irrelevant to the city. In the US, for the most part this refers to the black ghettos and in Europe to impoverished and migrant communities. Wacquant argued that this new form of marginalisation, which emerged in post-industrial societies, symbolised by the interfaces of colour, class and place, generates new stigmas, forms of dependency on welfare, long-term joblessness and territories of urban relegation. He argued that the current dynamics of global capitalism enable social inequality to persist in a context of economic prosperity. His thesis is that in the time of neoliberal capitalism, social welfare has been rolled back while punitive and criminalising aspects of the State have been rolled forward.

However, even though Wacquant has applied his punitive neoliberal thesis to Brazil (Wacquant 2003), as a case study, Brazil does not fit neatly into his concept of advanced marginality. Brazil never had a well-developed welfare state that could be rolled back. In fact, during most of the rule of the leftist Worker's party (2003–2016), there was an increase in state investments in welfare, particularly in the form of conditional cash transfers such as *Bolsa Família* (Hall 2008; Molyneaux 2008). Despite this period of improvements, Brazil has suffered from high levels of inequality over decades (pre- and post-neoliberalism). Deindustrialisation has been geographically uneven. So while some European and North American countries have seen the outward migration of manufacturing industries, the countries referred to as BRICS (Brazil, Russia, India, China and South Africa) had been receiving an influx of investment and industrial development (Naudé, Szirmai, and Lavopa 2013). Furthermore, unlike the American ghettos or French Banlieues that Wacquant speaks of, most households in favelas contain active people in the labour market (Perlman 2010), so they are not the jobless ghettos that they may appear to be.

Wacquant proposes that "advanced marginality" is characterised by spatial and racial segregation, the stigmatisation of territories and a diminishing sense of community life. While some of these characteristics are visible in Brazilian favelas, particularly the stigmatisation of residents and a diminishing sense of community life as a result of the fear of violence (Perlman 2010; Zaluar 2013), it is important to note that favelas, the peripheries and low-income communities in Brazil are highly heterogeneous places, as illustrated in the previous chapter. Thus, northern theorising is often unable to grasp the intricacies of southern contexts.

Southern perspectives

Much of the discussion about violence in Brazil in the 1980s and 1990s was centred on the debate about the relationship between poverty and crime. A review of this Brazilian literature can benefit from a discussion of the work of key academics, such as Alba Zaluar, Michel Misse and Luis Eduardo Soares. It is important to examine some of the theoretical frameworks that have already been developed in this field, including the causes of violence and its potential connections – or lack of – with poverty, so as to make possible an analysis of public security interventions that are intended to address these problems. Debates about the connections between poverty and crime remain central in the public sphere and in the narratives of members of the public security system.

There is a body of research that shows an implicit connection (albeit not a casual connection) between poverty and crime, insofar as it reveals that homicide rates are higher in low-income communities and that most victims of homicide are poor young black and mixed-race males (Zaluar 1999; Waiselfisz 2014). However, most Brazilian academics rejected the thesis that poverty and crime or poverty and urban violence are directly correlated or even that there is a causal relationship between poverty and violence (Coelho 1978; Paixão 1982, 1983; Adorno and Bordini 1989; Zaluar 1994, 2004; Misse 1995, 2011a, 2011b). The resolution of cases of homicide in Brazil is very low, thus it becomes difficult to establish even the most basic causal factors or the culprits. The rising death toll has been linked to the availability of firearms (Rangel and Bourgois 2005), although that alone cannot explain why some countries with even more firearms (e.g. the USA) have lower homicide rates than Brazil. A more complex analysis of the gun debate highlights that it is not just the number of firearms that matter, but the social role they play in societies with diverse gun cultures (Squires 2014).

Southern academics argue that there are no empirical grounds for explaining violence as the consequence of poverty per se. They suggest that the popular discourse that associates violence with poverty is based on a stereotype of poor populations, which criminalises poverty. This does not mean that there is no connection between poverty and crime, or that the connection is *only* a stereotype. Moreover, they rightly point out that crime happens among all social classes, although there is historical evidence that certain populations tend to be targeted and designated as "criminal". Causality is difficult to establish and there are numerous compounding factors that cannot always be accurately controlled for (e.g. gender, accessibility of firearms, opportunities to commit crime). The paradox of rising crime, for instance, in the 2000s when economic conditions were improving and poverty levels decreased in Brazil illustrates the complexity of this debate and the invalidity of any simplistic causal association of poverty with criminality.

The work of criminologist David Garland (2000, 2001) can be helpful in this debate. Garland explained that wealth and inequality (instead of poverty per se) are key characteristics of societies with high crime rates. Various phenomena, he argued, have all contributed to a complex vicious circle of expanding crime rates and extensive punitive measures: increasing opportunities for crime caused by booming consumption and the availability of desirable goods such as cars and mobile phones, coupled with the abandonment of the rehabilitative model of punishment; increasing fear of crime; the growing politicisation and populism associated with crime, whereby counterproductive punitive policies are endorsed in an attempt to appear "tough on crime" and gain votes; and the amplification of the privatisation and commercialisation of crime control. However, even if Garland's northern theorising can add value to understandings of broader global trends, it cannot fully encompass an understanding of the challenges of violence in the context of post-colonial societies with different cultures, criminal justice systems, histories of military authoritarian governance and fluctuating trends in crime and violence. This book will focus on expanding a southern perspective to address these challenges.

The southern theoretical debate of discourses that directly link poverty and crime, led to the challenge of the idea that without significantly reducing poverty and inequality, public security interventions could not succeed in reducing violence (Soares 2000; Ratton 2012). This contestation seeks to avoid determinism and defeatist approaches, since addressing poverty and inequality could take a lifetime while there are other shorter-term measures that can be taken to curb violence, such as increasing the control of firearms. Rather than directly linking poverty to violence, southern researchers have emphasised the multifaceted and complex causes of various forms of violence and the connections: for example, since the 1980s between the proliferation of firearms and the increasing rates of violence in Brazil (Briceño-León and Zubillaga 2002; Dreyfus, Lessing, and Purcena 2005; Rangel and Bourgois 2005; Beato and Marinho 2007; Cerqueira, Lobao, and Carvalho 2007; Cavalcanti 2016). Such armed violence, significantly reduces the life expectancy of poor young black males in Brazil.

> Firearm-related mortality in Brazil has increased significantly for all age groups since 1991, but death rates due to firearms have risen the most among children and adolescents aged 10 to 19. In 1991, 55.7% of homicides involving 15–19-year-olds were firearm-related, while in 2000 the proportion amounted to 77%. In the state capitals with the highest adolescent firearm-related mortality rates (between 102 and 222 per 100,000), rates are 5 to 11 times those of the overall rate for all age groups.
>
> (Pinheiro 2006, 302)

The expansion of the global economy, revolutions and improvements in technology, transportation and communication and free-market reforms such as deregulation, privatisation and liberalisation, have all heightened opportunities for legal and illegal international economic activities and consequently enhanced the flow of illegal goods and services (Penglase 2008, 121), including firearms and drugs. The growth of the international trade in firearms has increased the likelihood of people resorting to armed violence to settle private disputes (Kruijt and Koonings 1999).

The expansion of organised crime brotherhoods such as the PCC gang has also played a role in fluctuating levels of violence (Manso and Dias 2018). In some Brazilian states, such as São Paulo, the PCC established a peaceful truce with the police, monopolising criminal activities and the drug trade and ultimately contributing to reductions in levels of homicide (Feltran 2011; Denyer Willis 2015). In the northeast, competition and conflict between different gangs such as the expanding PCC and CV, have led to a series of prison riots and deadly disputes over the monopoly of criminal activities (Manso and Dias 2018). An approach that examines and acknowledges the roles played by a plurality of social actors – civil society, organised crime, corporate actors and the state – is therefore paramount for understanding the milieu in which new technologies and discourses of securitisation proliferate.

Police violence

Most of the police violence in low-income communities is committed by the military police (Perlman 2010, 168). The slowness of the Brazilian courts and the inadequacy of mechanisms of police accountability prompt the military police to act coercively in the streets instead of arresting suspects (Pereira 2008). The criminal justice system notably contributes to producing and expanding a cycle of violence through institutional failure, by deploying extrajudicial violence, aggressive raids and lethal force. Another notorious source of violence in favelas has been armed militias formed by self-appointed, off-duty or retired police officers who take law-and-order problems into their own hands (Huggins 2010; Perlman 2010; Garmany and Galdeano 2018). Militias have been known to extort money from favela residents, demanding regular payments for the delivery of goods, taxing taxi and motorbike-taxi businesses and even charging people for entering or leaving the favela (Perlman 2010, 168). As argued by Scheper-Hughes (2004) and Pinheiro (2006), militias and the police contribute to the disproportional mortality of the poor young black males.

The police force is deeply resistant to change (Soares 2000). Some studies, based on data about death occurring in conflict with the police, particularly *autos de resistência* ("resistance to arrest", cases of lethal police violence which are not registered as homicide) have shown that the degree of police violence is still very high and hard to measure (Bueno and Lima 2012). For instance, in Rio de Janeiro and São Paulo, Bueno and Lima estimate that 22,525 people were killed in confrontation with the police between 1993 and 2011. There is still no standard register for data about cases of police violence in the country, and since the restoration of democracy in Brazil, basic civil rights such as safety remain insufficiently consolidated (Possas 2012), both in practice and in the public perception. For instance, despite the difficulty in accessing this type of data, there is ample evidence that human rights violations, including by the State, continue to happen routinely in Brazil (Possas 2012).

A study of ten Brazilian state capitals (Cardia 2012) found that 47% of participants thought it appropriate for a police officer to be violent towards an incarcerated person who tried to escape; 62% thought that the criminal justice system overprotects the rights of the accused; and 29% thought it acceptable for courts to accept evidence extracted via torture. The "paradox of democracy" is that, despite the end of military dictatorship, human rights violations continue to occur routinely in large scale (Possas 2012). The persistence of extra-legal violence fuels the population's fears and sense of insecurity. Moreover, high crime rates have led to a sense of insecurity and fear that engender punitive attitudes towards the "other" – the offender – and provides support for regressive policies and practices which are incompatible with a human-rights agenda, such as arbitrary sentencing and the excessive use of imprisonment.

Ethnographic studies of policing and judicial practice in Rio de Janeiro have argued that the deviance and distortions of these institutions are not merely occasional or isolated cases of staff and institutional failure, but rather that they reveal mass adherence (even if not explicitly) to a deviant system of conflict management typical of segregated and hierarchical societies (Kant de Lima 1989). Brazil's justice system is replete with loopholes that perpetuate inequalities and generate widespread dissatisfaction. Those who have access to good lawyers can manipulate endless and innumerable delays in prosecution (Kant de Lima, Misse, and Miranda 2000). At the same time, extrajudicial punishment is routinely applied both by the agents of the public security apparatus and by the population, which, largely condones the humiliation, torture and even the killing of those considered criminals, before or after their official sentence (Singer 2000; Feltran 2011).

Despite the creation of new police institutions, and the formation of some community policing initiatives and programmes of police education organised by public universities, criminal justice and police reforms have been partial (Tavares dos Santos 2009). The impact, extent and suitability of public security initiatives in Brazil remains under-studied and it is unclear whether they are appropriate to provide safety, reform the police and provide lasting results. It was in this context of high levels of crime, and contested explanations for rising violence, that debates about what needs to be done to curb violence emerged. It was in this milieu that Pernambuco's new security programme was developed.

The genesis of new securitising interventions

The governor of the state of Pernambuco, Eduardo Campos (2007–2014) contracted a sociologist from the federal university of Pernambuco (UFPE), Professor José Luiz Ratton, to work as his public security advisor. Between March and April 2007, an initial set of consultations and events was organised as part of a forum of public security (*Fórum Estadual de Segurança Pública*) where the topic of public security was debated and the plan that informed PPV was drawn up. For Ratton, Galvão, and Fernandez (2014, 2) PPV was the first institutional reform of the Pernambucan police. They describe in more detail the process of developing the policy. The initial security plan proposed over 100 projects (PESP-PE 2007) organised into six lines of action: "qualified repression; institutional enhancement; information and knowledge management; training and capacity-building; crime and social violence prevention; and democratic management" (Ratton, Galvão, and Fernandez 2014, 2). However, only some of those were implemented. Ethnographic work, interviews and observations in the communities studied revealed that the social crime prevention measures initially proposed and the mediation of conflicts in communities were not implemented. The implemented changes focused, for the most part, on the governance of police work (interview with Ratton, July 2013, see also Macedo 2012).

As outlined in Chapter 2, evidence from interviews with sociologists involved with the design of PPV shows that the programme was inspired by homicide reduction programmes deployed in cities such as Bogotá, Minas Gerais and New York. The idea that these cities were "successfully" securitised after the implementation of managerial police reforms became widespread in academic and policy circles (see for instance the edited collection by Veloso and Ferreira 2008). Proponents of managerialism in Brazil, unlike those in the US and UK, are among critical social scientists from the "left" who also propose ideas around social justice. They perceive managerial reforms not only as a tool to reduce violence, but also to make police accountable to the most disadvantaged sectors of society (Soares 2008, 12–15). Whether the latter is possible through those means – managerial police reforms – is yet unclear in practice. In Chapter 5, I discuss the fallacies of the New York miracle by exploring research that challenges crime reduction claims grounded in COMPSTAT, managerial reforms, Broken Windows Theory and Zero Tolerance policing. This is not to say that managerial reforms have no value, but rather that they have limits and often involve further risks, as the following chapters illustrate.

The Minas Gerais programme known as Stay Alive, for example, was explicitly influenced by US violence-reduction programmes, such as Operation Ceasefire and hotspot policing (Beato Filho 2013, 1 and 5). Nonetheless, it combined managerial police reforms with important social crime prevention measures (e.g. youth sports programmes and conflict mediation). PPV's design also has clear similarities with US homicide reduction programmes, including similarities with the (in)famous American police performance management programme known as COMPSTAT (Macedo 2012). For instance, both the New York programme and PPV territorialised police work by enforcing responsibility for policing particular geographical areas. In the PPV case, these areas are known as AIS (*Áreas Integradas de Segurança*) and the state of Pernambuco now has 26 of them. Other similarities are the emphasis placed on police performance targets, monitoring levels of homicide and demanding reductions. This does not mean a clear and simple reproduction of US models but rather the emulation of some aspects of these security programmes.

Ratton's academic work before becoming involved with the design of PPV was influenced by situational crime prevention (SCP) theories (Ratton et al. 2011). The situational approach, which originated in the work of Felson (2002) and Clarke and Felson (2004) in the Global North, proposes addressing environmental causes of crime such as increased opportunities for crime. This approach relies on a narrow legalistic conceptualisation of crime, as defined by the State, ignoring mismanagement of data by State and wider harms, including those committed by state actors. The State has the power to define what a crime is, what counts as a homicide and it has the tools to manipulate this data. Ratton et al.'s (2011) study was based on an analysis of 78 homicide *inquéritos* (police investigation registers) between 2002 and 2007, and argued that, among other things, in over 88% of cases victims and perpetrators were known to each other. There is a clear bias in the study in that it deployed only data produced by the police (homicide investigation registers). The study argued that homicides in Recife happen more often in routine daily interactions in socially disorganised and deprived environments; it most frequently involves young males (93% of victims were male and 98% of perpetrators were male) who are black or mixed race, know each other and have easy access to firearms; and more often occurs at night, at weekends, in public spaces. The key motivation is the resolution of conflicts through violence, invariably using a firearm and resulting in the death of at least one of the individuals involved. A significant limitation of their study is that it does not consider the impact of institutional factors on the "diagnosis" of homicide. Firstly, while many homicide cases may occur between people who know each other, it is important to acknowledge that these data look at cases where a suspect was identified and sometimes convicted. As such, it neglects data and cases where the police were unable or unwilling to adequately identify the accused, which in Brazil is the case for most incidents of murder. Thus, easy-to-accuse and "usual suspects" are more likely to be included in official police registers.

Secondly, such interactional studies fail to acknowledge the structural, institutional and systemic disparities that contribute to their conclusions. They make claims of a diagnosis of where and who the victims and perpetrators of homicide are, concluding that these are mostly poor young males. They claim to reveal how and when these homicides occur. However, if most cases of homicides are not resolved, the actual perpetrators are difficult to label. The evidence emerging from police records is unlikely to suggest that the police perpetrated homicides. Situational studies can portray a blame-the-victim view in which the poor are blamed for the everyday violence they encounter as a consequence of wider structural inequalities. Moreover, while middle- and upper-class individuals in Brazil often benefit from private security – including security guards, alarm systems, private transport, gated communities – and better access to the formal justice system, the poor are left to provide security and conflict resolution with "their own hands". These dynamics reveal, among other issues, a lack of adequate public security provision. The situational crime prevention approach is centred on state interventions such as increased surveillance through CCTV cameras and increased policing and control of those marginalised populations perceived as criminal. The interventions that are justified under the situational crime prevention framework have had perverse social control effects. These include the reproduction of inequalities in the criminal justice system, as seen in the overrepresentation of poor people in prisons, the deterioration or continuation of poor police-community relations, the displacement of certain crimes to areas that are unsupervised, to the further disadvantage of the most marginalised groups.

Some studies address the limitations of situational and managerial criminology by engaging with the cultural and emotive aspects that lead a conflict to result in death. These include attempts to maintain a version of masculine honour (Polk 1994; Bourgois 2003; Zaluar 2010; Drybread 2014) and fear of victimisation when faced with a situation where all those involved are armed, leading one of the individuals to "pull the trigger" first (Wilkinson and Fagan 2001). In such circumstances violence and fear become key elements of daily life, a currency of survival (Fagan and Wilkinson 1998; Rodgers 2009; Zubillaga 2009) and one means by which people negotiate their place and identity. Managerial criminology, and its emphasis on target monitoring, surveillance and arrests, is not able to capture or address these cultural and emotive aspects of a society with high levels of violence.

Monitoring police statistics and focusing on performance evaluations based solely on statistics fail to acknowledge the profoundly socially constructed nature of what is defined as a crime and who is defined as a criminal, a critique which is well elaborated by Young (2011). Statistical counts (even when they emerge from victimisation surveys) often fail to capture harmful practices (Raymen 2015, 14) and hidden crimes such as corporate crimes, domestic violence and police misconduct. Social constructions of criminals tend to reinforce conventional stereotypes and the criminalisation of those perceived as undeserving "others". Structural and social inequalities affecting offenders are ignored. Instead, those criminalised are depicted "as culpable, undeserving and somewhat dangerous individuals who must be carefully controlled for the protection of the public and the prevention of further offending" (Garland 2001, 175).

These criticisms of the theoretical rationale underpinning PPV do not mean that there were no positive aspects of this public security programme. The emphasis on monitoring certain police targets offers potential benefits to society as a whole. For example, PPV monitors firearms apprehensions by police, which encourages the control of firearms. As firearms are a key element in the increase of lethal violence (Squires 2000; Dreyfus, Lessing, and Purcena 2005; Rangel and Bourgois 2005; Cavalcanti 2016), this aspect of PPV can be seen as having beneficial effects to society. The same could not be said about PPV's emphasis on monitoring the amount of drugs apprehended by police. The latter tends to reinforce issues associated with the war on drugs, such as old problems of criminalisation of the marginalised, while having no proven effect on the reduction of violence (Simon 2007). It is therefore important that critical criminological and security studies consider the ways in which securitisation models can affect the dynamics of violence and safety in poor communities, from the perception of the marginalised themselves.

Conclusion

This chapter introduced English-speaking readers to the work of Brazilian ethnographers such as Alba Zaluar (2004, 2010) and Michel Misse (2011a, 2011b). It deployed the work of southern theorists (e.g. Gabriel Feltran; Sergio Adorno), critical criminologists (e.g. Garland) and comparative urban ethnographers (e.g. Loïc Wacquant) to examine competing understandings of violence, security and security policy transfer. The chapter introduced the genesis of a new security intervention, known as "Pact for Life", which emerged in the region in 2007, while exploring the extent to which such interventions emulate Global North criminological theories. This discussion suggests that (a) critical southern theorists have contested victim-blaming theoretical accounts that correlate violence with the poor; and (b) northern criminological models such as situational crime prevention and managerial criminology risk exacerbating the marginalisation of poor communities.

References

Adorno, S., and E. Bordini. 1989. "Reincidência e reincidentes penitenciários em São Paulo, 1974–1985." *Revista Brasileira de Ciências Sociais* 9 (3): 70–94.

Beato, C., and F. C. Marinho. 2007. "Padrões regionais de homicídio noBrasil." In *Homicídios no Brasil*, edited by C. a. Batitucci, 177–190. Rio de Janeiro: FGV.

Beato Filho, C. C. 2013. *Estudio de caso: Programa Fica Vivo en Brasil.* CAPSI Iniciativa Centroamericana del Sector Privado. www.capsinitiative.net/wp-content/uploads/2014/07/Caso-Fica-Vivo-Version-final-Claudio-Beato-Espanol.pdf.

Beato Filho, C. B., L. M. L. Ribeiro, V. C. de Oliveira, and S. C. F. Prado. 2017. "Reducción de homicidios en Minas Gerais un análisis del programa 'Fica Vivo!'" *Revista CIDOB d'afers Internacionals* 116: 129–157. ISSN 1133–6595. doi:10.24241/rcai.2017.116.2.129.

Bourgois, P. I. 2003. *In Search of Respect: Selling Crack in El Barrio.* 2nd ed. Cambridge: Cambridge University Press.

Briceño-León, R., and V. Zubillaga. 2002. "Violence and Globalization in Latin America." *Current Sociology* 50 (1): 19–37.

Bueno, S., and R. S. D. Lima. 2012. *A opaca estética da indiferença.* São Paulo. 5° Relatório Nacional sobre os Direitos Humanos no Brasil 2001–2010. www.usp.br/imprensa/wp-content/uploads/5%C2%BA-Relat%C3%B3rio-Nacional-sobre-os-Direitos-Humanos-no-Brasil-2001-2010.pdf.

Cardia, N. 2012. *Os direitos humanos segundo a pesquisa 'Atitudes, normas culturais e valores em relação a violação de direitos humanos e violência'.* São Paulo. 5° Relatório Nacional sobre os Direitos Humanos no Brasil. www.usp.br/imprensa/wp-content/uploads/5%C2%BA-Relat%C3%B3rio-Nacional-sobre-os-Direitos-Humanos-no-Brasil-2001-2010.pdf.

Cavalcanti, R. P. 2016. "Armed Violence and the Politics of Gun Control in Brazil: An Analysis of the 2005 Referendum." *Bulletin of Latin American Research*, Online (March): 1–16. doi:10.1111/blar.12476.

Cerqueira, D., W. Lobao, and A. Carvalho. 2007. *O jogo dos sete mitose a miséria da segurança pública no Brasil.* Rio de Janeiro: IPEA. Accessed 08 January 2020. http://www.ipea.gov.br/portal/images/stories/PDFs/TDs/td_1144.pdf.

Clarke, R. V. G., and M. Felson. 2004. *Routine Activity and Rational Choice.* New Brunswick, NJ: Transaction Publishers.

Coelho, E. C. 1978. "A criminalização da marginalidade e a marginalização da criminalidade." *Revista de administração Pública* 12 (2): 139–161.

Denyer Willis, G. 2015. *The Killing Consensus: Police, Organized Crime, and the Regulation of Life and Death in Urban Brazil.* Berkeley: University of California Press.

Dreyfus, P., B. Lessing, and J. C. Purcena. 2005. "The Brazilian Small Arms Industry: Legal Production and Trade." http://s3.amazonaws.com/zanran_storage/www.vivario.org.br/ContentPages/762566710.pdf.

Drybread, K. 2014. "Murder and the Making of Man-Subjects in a Brazilian Juvenile Prison." *American Anthropologist* 116 (4): 752–764. doi:10.1111/aman.12147.

Fagan, J. A., and D. L. Wilkinson. 1998. "Guns, Youth Violence and Social Identity in Inner Cities." In *Crime and Justice: Annual Review of Research*, edited by M. Tonry and M. Moore, Vol. 24, 105–188. Chicago, IL: University of Chicago Press.

Felson, M. 2002. *Crime and Everyday Life.* 3rd ed. Thousand Oaks, CA: Sage Publications.

Feltran, G. d. S. 2011. *Fronteiras de Tensão: Política e Violência nas Periferias de São Paulo.* São Paulo: Unesp.

Garland, D. 2000. "The Culture of High Crime Societies: Some Preconditions of Recent 'Law and Order' Policies." *British Journal of Criminology* 40 (3): 347–375.

Garland, D. 2001. *The Culture of Control: Crime and Social Order in Late Modernity.* Oxford: Clarendon.

Garmany, J., and A. P. Galdeano. 2018. "Crime, Insecurity and Corruption: Considering the Growth of Urban Private Security." *Urban Studies* 55 (5): 1111–1120. doi:10.1177/0042098017732691.

Hall, A. 2008. "Brazil's Bolsa Família: A Double-Edged Sword?" *Development and Change* 39 (5): 779–822.

Huggins, M. K. 2010. "Systemic Police Violence in Brazil." In *Police Use of Force: A Global Perspective*, edited by J. B. Kuhns and J. Knutsson, 73–82. Santa Barbara, CA, Denver, CO, and Oxford: Praeger.

Kant de Lima, R. 1989. "Cultura Jurídica e Práticas Policiais: A Tradição Inquisitorial." *Revista Brasileira de Ciências Sociais* 4 (10): 66–84.

Kant de Lima, R., M. Misse, and A. P. M. d. Miranda. 2000. "Criminalidade, Violência Urbana, Justiça Criminal e Segurança Pública: uma Bibliografia." *BIB – Revista Brasileira de Bibliografia em Ciências Sociais* 50: 45–96.

Kruijt, D., and K. Koonings. 1999. "Introduction: Violence and Fear in Latin America." In *Societies of Fear: The Legacy of Civil War, Violence and Terror in Latin America*, edited by K. Koonings and D. Kruijt. London: Zed.

Macedo, A. d. O. 2012. "'Policia, quando quer, faz!' Analise da Estrutura de Governanca do 'Pacto pela Vida' de Pernambuco." Masters, Universidade de Brasilia.

Manso, B. P., and C. C. N. Dias. 2018. *A guerra: a ascensão do PCC e o mundo do crime no Brasil.* São Paulo: Todavia.

Misse, M. 1995. "Cinco Teses Equivocadas Sobre A Criminalidade Urbana No Brasil." *Estudos* 91: 23–40.

Misse, M. 2011a. *Crime e Violência No Brasil Contemporaneo: Estudos de Sociologia do Crime e da Violencia Urbana*. 2nd ed. Rio de Janeiro: Lumen Juris.
Misse, M. 2011b. "Crime organizado e crime comum no Rio de Janeiro: diferenças e afinidades." *Revista de Sociologia e Política* 19 (40): 13–25.
Molyneaux, M. 2008. "The 'Neoliberal Turn' and the New Social Policy in Latin America: How Neoliberal, How New?" *Development and Change* 39 (5): 775–797.
Naudé, W., A. Szirmai, and A. Lavopa. 2013. "Industrialization Lessons from BRICS: A Comparative Analysis." http://ftp.iza.org/dp7543.pdf.
Paixão, A. L. 1982. "Crimes e Criminosos em Belo Horizonte: Uma Exploração Inicial das Estatísticas Oficiais da Criminalidade." In *Violência e Cidade*, edited by R. Boschi, 75–98. Rio de Janeiro: Zahar.
Paixão, A. L. 1983. "Sociologia do Crime e do Desvio: Uma Revisão da Literatura." *Mimeo*.
Penglase, B. 2008. "The Bastard Child of the Dictatorship: The Comando Vermelho and the Birth of 'Narco-Culture' in Rio de Janeiro." *Luso-Brazilian Review* 45 (1): 118–145.
Pereira, A. W. 2008. "Public Security, Private Interests, and Police Reform in Brazil." In *Democratic Brazil Revisited*, edited by P. R. Kingstone and T. J. Power, 185–208. Pittsburgh, PA: University of Pittsburgh Press.
Perlman, J. E. 1976. *The Myth of Marginality: Urban Poverty and Politics in Rio de Janeiro*. Berkeley and London: University of California Press.
Perlman, J. E. 2010. *Favela: Four Decades of Living on the Edge in Rio de Janeiro*. Oxford and New York: Oxford University Press.
PESP-PE. 2007. *Plano Estadual de Seguranca Publica: PACTO PELA VIDA*. Recife: Cultura. www.seres.pe.gov.br/index/pacto_pela_vida.pdf.
Pinheiro, P. S. 2006. *World Report on Violence against Children*. Geneva: United Nations Secretary-General's Study on Violence against Children. ISBN-13 978-92-95057-51-7. Accessed 9 January 2020. https://resourcecentre.savethechildren.net/node/2999/pdf/2999.pdf.
Polk, K. 1994. "Masculinity, Honour and Confrontational Homicide." In *Just Boys Doing Business? Men, Masculinities and Crime*, edited by T. Newburn and E. A. Stanko, xii, 290. London and New York: Routledge.
Possas, M. T. 2012. *Introdução*. São Paulo. 5º Relatório Nacional sobre os Direitos Humanos no Brasil (2001–2010). www.usp.br/imprensa/wp-content/uploads/5%C2%BA-Relat%C3%B3rio-Nacional-sobre-os-Direitos-Humanos-no-Brasil-2001-2010.pdf.
Rangel, A. B., and J. Bourgois. 2005. *Armas de Fogo: Proteção ou Risco? Guia Pratico – 100 Perguntas e Respostas*. Rio de Janeiro: Viva Rio/ISER.
Ratton, J. L. 2012. "Apresentação Seminário Políticas Locais de Prevenção da Violência." In *A Segurança Cidadã em debate. Cadernos sobre Segurança e Prevenção da Violência na América Latina*, edited by J. L. Ratton, G. Costa, C. Romero, and L. E. Soares, Vol. URB-Al III, 10–23. Recife: Provisual.
Ratton, J. L., C. Galvão, R. Andrade, and N. Pavão. 2011. "Configurações de Homicídios em Recife: um estudo de caso." *Segurança, Justiça e Cidadania, Ano* 3 (6): 73–89.
Ratton, J. L., C. Galvão, and M. Fernandez. 2014. "Pact for Life and the Reduction of Homicides in the State of Pernambuco." *Stability: International Journal of Security & Development* 3 (1): 1–15.
Raymen, T. 2015. "Designing-In Crime by Designing-Out the Social? Situational Crime Prevention and the Intensification of Harmful Subjectivities." *British Journal of Criminology*. doi:10.1093/bjc/azv069.

Rodgers, D. 2009. "Living in the Shadow of Death: Gangs Violence and Social Order in Urban Nicaragua: 1996–2002." In *Youth Violence in Latin America*, edited by G. A. Jones and D. Rodgers, 25–44. New York: Palgrave Macmillan.

Scheper-Hughes, N. 2004 "Dangerous and Endangered Youth: Social Structures and Determinants of Violence." *Annals of the New York Academy of Sciences* 1036: 13–46. doi:10.1196/annals.1330.002.

Simon, J. 2007. *Governing through Crime : How the War on Crime Transformed American Democracy and Created a Culture of Fear.* Oxford and New York: Oxford University Press.

Singer, H. 2000. "Discursos Desconcertados: Linchamentos, Punições e Direitos Humanos." Doutorado em Sociologia, USP, São Paulo.

Soares, L. E. 2000. *Meu casaco de general: 500 dias no front da segurança pública do Rio de Janeiro.* São Paulo: Companhia das Letras.

Soares, L. E. 2008. "Pausa para reflexão como um convite à ação." In *É Possível: Gestão sa Segurança Pública e Redução da Violência*, edited by F. Veloso and S. G. Ferreira, 9–15. Rio de Janeiro: Contra Capa/Instituto de Estudos de Política Econômica (IEPE).

Squires, P. 2000. *Gun Culture or Gun Control?: Firearms and Violence: Safety and Society.* Abingdon, UK and New York: Routledge.

Squires, P. 2014. *Gun Crime in Global Contexts.* 1st ed. London and New York: Routledge, Taylor & Francis Group.

Tavares dos Santos, J. V. 2009. *Violências e Conflitualidades.* Porto Alegre: Tomo.

Veloso, F., and S. G. Ferreira. 2008. "Introdução." In *É Possível: Gestão sa Segurança Pública e Redução da Violência*, edited by F. Veloso and S. G. Ferreira, 17–21. Rio de Janeiro: Contra Capa/Instituto de Estudos de política Econômica (IEPE).

Wacquant, L. c. J. D. 1996. "The Rise of Advanced Marginality: Notes on Its Nature and Implications." *Acta Sociologica* 39 (2): 121–139.

Wacquant, L. c. J. D. 2003. "Toward a Dictatorship over the Poor? Notes on the Penalization of Poverty in Brazil." *Punishment & Society-International Journal of Penology* 5 (2): 197–205. doi: 10.1177/146247450352004.

Waiselfisz, J. J. 2014. *Mapa da Violencia 2014: Os jovens do Brasil.* www.mapadaviolencia.org.br/pdf2014/Mapa2014_JovensBrasil_Preliminar.pdf

Wilkinson, D. L., and J. Fagan. 2001. "A Theory of Violent Events." In *The Process and Structure of Crime: Criminal Events and Crime Analysis*, edited by R. F. Meier, L. W. Kennedy, and V. Sacco, Vol. 9, 169–196. New Brunswick, NJ: Transaction.

Young, J. 2011. *The Criminological Imagination.* Cambridge and Malden, MA: Polity.

Zaluar, A. 1994. *A máquina e a revolta. As organizações populares e o significado da pobreza.* 2nd ed. São Paulo: Editora Brasiliense.

Zaluar, A. 1999. "Um debate disperso: violência e crime no Brasil da redemocratização." *Um debate disperso: violência e crime no Brasil da redemocratização*, 13(3): 3–17. doi:10.1590/S0102-88391999000300002.

Zaluar, A. 2004. *Integração Perversa: Pobreza e Tráfico de drogas.* Rio de Janeiro: FGV.

Zaluar, A. 2010. "Youth, Drug Traffic and Hypermasculinity in Rio de Janeiro." *Vibrant – Virtual Brazilian Anthropology* 7 (2): 7–27.

Zaluar, A. 2013. "Warrior Ethos and Cruelty among Drug Dealers in Favelas of Rio de Janeiro." SLAS 2013 Annual Conference, University of Manchester.

Zubillaga, V. 2009. "'Gaining Respect': The Logic of Violence among Young Men in the Barrios of Caracas, Venezuela." In *Youth Violence in Latin America*, edited by G. A. Jones and D. Rodgers, 83–103. New York: Palgrave Macmillan.

Chapter 4

Policing the poor

This chapter introduces the particular context of policing in Brazil. It considers the issues that cultural and structural systems generate. Such issues, I argue, are illustrated by recurrent police strikes, the politicisation of the police, inefficient fragmentation of their work and result in attitudes and pressures that make policing by consent highly unlikely. The chapter draws on ethnographic data acquired through interviews with low and high-ranking members of two different police forces: the civil and the military police (*polícia civil* or PC, and *polícia militar*, or PM). Such unique first-hand data in this region of Brazil sheds light into the challenges and opportunities for changing institutions that are meant to provide an important public emergency service: the protection of the public (above all other social control and order maintenance roles).

In contrast to the dominant discourse of "success" presented by high-ranking state actors, this chapter reveals critical and counter-hegemonic narratives on the part of other state actors, namely low-ranking police officers. The chapter scrutinises inherent and enduring problems in the security apparatus, which are noticeable in the narratives of state actors, including classism, racism and brutalising training. These matters manifest themselves on the streets as a highly coercive and authoritarian style of policing. I argue that these problems, and the unequal social relations in which they are embedded, hinder the application of democratic principles in security interventions and erode the legitimacy of the State and its interventions. In doing so, this chapter complements a growing body of literature on policing and criminology in the Global South (Chevigny 1995; Huggins 1998; Bayley 2001, 2006; Tavares Dos Santos 2009; Denyer Willis 2015; Carrington, Hogg, and Sozzo 2016).

The structure and politics of the Brazilian police

The Brazilian police are divided into two major forces: the military police and the civil police. Other smaller forces exist, such as the federal police, with functions similar to the American FBI. The military police patrol the streets, while the civil police are responsible for investigations. The rigid military hierarchy and structure of the military police limits interaction with the public and distances them from the communities they patrol. The civil police on the other hand spends most of its time in police stations *(delegacias)* dealing with paperwork (Pereira 2008), supposedly conducting investigations. This structure contributes to the ineffectiveness of both forces. The division of policing work means that no single force is responsible for the full cycle of policing, generating inter-agency rivalry and difficulties in cooperating between the forces.

There are also clear differences in the training, culture, recruitment criteria and career prospects of each force. For instance, the chiefs of civil police *(delegados)* must have a law degree to be in office and do not wear uniforms. Meanwhile, the military police are uniformed, go through military training and abide by military codes of conduct. The military police are no longer under army control, but they are still divided into military ranks, institutionally beset by rigid military ideologies and subjected to a military penal code. Soldiers – the lowest rank in the military police – cannot progress to the highest ranks in the military police through work. The highest ranks in the military police go through a separate recruitment process and are often politically connected. Police culture in Brazil resembles the logics of Brazilian culture, as synthesised by Roberto da Matta: when personal relations are established, they supersede formal and institutional norms and associations, allowing for every kind of benefit, potentially opening the way to various forms of discrimination and the giving and receiving of illicit favours (Soares 2000, 62).

The Brazilian military also continue to be influential in the country's security provision, with many generals occupying positions of leadership in the secretariats of public security of various states and the army being increasingly present in public life and called in to control public order (Soares 2000; Zaverucha 2000; Mesquita Neto 2011, 258; Fernandes 2013; Harig 2014). One example of this occurred during the police strikes in May 2014 in Pernambuco, when the army was called in to control rioting and looting in the larger cities of the metropolitan region.

The reliance of the Brazilian federal and state governments on the armed forces to contain short-term crises in the public security apparatus, such as police strikes, postpones and hinders reform proposals and the demilitarisation of the public security system. In this context, fighting those perceived as internal enemies and threats take precedence over consensual policing, equality before the law and the protection of citizens' safety and rights. The military ethos and mission is distinct from that of the police. As argued by Chevigny (1995, 255):

> Military forces are organised primarily to use violence against a well-defined enemy, and although they can patrol, they are ill-suited to turn to the police jobs of service, peaceable order keeping, or even arresting suspects for crime. A soldier is trained to solve many problems by shooting someone, and the police if they think of themselves as an army, are likely to do the same.

Soldiers obey orders from above instead of responding to citizens' demands and their use of force is less restrained. Military police soldiers tend to obey orders from above, rather than respond to citizens' demands, in the same ways as an army soldier would.

Beyond the structure of policing, the politicisation of the institution also affects the securitisation apparatus. Most high-ranking positions in the police and in the National Secretariat for Public Safety (SENASP) are staffed with political appointees, so political patronage and loyalty continue to be a problem (Pereira 2008). This also leads to a discontinuation in policies and practices when new governments are elected. Members of the police are also able to deploy their contacts and police associations to run for office and despite it being illegal, the police often use strikes as political weapons. Thus the politicisation of the security system obstructs its effectiveness in curbing violence.

Finally, the privatisation of security challenges the notion that security is a public good. Commercial and private interests rather than the collective good are prioritised. Private security has been a thriving industry in Brazil for a number of years (Cubas 2002). It is widely tolerated, although illegal, for police officers to supplement their income by taking second jobs in the private security sector. Public resources are therefore employed to protect private interests. Some contractors have even been known to perpetrate massacres so as later to be able to sell their security service to the affected communities demonstrating how the industry can be parasitic in nature (Pereira 2008). It is a business that thrives on the failures of the public security system and profits from the context of an intense fear of crime, while itself generating yet more inequalities (e.g. in access to safety), mistrust, and segregation in society. Such structural, political and cultural characteristics of policing generate diverse, often contradictory narratives and experiences of securitisation.

Security for whom?

High-ranking government officials and high-ranking police made the case that the new security agenda had been innovative and successful in reducing crime, particularly homicide, and that this had benefited all citizens. However, this narrative obscures the perverse effects of securitisation, masking the ideologies that this agenda is based on. While the reform of state institutions, in particular the security apparatus, is desirable in order to foster the protection of the population, these institutions exist within a particular set of unequal social and power relations that repeatedly hinder or undermine reforms.

When particular methods of security are enforced, such as those that have embedded some of the ideals of modernisation and zero-tolerance policing, they can have spatial and social class implications (Davis 2013). Attempts to cleanse the streets of groups and communities who are perceived as disorderly, socially undesirable (e.g. the poor and marginalised) can be attractive to businesses and profit-seeking real estate developers, though ultimately this approach segregates social space and the polity along class and ethnic lines. Real estate developers have pressured residents in poor communities to sell their properties and relocate, especially where the communities have become desirable spaces for wealthy professionals, being close to the city centre and upper-class neighbourhoods by the seafront. The phenomenon of securitising the city through policing the poor has accompanied the growth of real estate developments and spreading skyscrapers in the city.

Moreover, securitisation poses challenges in the context of inadequate community-police relations, including lack of trust in the police, resulting in impediments to investigations, as seen in community's "law of silence". Issues of police corruption, class and ethnic discrimination revealed in the narratives of members of the security apparatus generate dilemmas when policing is rolled out to the poor. In the Brazilian context, low-ranking officers themselves identified the inadequacy of their training and the brutalising processes that they have encountered in the force as fundamentally incompatible with the principles of intelligence-led, consensual policing. As a result, new security interventions have not produced a sense of "security" or policing that is respectful of citizens' rights.

Blaming the poor: crack, social class and violence

The narratives examined in this section reveal the development of a counter-narrative to the punitive rhetoric about crime and criminals. In these narratives, criminals are not portrayed as outsiders who need to be incarcerated and eliminated from the public sphere. They are constructed as socially excluded and impoverished people with drug addictions, who ultimately epitomise public health problems in the country. This construction is paradoxical, as it "others" criminals along class lines since the police present classist understandings of the causes of crime. In this narrative, crime and poverty are inherently conflated.

State actors interviewed repeatedly made claims that blamed the poor for violence. Chief officers in the civil and military police argued that the problem of homicide in Pernambuco is caused by poverty and drug addiction. However, even official police data from the Department of Homicide and Protection to the Person in Pernambuco (DHPP-PE) show that only 32% of cases of homicide are drug-related (Nóbrega 2012, 129), leaving the majority of cases brought to the police classified as unrelated to drugs. Moreover, given that the police in Brazil only resolve few cases of homicide each year, with estimates that only 8% of homicide investigations are successfully completed (Costa 2015), it is difficult to make an accurate association between cause and effect.

Police interviewees argued that although in their view the new security agenda (*Pact for Life*, PPV) could reduce homicide rates through policing, it was necessary to do more to prevent the causes of crime. However, this would not be achieved simply through policing. Interviewees called for a less symptomatic approach. While the police claimed to be doing their job, which in their view was to arrest criminals, they did not believe this was the long-term solution to violence and crime in the city. As a securitisation approach, members of the police argued that PPV did not succeed in providing any type of social intervention – such as adequate drug rehabilitation or social assistance in the poor communities targeted by the program.

> The problem here is mainly related to the situation in poor communities. If you ask me today how many people I have arrested in middle class areas, I will tell you almost none. The crimes that we focus on today, like homicide, robbery followed by murder, mostly originate in poor communities in the periphery. The protagonists are from the periphery. Sometimes, they live in a house with no lighting, no food. If it weren't for these conditions, people wouldn't have the reduced moral values to point a gun at someone else to steal handbags. These people are excluded from society. This generates a revolt against our society. They will try to include themselves in their own way. We have a beautiful seafront, posh neighbourhoods. Then you go into the periphery they haven't even got pavements or paved roads. [...] The kids I see looking for food in the saucepans in their houses, and crying because there is no food – unfortunately they'll be my "clients" [arrested criminals] in the future. *Pact* [*for life*] is achieving results but not in relation to the causes of crime – in some cases it is not even poverty, it is *miséria* (extreme poverty)! [...] Often these crimes are related to the use of crack cocaine. We need preventative policies at the federal, state and local government level to deal with this. We also don't have enough rehabilitation centres in Pernambuco. They are all over-crowded. Ninety per cent of the homicides are linked to drug trafficking, either as dealers or as users, sometimes it is caused by a dispute, drug debt. Once we reduce the population of drug addicts we will also reduce homicides, because we will reduce the problem of drug debt and the demand for crack. I don't know if you have ever met a crack addict ... they have lost their lives and the ability to make decisions. If you ask them any questions, all they will tell you is "I want another rock [of crack cocaine]". Crack is a disease. This is a public health problem. If we treat it as a problem for the police, we will simply overflow prisons. This is not what we intend. But *Pact* [*for life*] is doing what it can within the limits of the police.
>
> (*Delegada*, civil police, Recife, 24 September 2013)

Here we see the association of the problem of violent mortality as one caused by poverty and drug addiction. Addicts accrue debts and pay with their lives. If only there were fewer addicts, there would be less drug debt and less demand for crack cocaine. In this way, broader, structural and institutional issues connected to drug trafficking – which is organised from outside poor communities, facilitated through financial institutions and political actors (Nóbrega 2012, 60) and enriches people higher up the scale – become marginal, and the only culprit to be targeted is the drug addict living in poverty.

In a context where firearms are readily available, where there is a population in either poorly paid work or unemployed, and where young people have access only to poor quality education and inappropriate policing, the problem of crime is individualised to an extent and the scapegoats are drug addicts. A wide international literature discusses the problems of individualising crime and placing blame on certain social groups, particularly young black men (Hall et al. 1978; Misse 1995, 2011; Young 1999, 2011; Caldeira 2000; Wacquant 2008; Fernandes 2013, 2014; Sousa Silva 2016). The point here is not to dismiss the destructive impact that the spread of crack cocaine can have in a community, or to explore the process of individualisation of crime, since this has already been written about. Instead, the objective is to examine the problematic contradictions within the narratives that focus on structural problems and yet simultaneously individualise these problems by placing the onus for crime on individual addicts. These explanations rely on opposing sets of values. Ultimately, the emphasis on locating the causes of crime at the level of individual failure (addiction) makes intelligible the punitive discourse that is deployed to justify repressive policing and incarceration and relegates compassion, restorative justice and rehabilitation to the periphery.

The *delegada* rightly points out the significance of the crack-cocaine epidemic in current levels of homicide in Brazil, as well as some of the continuing structural problems in Brazilian society – such as poverty, social inequality and inadequate infrastructure in poor communities – "they haven't got pavements or even paved roads". But there is no consideration of the fact that somewhere further up the ladder decisions were made to invest in repressive policing ("arresting criminals") as the main method of crime control instead of investing, for instance, in drug rehabilitation or in other social crime-prevention methods, such as demilitarised community policing, youth clubs, apprenticeships and employment opportunities.

According to Wolff (2014) the spread of crack cocaine in Recife brought instability to low-income communities with increases in violence associated with crack addiction. In Rio de Janeiro traffickers have been able to become organised and coercively establish their authority, informal law and social control over communities because they have access to more wealth, in comparison with Recife. Rio has a higher demand for cocaine from upper- and middle-class clients, and because of the geography of low-income communities in the city (which are often located in hilly areas with narrow alleyways) police and motorised access is more difficult and drug hiding-places more numerous. The case in Recife is dissimilar to Rio in many ways. Most of Recife's low-income communities are smaller, located on flat land and accessible by car, which facilitates motorised police action. Furthermore, while marijuana was the predominant drug in the northeast's drug market, the profits it provided were significantly smaller than those associated with the crack/cocaine trade. All these factors have made drug traffickers less powerful and less influential in Recife than in Rio de Janeiro, including in their degree of control over the local trade, thus enabling more competition and small-scale (albeit lethal) disputes.

The cocaine trade was never really established in Recife to the same extent as in Rio partly due to lower demand and because Recife's gangs are less wealthy and less organised (Koster 2009; Wolff 2014). As argued by Garmany (2011), the greater concentration of wealth in Brazil's south and southeast regions ensured that these regions had higher demand and a more thriving market for illicit drugs in comparison with the northeast region. Additionally, by being better connected in terms of transport, communication and technology, the drug market developed earlier in the southeast of the country. But by the late 1990s crack cocaine had started to spread in Recife, with the consequence that the city began to experience much higher rates of homicides than Rio de Janeiro. A cheaper and highly addictive drug, crack became widespread in poor communities. This analysis, which connects increasing homicide rates with a single factor – the spread of the crack market – is based on interviews with members of the police and therefore provides only a partial account of the dynamics of a high-homicide society. It is a skewed version of reality, which ignores the deaths that are seldom investigated and barely accounted for.

Regional differences in violence are important because the type of public security policy that needs to be provided must address those differences. Data from the Department of Homicide and Protection to the Person in Pernambuco (DHPP-PE) show that almost 32% of cases of homicide are related to drug trafficking, 28.2% are associated with vengeance, 20.5% are linked to interpersonal relations, 7.9% are considered crimes of passion, 7.16% are connected to death squads and 4.14% with fights (Nóbrega 2012, 127–129). These data refer to registered homicides. There is scope for inadequate categorisation or overlap, for example, if a person was killed by a death squad hired by drug traffickers or if the same criminal group operates as a death squad and drug trafficking organisation, how should the crime be categorised? Quantitative classifications can be somewhat blurred. One important point is that whether or not crack cocaine is the leading cause of lethal death in Recife, security interventions (such as PPV) do not seem equipped to deal with the root causes of crack addiction, neither are they able to deal with crime problems symptomatically. The expansion of repressive policing and incarceration as methods of crime control – part of the war on drugs in which it becomes the norm to blame the poor and drug-addicted for violent relations – obstructs understandings of the causes of crime and generates a skewed mode of control in which young and marginalised citizens are oppressed.

Silencing the poor?

Accountable problem-solving policing requires the public's cooperation, and information emanating from citizens (Lea and Young 1993; Jackson et al. 2013; Shiner 2016). So, in the context in which only the poor are being targeted by the securitisation apparatus, a key challenge is the "lei do silêncio" (or law of silence), that is, an unwritten rule in poor communities that residents will not talk to or inform the police, in other words, "no grassing". If, as according to residents in the communities studied, the police spend their time mostly in their cars or inside police stations, instead of establishing connections in the community, it is not surprising that people will not inform or trust the police. Police brutality, corruption and inefficiency are also factors leading to mistrust, so is residents' fear of revenge:

> One of the main challenges we face is the predominance of fear. I will give you a very clear example. There is a community, in area 5, Alto Jose Bonifácio, where an 11-year-old boy was playing on the steps leading up the hill. A guy on a motorbike is going up the steps [riding the motorbike actually on the steps] and shoots the boy. His mum and neighbours see it all, and the mum runs to him. The man in the motorbike threatens her: "You'll let him bleed to death there, you won't save him. And tell your other son to stop messing around in the area". This mother would not talk. She would not say anything about who did this. In a place like this, you'd never get any witnesses. If it wasn't for the investigations, phone taps and intelligence-led policing, we'd be immobilised. The way we investigate has improved.
>
> (*Delegada*, Civil Police, 7 October 2013)

How do the police obtain information if people refuse to talk to them? According to police interviewees, there is a need for covert police operations, such as telephone tapping, because people in poor communities are too scared to inform the police. As well as fear, lack of trust in the Brazilian justice system discourages witnesses from stepping forward, making it difficult to resolve cases, particularly homicide, leaving investigations either obstructed or reliant on indisputable evidence such as security camera footage, where this is available. But hard scientific evidence, such as fingerprints and DNA samples, are hardly reliable in Brazil, given that the police generally hear about cases long after the crime has occurred, are slow to respond to calls and usually do not bother to isolate the crime scene with cordons (Garmany 2011; Denyer Willis 2015).

In authoritarian regimes the police enforce security and conduct investigations by instilling fear, through brute and unrestricted force, often using torture, but these methods are unwarranted in democratic regimes, although they continue to be used (Zaverucha 2004; Huggins 2010). In a democratic society the police can only attempt to provide security and carry out investigations through means that are respectful of citizens' human rights, in cooperation with the public and with their consent (Uildricks 2009, 16; Shiner 2016). So the lack of dialogue between the police and the public, and the factors and relations that silence the poor – fear of retaliation, sporadic police presence, motorised distant policing, mistrust – are some of the problems that obstruct cooperative police-citizen relations and the implementation of democratic public safety interventions.

Ethnic, gender and class discrimination

Instead of addressing long-standing problems of segregation and discriminatory policing, securitisation has aggravated these issues, further restricting access to public space and reproducing social relations delineated by class, gender and ethnic lines. A moralising narrative about the poor is observed in interviewees' opinions about crime. Poverty and crime are discursively linked in discriminatory narratives that directly criminalise poor black people. Social class and "race" were mobilising factors in police-community interactions. This is not a surprising finding – it is well backed up by Brazilian and international literature (Hall et al. 1978; Zaluar 2004; Bowling and Phillips 2007; Barros 2008; Goodman and Ruggiero 2008; Wacquant 2008) – but nevertheless it is a rather enduring and bleak one. What is distinctive in the evidence here presented is the extent of discrimination, disdain and ethnic and social class divisions in the ways in which community-police relations took form, despite securitisation efforts.

The police are the most visible state institution, the "State on the streets" (Hinton 2006). Yet, the very nature of police work can enforce social distinctions and social divisions by enforcing the law against certain citizens in order to protect others. This generates an unequal distribution of safety. While some citizens receive police protection, others are the targets of police repression. This imbalanced provision of security and the way it affects diverse social groups is what González (2014, 24) calls "micro-citizenships", which is to say constrained or fragmented citizenships. The concept refers not only to the imbalance in the receipt of security provision, but also to its consequences, such as the likelihood that some citizens will refrain from public space and community participation due to fear of crime and inadequate protection, and also the likelihood that some groups will resort to extra-legal measures or "take the law in their own hands". At the very least, the unequal distribution of policing and disproportionate policing tactics – such as police racial profiling, verbal and physical confrontation with residents of poor communities – generate resentment and hostility towards the methods of the police. Residents, who demanded to be treated with respect and dignity, felt vulnerable to discriminatory and disproportionate policing practices.

Although in theory the police have the job of protecting any citizen in need and enforcing the law against perpetrators, in reality by targeting specific groups – for instance due to societal or institutional misconceptions and prejudice against particular groups or because a particular type of crime, prominent among certain social groups (e.g. drug-related offences instead of tax evasion or police violence) is targeted – the State and its repressive arm, the police, generate the fragmentation of citizenships (Neocleous 2000; González 2014). However, this fragmentation is not simply caused by enforcing the law to protect some groups of citizens against other citizen groups, but also by societal prejudice and decisions about enforcing *certain* laws and prioritising certain crimes.

Class discrimination is embedded into everyday interactions, in everyday talk, in the way spaces in the city are organised. It is widespread in Brazilian society in a way that is taken for granted by Brazilians. This is illustrated in the narrative of a high-ranking officer from the military police, who complained that a trendy new musical style in the community only attracted poor people to the area. He was nostalgic about the days when the clubs in the community played samba and attracted an upper-class clientele. He directly associates violence with poverty. Even the personal taste of the poor (e.g. *brega* music) is allegedly a cause for violence:

> We have this disorderly occupation [housing] in the *morros* [hillside communities], abandoned by the State. […] There is a lack of structure, lack of investment, lack of culture. They have a life that is different to the rest of the city. It is a different reality. If you walk past, [you will see that] these are party people. Sunday to Sunday there is always beer on the bar tables, the music is created in the community, those *bregas* [type of music]. It is mostly young people who are out and about. The other thing is that now it is natural here for women to be the mother *and the father* in the household. They get pregnant and they themselves raise the kids. So, what happens is, in these parties, there are a lot of drugs, some people are addicted, others use them regularly. In the past, the clubs in these communities played samba, now it is just *brega.* I have already talked to them to put the samba back on but they choose *brega.* It is a culture shock really. In the past, we had Martinho da Villa, Zeca Pagodinho [famous samba artists], the people that would come to these parties were upper class, you could tell, because they were coming from Boa Viagem [upper-class neighbourhood], and you could tell by their nice cars. With these people, there is no type of violence, no fights, no theft. But some people are seduced into the hill by young women that have active sexual lives, and then there are the traffickers, this is when violence occurs.
>
> (Major, military police, 1 August 2013)

Many Brazilian low-income communities and favelas operate as areas of symbolically creative and socially infamous encounters between classes, ethnicities and bohemian popular culture. The hallmarks of neoliberal literacy – such as entrepreneurialism and participation in new (musical) trends – are interestingly identified as evidence of immorality in places perceived as "vulgar" spaces targeted in urban-cleansing operations. Police narratives locate the blame for violence on poor young women and families seen as dysfunctional and therefore immoral. As he puts it, first, these women get pregnant (almost mysteriously, as the role of men in reproducing is neglected here), then they raise the children themselves – implicitly, these are the children who then become offenders. Then, these women, in his narrative, seduce people into the community, where once again, mysteriously violence occurs when presumably "seduced" people encounter drug traffickers. This moralising rhetoric quite unsubtly hints to the fact that these women are apparently "sexually irresponsible" and "single parents". Young women are thus constructed as a "moral danger" and young men as "criminals". The interstices of the asymmetrical power relations with regard to gender, class and age are mixed and meshed in a narrative that simply criminalises people in the peripheries of the city. But the nature of the *major*'s rhetoric does little to explain crime and much to place culpability on the victims of multiple forms of structural violence.

Even the musical taste of these populations, or any expression of their culture, is blamed and associated with violence. As social scientists have argued judging the tastes of the working class and the poor is a method of enforcing social distances and segregation by the dominant social classes (Bourdieu 1984; Skeggs 1997, 2004). For Bourdieu, the mechanism through which the dominant classes naturalise their representations and ideas is defined as "symbolic violence" and is developed by institutions and agents of authority. However, the association of crime with poverty, and the repression and criminalisation of activities associated with the poor, is not new in Brazil, as illustrated by the work of Holloway (1989) on the criminalisation of *capoeira* and the work of Chazkel (2011) on the *jogo do bicho* (a form of informal gambling known as "the animal game"). The behaviour and activities of lower classes in Brazil have historically been perceived by elites as distasteful and threatening, often leading to brutal reactions, surveillance and control by police (Holloway 1993). Poor black people are the subjects of the social practices that criminalise bodies and spaces, subjected to processes of structural, routine, institutionalised and symbolic violence.

Some officials admitted the problems of class and ethnic discrimination in the police at an institutional level, as well the problem of police corruption, and argued that more police are now dismissed due to this. While other officers denied discrimination or dismissed its extent, every official interviewed associated crime with poverty, and often with one's ethnicity, as shown in the extract below, where a homicide detective, a *delegada* at the Department of Homicide and Protection of Persons civil police station, argues that poor black people are the main "recruits" for criminal lifestyles.

> Nobody likes the police. *If I said that there is no corruption in the police and no discrimination in relation to race and class, I would be lying.* But now we have a lot more officers being dismissed. There is prejudice everywhere. But here today the "marginal" [criminal] doesn't have a stereotype anymore, a stereotype of colour. [...] But If I said that this is not a problem anymore

> I would be lying; it is the poor and black people that are still victims of this recruitment [into crime], unfortunately *they are still the main actors in the practice of crime*. If the police were just walking about the streets wearing uniforms, preventative police, people would like that. But if you go to make arrests, invade a community at night, knock down some doors to make an arrest, nobody likes that. There is no harmony in this relationship – of course not! But there is no guerrilla. There are exchanges of bullets between criminals and police but more in cases of retaliation, not simply because the police went into the community, this is rare.
>
> (Chief of civil police, 7 October 2013)

Crimes of the powerful, white-collar crimes and crimes committed by the police themselves are not considered. According to the police, "poor and black people" are "still the main actors in the practice of crime". This social representation is often used to justify the type of policing that is delivered to those perceived as criminal, which is repressive heavy-handed policing. As the chief of police put it, making "arrests, invading a community at night, and knocking down doors", all of which causes friction and disdain for the police.

In a study of racial profiling in the Pernambucan police, Barros (2008) conducted a survey with 923 participants (454 in training and 469 already working for the military police), 24 interviews and looked at 1,538 *Boletins de Ocorrência* (registered police crime records), finding that most officers (65%), most trainee officers (76.9%) and students in the school for non-commissioned officers (74%) believed that black or mixed race people are targeted during stop-and-searches. In line with the *delegada*'s views above, this approach (targeting on ethnic and class grounds) generates widespread distrust and dislike for the police. But rather than being unique to the police, such problems are endemic at most levels of the Brazilian state (Hinton 2006, 11) and, it could be argued, at most levels of Brazilian society. Police reforms and the implementation of PPV have not dealt with these issues. Although according to interviewees a number of dismissals due to corruption have occurred, the training of police and current internal oversight systems have not focused on addressing the lack of police accountability, institutional racism, classism and corruption in the force.

Rolling out policing

> We don't have enough officers. I have 740 officers in my battalion. Just one of the neighbourhoods we police has 11,000 inhabitants. We should have at least one officer for every 100 inhabitants to be able to act. In total my battalion polices an area of nearly 200,000 people. Also bear in mind that officers also take holidays, get ill and pregnant, so effectively, we have even fewer.
>
> (*Major*, military police, 1 August 2013)

Complaints about the insufficient number of police officers were common in interviews with the civil police. But the expansion of policing has the potential to drain state capacity and resources, while funnelling more investment into control and repressive practices. An issue that was emphasised in many experts' narratives was the need to recruit more and new staff since the new securitisation programme (PPV) had allegedly achieved results by focusing on cases of homicide and dealing with cases of murder within 24 hours of their occurrence. For experts, the regular monitoring of police targets and the bonus system for achievement were central to securitisation, but the achievement of targets depended on the police being well staffed.

Yet, policing has increased, and armed militarised police are even present inside public schools. This topic has raised much debate in Pernambuco, as well as internationally (Kupchik 2016). Research studies in the US have found that bringing police inside schools tends to increase the chances that young people will be arrested for minor behaviours and leads to poorer care for young people (ibid). In other words, more policing means more criminalisation. Moreover, police officers end up being asked to provide wider services, such as dealing with family crises and the effects of childhood trauma, without being adequately trained for this. One interviewed *major* chose a medical metaphor to explain his view of the need for armed policing in schools:

> Look, the gun is the tool of work for the police, just as the scalpel is a tool for the surgeon.
>
> (Major, school patrol, military police, 16 October 2013)

According to the *major*, the school patrol had been established prior to PPV and was seen as an essential aspect of policing. Schools, in particular state funded schools, had become besieged with firearms and with the spread of the drug trade – students were both dealing and using drugs at school – often this led to violent, and sometimes lethal, conflict at schools, generating a perceived need for policing. Yet, for the *major*, the school patrol did not just provide repressive law enforcement, it also became involved with educational work, including preventative talks to discourage young people from using and dealing drugs and encouraging them to participate in artistic and sport activities instead. These non-adversarial dialogues were seen as necessary to create opportunities to befriend young people and build positive relationships between the police and the young.

> [The school patrol] started a few years before *Pacto* [*pela vida*], around the year 2000, during the government of Jarbas. We provide motivational talks at schools, sometimes music, many of our officers are musicians or sports people. We try to dissuade young people, as parents ourselves, from becoming involved in a life in drugs.
>
> (Major, military police, 16 October 2013)

Despite the "armed police at school" polemic, young people in the schools that I visited during the fieldwork enjoyed the art and sport activities provided by the school patrol. In one particular school, young people had developed strong relationships with two well-liked officers who visited the school unarmed to provide talks and anti-drug motivational courses, but this was a small initiative with only two officers involved. What is deeply concerning here is the way in which securitisation tactics and processes gradually proliferate and become normalised. So deadly weapons in the hands of poorly trained, sometimes corrupt and violent police become justified and present even in spaces denominated for the purpose of educating children.

Becoming a soldier

This section explores the strongest self-critique of securitisation, which emerged from interviews with *soldados* ("soldiers"), those who are at the lowest and initial rank in the militarised police force and who patrol the streets. Their critique was centred on the inadequacies of the methods and ethos of policing in use, on the fallacies of brutalising training and working conditions, which they viewed as a form of socialisation of police to be violent. Among the interviewees, while the high-ranking officials involved in securitisation processes praised the government and PPV itself, officials further down the hierarchy tended to be more critical of the programme. Interviews conducted with low-ranking military police officers were arranged through a contact established a few years ago in one of the case-study communities. The interviewees were more critical of the government's approach to crime control. At times, the officers asked to stop voice-recording them, especially when they wanted to talk about issues that could lead to their detention for disciplinary action, since the militarised police continue to abide by a military code of conduct. This was most evident when they discussed data mishandling, violence and corruption in the police:

ROXANA: "How has the programme *Pact for Life* changed the work you do?"

OFFICER JÚLIA: "We have targets, like reducing homicides, but the ethos is still the same. Our boss wants us to be out on the streets slapping people, they don't understand that a lot of the work we could do is preventative, we could instead be talking to young people and doing some educational work about drugs and guns. Our boss is not interested in that. How can we reduce homicide with oppressive work? We are hardly trained to use a gun. I think I got a chance to try using one once in my training".

Interviewees claimed to have had hardly any firearms training and yet were given a gun to carry. Júlia's partner also said "I think I got to shoot a gun once during training, some people didn't even get one chance as there wasn't enough ammunition" (military police *soldado* Júlio, July 2013). While researchers have debated the variation in the training and use of armaments across nations, for instance, in the US officers are taught to shoot at the centre of mass and in Sweden police are taught to shoot at a suspect's legs (Maguire 2010, 200), the idea that a military police officer in Brazil can receive a gun to work with after having had hardly any training handling firearms raises concerns about the potential for more widespread and serious misuse of force. Furthermore, there is a danger that State use of violence can fulfil the "brutalisation hypothesis", which is the idea that state violence can encourage or be used to justify more violence by the general population (Shepherd 2005; Maguire 2010).

ROXANA: "Really? So what was the rest of the training like?"

OFFICER JÚLIA: "We have had hardly any training. I think we had about 4 months when we started a few years back. Most of the people who started with me have dropped out. One attempted suicide. We didn't get our pay for a while; some people couldn't afford the bus or food during training. It was quite a brutalising experience. You are treated with very little respect, you are shouted at, and your skills are not really put into use. I have a degree but have never used these skills at work".

While officers like Julia criticised police training – both its quality and availability – higher-ranking officials had claimed that the police were no longer trained to be brutal and violent, and that they were now in the service of communities rather than the State. There is a stark contrast between the claims made by the less powerful low-ranking and the more powerful and politically connected high-ranking officers.

> In the past we focused on serving [interests of] the State. So if we caught someone on the streets we would give them a beating. I am saying this because it is the reality. The police would kill. "Ah [if we come across] bandits we kill them", and that [approach] was seen as OK. People themselves would celebrate if a bandit was killed. But there has been an evolution in society. Things have changed with *Pacto*. Before, alcoholism was very common in the force, even in high-ranks. But, in 2004, we had this national training, which included a human-rights module. In 2007, *Pacto* started and it aims at preserving life, not killing. Today you have a different type of police. The police battalion that hits targets [of reducing homicide] will get a prize, a bonus at the end of the semester, say R$3,000 (approximately £700 at the time of the interview) for an official, R$1,500 for a *soldado* (initial rank in the military police). Pacto has been saving lives. [...] If you ask me, how many people have been killed by the police in my battalion since the start of Pacto, I can tell you, less than 10 people. That is a large difference in comparison to the 1990s.
>
> (Major, military police, 1 August 2013)

As seen in the two extracts above, while many high-ranking officials had argued that the police had become more humane under PPV and that the ethos of the police was no longer to kill, eliminate or beat criminals, lower-ranking officers casted doubt on the impact of brutalising police training. The initial plan of public security in Pernambuco had proposed a number of reforms. This included police training, such as training in harm reduction and in courses about: human rights, firearms, public law, violence against women, ethnic and racial relations, prevention and mediation of conflict (PESP-PE 2007, 114). The data emerging from interviews with officers suggests that either training proposals were not implemented, or they failed to reach a significant or sufficient part of the police force. Given that officers are equipped with firearms and continuously deal with issues that affect human rights, these training courses and refresher courses should reach all relevant members of the police.

The warrior ethos within the military police training continues to take precedence over the development of skills in negotiation and respect for human rights. The experiences of suffering and physical punishment in police training instigate the military mentality that lauds values associated with masculinity and the use of force, thus contributing to the enactment of police violence on the streets. So when residents in low-income communities did have contact with the police, it was the military ethos of the patrolling police that prevailed – the police were violent and abusive towards residents – practices that resonate with the hazing in police training (Huggins, Haritos-Fatouros, and Zimbardo 2002, 148) that is still predominant as argued by the military police *soldiers* interviewed.

Hazing in police training is a significant aspect of the creation of acceptability of violence (Huggins, Haritos-Fatouros, and Zimbardo 2002). According to Huggins, physically and psychologically punishing exercises, detention for failure to obey to arbitrary authoritarian commands, abusive name calling and status degradation are all part of the dehumanising militarised police training in Brazil during the military dictatorship years (1964–1985). According to my research participants in low-ranks of the PM, beyond the re-democratisation of Brazil, these same aspects of police training remain present in the militarised police.

Officers argued that the training they were subjected to was brutalising and did not prepare them to deal with civil society. They argued that among the initial recruits who started with them, most had decided to leave the police before their training had ended, seeing that this type of work "was not for them". Some of their colleagues had committed suicide, most suffered from anxiety and stress related to the training, work and to bullying from superiors. Interviewees also reported that there were months of delay between starting their training and getting their first salary; many had to survive in a situation of severe poverty, with no money for transport, accommodation or food. One trainee had come from the interior of the state and having no payment, no family or friendship networks to support him in the city, he would walk miles after training until the nearest hospital where he would check himself in, this was both his accommodation and a place to receive some form of nutrition – he received *soro* (intravenous hospital serum), as he could not afford to buy any food. What these examples show is that the institution of a culture of brutalisation in the police as an institution is not generated on the streets, but rather it is present and ingrained from within, noticed in the very beginning of officers' recruitment and training. The provision of basic police rights is significant to any police force or state that wants to reform because "ultimately human rights values can only be expected to be internalised by police if, they are treated likewise" (Uildricks 2009, 14).

Another problem with their training, according to participants, was that it was inconsistent and not available for all officers. For example, some officers had not received any training for 4 years, since they started working for the police. However, some of their colleagues had been selected and sent to further training courses. This privilege, they explained, was not universal as there were not enough officers to patrol each area, so further training would take them away from urgent patrolling duties. They explained that there had been some changes in the curriculum of the last set of recruited police officers, including the addition of a module on community policing. The officers interviewed had not received this training. They did not believe that their training could prepare them for policing civilian communities.

While in Huggins, Haritos-Fatouros, and Zimbardo's (2002) *Violence Workers* many officers had accepted the status quo, and became executioners, torturers or atrocity facilitators, my low-ranking participants critiqued the police force's training and practices and viewed those as archaic and in need of reform. This does not deny the role of hazing in police training in shaping the outcomes of the type of policing that is enacted on the streets. Many residents indeed complained about police violence and brutality. Certainly, militarised dehumanising and brutal training plays an important part in shaping the identities and practices of many officers in the force. However, while Huggins et al. aimed to interview police that were involved in atrocities, it must be noted that our samples are clearly different. My police sample was established on the basis of access, experience of having worked during the PPV years and willingness to be interviewed. Nonetheless, what both my data and Huggins' et al. data show is that the training of Brazilian police remains inadequate and brutalising.

The critique made by low-ranking officers went beyond the inadequacies of training and extant police culture. They also questioned the accuracy and reliability of police and homicide statistics and raised questions about the unequal distribution of policing across neighbourhoods. Those issues are illustrated in the extract below:

> During carnival I worked in the office computing the homicide stats. Our boss wants to hit the targets so that he gets a bonus. We were told not to compute some of the deaths. There was not much we could do, otherwise we would be at risk of disciplinary action. We can even be imprisoned. I don't really believe that *Pacto* [*pela Vida*] has made much difference. I live in a low-income community myself, we have hardly any policing. I see a police car pass by but I don't see them do anything. The police don't know how to approach, or stop and search a citizen. The police are sent to particular areas where they are on "show" or when it is near an election. [...] *Pacto pela Vida* made some changes. They divided the city in different areas [áreas integradas de segurança, or AIS], some motivational plans were created to motivate officers. And more officers were contracted. We definitely have a lot more police officers than we did before *Pacto*.
>
> (Officer Júlia, military police)

Officer Júlia, just like other residents in the community, expressed a lack of satisfaction with the type of policing that is available in low-income communities. Many of Brazil's low-ranking officers, like Júlia and her colleague, live in the very low-income communities that are the subjects of police criminalisation, where much of the population is targeted as "suspect". The officers' complaints were very similar to those of the residents. They see a police car occasionally going past but they do not see any intelligence-led policing taking place or any actual policing on the streets. Just as the majority of interviews with officers and officials emphasised, securitisation is focused on repressive and sporadic policing action and very little on preventative work.

During an interview with two low-ranking police officers who both live in low-income communities, they asserted that despite the fact they are police officers living in the community, there is not enough policing actually taking place in their communities. They argued that the police are in fact rarely present, and even when they are present there is much corruption in the high-ranks of the police, so that if they arrest a drug trafficker, he will have important political allies or friends in the police and the case will be dropped. The continuation of trafficker power and violence in poor communities can be associated with extended networks between criminals, politicians, state actors and community actors.

The officers interviewed argued that they knew better than to interfere in their own community, where they felt vulnerable and where their families are exposed to arbitrariness and risk experiencing cruelty and vengeance from local criminals. Both officers claimed that most of the increase in police presence seen during the implementation of PPV focuses on protecting high-income neighbourhoods, especially during election periods. Throughout the last election period, the mayor extended the number of police cars and officers and asked them to go on "display" to upper-class neighbourhoods. In the officers' words: *Foi um puro circo* (literally, "It was a pure circus [show]").

Conclusion

This chapter's findings warrant at least two important contributions to the debate on security and the criminological literature. Firstly, they expose some of the ingrained and continuing forms of social and power inequalities extant in the security apparatus, as well as its institutional failure to address deep-seated and longstanding issues of corruption and discrimination, which primarily affect people living in low-income communities. Second, they enable an examination of a counter-narrative about securitisations emerging from state actors themselves. This counter-narrative illustrates concerns about the inadequacy of increased and repressive policing in resolving crime in Brazil, as well as concerns about the structure of the police and the type of police training that is available. As suggested in the introduction of this chapter, these findings complement a growing body of literature about policing in the Global South.

The enduring issues of classism, sexism and racism in the police, explored in this chapter, impede the possibility of consensual intelligence-led policing, raising questions regarding the suitability of the adopted approaches to make spaces safer. The absence of any attempt to improve the quality of police-community interactions, compounded by a lack of trust in the police, ultimately reinforces the "law of silence" (the informal rule of not informing on somebody, not "snitching") in poor communities. Problems in the training and brutalisation of officers before they start working also reduce the prospects for positive community-police relations. In other words, it was argued that continuing and unaddressed issues of classism, racism and training in the public security apparatus mar the application of safety policies and interventions, insofar as these policies cannot promote the safety of the most marginalised and vulnerable if these populations are continuously perceived and treated as criminal and undeserving of respectful treatment.

References

Barros, G. d. S. 2008. "Filtragem racial: a cor na seleção do suspeito." *Revista Brasileira de Segurança Pública* 2 (3): 134–155.

Bayley, D. H. 2001. "Democratizing the Police Abroad: What to Do and How to Do It." *Issues in International Crime*. June 2001. Number: NCJ 188742. Washington, D.C: U.S. Department of Justice Office of Justice Programs. p. v–132. Accessed 13 January 2020. https://ncjrs.gov/Pdffiles1/Nij/188742.Pdf.

Bayley, D. H. 2006. *Changing the Guard: Developing Democratic Police Abroad*. New York: Oxford University Press.

Bourdieu, P. 1984. *Distinction: A Social Critique of the Judgement of Taste*. Cambridge, MA: Harvard University Press.

Bowling, B., and C. Phillips. 2007. "Disproportionate and Discriminatory: Reviewing the Evidence on Police Stop and Search." *The Modern Law Review* 70 (6): 936–961.

Caldeira, T. P. d. R. 2000. *City of Walls: Crime, Segregation, and Citizenship in São Paulo*. Berkeley: University of California Press.

Carrington, K., R. Hogg, and M. Sozzo. 2016. "Southern Criminology." *British Journal of Criminology* 56 (1): 1–20.

Chazkel, A. 2011. *Laws of Chance: Brazil's Clandestine Lottery and the Making of Urban Public Life*. Durham, NC: Duke University Press.

Chevigny, P. 1995. *Edge of the Knife: Police Violence in the Americas*. New York: New Press.

Costa, A. T. M. 2015. "A (in)efetividade da justiça criminal brasileira: Uma análise do fluxo de justiça dos homicídios no Distrito Federal." *Civitas: Revista de Ciências Sociais* 15: 11–26.

Cubas, V. 2002. "A expansão das Empresas de Segurança Privada em São Paulo." Masters in Sociology, University of São Paulo, São Paulo.

Davis, D. E. 2013. "Zero-Tolerance Policing, Stealth Real Estate Development, and the Transformation of Public Space: Evidence from Mexico City." *Latin American Perspectives* 40 (2): 53–76. doi:10.1177/0094582x12467761.

Denyer Willis, G. 2015. *The Killing Consensus: Police, Organized Crime, and the Regulation of Life and Death in Urban Brazil*. Oakland: University of California Press.

Fernandes, F. L. 2013. "Youth Gang Members in Rio de Janeiro: The Face of a 'Lost Generation' in an Age of Fear and Mistrust." *Bulletin of Latin American Research* 32 (2): 210–223. doi:10.1111/blar.12030.

Fernandes, F. L. 2014. "The Construction of Socio-Political and Symbolical Marginalization in Brazil: Reflecting the Relation between Socio-Spatial Stigma and Responses to Violence in Rio de Janeiro." *International Journal of Humanities and Social Science* 4 (2): 52–67.

Garmany, J. 2011. "Situating Fortaleza: Urban Space and Uneven Development in North-Eastern Brazil." *Cities* 28: 45–52.

González, Y. M. 2014. "State Building on the Ground: Police Reform and Participatory Security in Latin America." PhD, Princeton University.

Goodman, A., and V. Ruggiero. 2008. "Crime, Punishment, and Ethnic Minorities in England and Wales." *Race/Ethnicity: Multidisciplinary Global Contexts* 2 (1): 53–68.

Hall, S., C. Critcher, T. Jefferson, J. Clarke, and B. Roberts. 1978. *Policing the Crisis: Mugging, the State, and Law and Order*. London: Macmillan.

Harig, C. 2014. *The Paradox of Brazil's Militarised Public Security*. Strife. Accessed 10 April 2015. http://strifeblog.org/2014/07/11/the-paradox-of-brazils-militarised-public-security/.

Hinton, M. 2006. *The State on the Streets: Police and Politics in Argentina and Brazil*. Boulder, MA and London: Lynne Rienner.

Holloway, T. H. 1989. "'A Healthy Terror': Police Repression of Capoeiras in Nineteenth-Century Rio de Janeiro." *The Hispanic American Historical Review* 69 (4): 637.

Holloway, T. H. 1993. *Policing Rio de Janeiro: Repression and Resistance in a 19th-Century City*. Stanford, CA: Stanford University Press.

Huggins, M. K. 1998. *Political Policing: The United States and Latin America*. Durham, NC: Duke University Press.

Huggins, M. K. 2010. "Systemic Police Violence in Brazil." In *Police Use of Force: A Global Perspective*, edited by J. B. Kuhns and J. Knutsson, 73–82. Santa Barbara, CA, Denver, CO, and Oxford: Praeger.

Huggins, M. K., M. Haritos-Fatouros, and P. G. Zimbardo. 2002. *Violence Workers: Police Torturers and Murderers Reconstruct Brazilian Atrocities*. Berkeley, Los Angeles, and London: University of California Press.

Jackson, J., B. Bradford, B. Stanko, and K. Hohl. 2013. *Just Authority? Trust in the Police in England and Wales*. London and New York: Routledge.

Koster, M. (2009). "In Fear of Abandonment: Slum Life, Community Leaders and Politics in Recife, Brazil." PhD, Wageningen University, Netherlands.

Kupchik, A. (2016). "Why Are Police Inside Public Schools?" *The Conversation*, September 7.

Lea, J., and J. Young. 1993. *What Is to Be Done about Law and Order? Crisis in the Nineties*. London: Pluto.

Maguire, E. R. 2010. "Conclusion: A Journey through the World of Police Use of Force." In *Police Use of Force: A Global Perspective*, edited by J. B. Kuhns and J. Knutsson, 199–212. Santa Barbara, CA, Denver, CO, and Oxford: Praeger.

Mesquita Neto, P. d. M. 2011. *Ensaios sobre segurança cidadã*. São Paulo: Quartier Latin; Fapesp.

Misse, M. 1995. "Cinco Teses Equivocadas Sobre A Criminalidade Urbana No Brasil." *Estudos* 91: 23–40.

Misse, M. 2011. *Crime e Violência No Brasil Contemporaneo: Estudos de Sociologia do Crime e da Violencia Urbana*. 2nd ed. Rio de Janeiro: Lumen Juris.

Neocleous, M. 2000. *The Fabrication of Social Order: A Critical Theory of Police Power*. Sterling, VA: Pluto Press.

Nóbrega, J. M. J. 2012. *Homicídios no Nordeste: Dinamica. Relações causais e desmistificação da violência homicida*. Campina Grande: EDUFCG.

Pereira, A. W. 2008. "Public Security, Private Interests, and Police Reform in Brazil." In *Democratic Brazil Revisited*, edited by P. R. Kingstone and T. J. Power, 185–208. Pittsburgh, PA: University of Pittsburgh Press.

PESP-PE. 2007. *Plano Estadual de Seguranca Publica: PACTO PELA VIDA*. Recife: Cultura. www.seres.pe.gov.br/index/pacto_pela_vida.pdf

Shepherd, J. M. 2005. "Deterrence versus Brutalization: Capital Punishment's Differing Impacts among States." *Michigan Law Review* 104 (2): 203–256.

Shiner, M. 2016. "Drug Policing: What Is It Good for?" After the Drug Wars: Report of the LSE Expert Group on the Economics of Drug Policy. www.lse.ac.uk/IDEAS/publications/reports/pdf/LSE-IDEAS-After-the-Drug-Wars.pdf.

Skeggs, B. 1997. *Formations of Class and Gender: Becoming Respectable*. London: SAGE.

Skeggs, B. 2004. *Class, Self, Culture*. London: Routledge.

Soares, L. E. 2000. *Meu casaco de general: 500 dias no front da segurança pública do Rio de Janeiro*. São Paulo: Companhia das Letras.

Sousa Silva, E. 2016. "Reflections on Favelas and Public Security: Maré as a Point of Reference". Dialogues on Public Security: Experiences in Brazil and in the UK, on 26th February 2016, Queen Mary University of London.

Tavares Dos Santos, J. V. 2009. *Violências e Conflitualidades*. Porto Alegre: Tomo.

Uildricks, N. 2009. *Policing Insecurity: Police Reform, Security, and Human Rights in Latin America*. Lanham, MD and Plymouth: Lexington Books.

Wacquant, L. c. J. D. 2008. *Urban Outcasts: A Comparative Sociology of Advanced Marginality*. Cambridge and Malden, MA: Polity.

Wolff, M. J. 2014. "Criminal Authorities and the State: Gangs, Organized Crime, and Police in Brazil." PhD, University of New Mexico, USA.

Young, J. 1999. *The Exclusive Society: Social Exclusion, Crime and Difference in Late Modernity.* London: SAGE.

Young, J. 2011. *The Criminological Imagination.* Cambridge and Malden, MA: Polity.

Zaluar, A. 2004. *Integração Perversa: Pobreza e Tráfico de drogas.* Rio de Janeiro: FGV.

Zaverucha, J. 2000. "Fragile Democracy and the Militarization of Public Safety in Brazil." *Latin American Perspectives* 27 (3): (Violence, Coercion, and Rights in the Americas) 8–31.

Zaverucha, J. 2004. *Policia Civil de Pernambuco: O Desafio da Reforma.* Recife: Editora Universitaria UFPE.

Chapter 5

Reforming the system

This chapter continues to interrogate the nature of the regional criminal justice system by exploring in more detail the changes that occurred since the implementation of the *Pact for Life* programme. It deconstructs official narratives about "success", questioning the ways in which such success is framed, who it affects and how it changes the region's landscape. Such an approach, when critically informed by – and engaged with the limitations of – the work of critical criminologists reveals similarities in the penal management of poverty around the globe. Investigating the spread of managerial criminology to Brazil, drawing on statistical data and on my own field notes, I challenge dominant approaches to crime control by illustrating their perverse effects in the Brazilian context. Some of these include the exacerbation of inequalities, the fallacious idea that the modernisation of the criminal justice system and a focus on public management can control crime, the unsustainable growth of prison populations and the expansions of burdens on the criminal justice system, when solutions to crime problems may be better found elsewhere.

Some of the chapter's guiding questions are as follows: What practical changes have occurred in the field of public security since the implementation of securitisation programmes (*Pacto pela Vida* programme, PPV)? How do experts (policy-makers and practitioners) explain the decline in homicides in Pernambuco? What, in their opinion, are the current challenges in the field of public security? These questions are important and are worth analysing not only because they examine recent developments in an understudied geographical area but also because they refer to the relation between state and society, which exposes the effectiveness of civic rights – such as the right to safety, protection from arbitrary arrest and police brutality and access to a fair trial – as they have been enforced in Northeast Brazil.

First, the chapter provides an overview of this current programme of public security and police reform in Pernambuco. Second, it begins to examine the narratives of state agents involved with this programme, focusing on their alleged achievements and the challenges that they face. This leads to a discussion of the perverse effects that can be seen in instances where crime control policies from the Global North have been emulated in the Global South. It concludes with an analysis of the theoretical implications of these developments.

Overview of public security reforms

Most Latin American police forces are notoriously corrupt, inefficient and militarised (Chevigny 1995; Huggins, Haritos-Fatouros, and Zimbardo 2002; Macaulay 2007; Mesquita Neto 2011). In the last two decades, a number of police reform initiatives have been developed and implemented in Latin American countries (Frühling 2009; Husain 2009), often in response to growing perceptions that the police and criminal justice systems are not adequately responsive to citizens, do not provide security and justice and are not accountable to the law or to the communities they serve (Mesquita Neto 2006, 153). The system lacks legitimacy, professionalism, accountability and respect for human rights – essential parts of an internationally visible police reform agenda. Increasingly high crime rates have led to demands for improved security policies and policing (Tulchin and Ruthenburg 2006). It is in this context that PPV emerged.

State actors who were interviewed explained that PPV had emerged in response to the extreme levels of violence and high homicide rates in Pernambuco, and the growing perception that the public security apparatus and the police urgently needed to address the situation. Although over 100 project ideas were proposed in the initial PPV plan (PESP-PE 2007; Ratton, Galvão, and Fernandez 2014), only some were implemented. The implemented parts of the programme had been focused on the governance of the police (interview with sociologists involved with the design of PPV, July 2013).

It is unclear how the process of policy implementation took place and why only certain lines of action were implemented. Neither State actors nor members of civil society involved with the programme could provide a justification for this. Some claimed that there were some social crime prevention programmes, such as the project "Atitude", which provides arts training for ex-offenders trying to overcome addiction. Such programmes were very small in size and unable to cope with the demand. A key critique of the securitisation agenda is the State's failure to implement a social or humanised version of security (Amar 2013). The perceived setbacks of PPV, such as the return of rising homicide rates, were perceived as a result of the lack of implementation of all projects initially proposed (Maciel 2015). Some of the important and not implemented projects relate to the failure to create a council of public security responsible for the democratic management of PPV; improvements to the quality of life in low-income communities, such as improvements to the health service and measures to tackle racial violence (ibid).

The implemented projects displayed similarities to the violence and crime-reduction strategies deployed in cities such as New York, Bogotá and Belo Horizonte, insofar as they focused on the application and management of information, crime statistics and police targets. This led Macedo to argue that the programme suffered from "institutional isomorphism" (2012, 28), because it mimicked and appropriated governance and social control measures developed elsewhere. Overall, PPV's model of securitisation focuses on the expansion of the use of institutions of social control such as the police and the prison, thus emphasising the panoptic model of governance long ago noted by Foucault (1979).

Even though many of the projects originally proposed were not implemented, investment in security grew rapidly. Using data from the federal government system of integrated financial administration (SIAFI), Macedo (2012, 84) estimated that investment in public security in Pernambuco grew by 717.4% from 2006 to 2010. Detailed information about the distribution of this investment does not exist. However, interview data and initial evaluations of PPV (Macedo 2012; Wolff 2014) show that the intervention focused far more on repressive policing than on the social and economic projects originally proposed.

One of the most visible changes with the implementation of PPV is the establishment of a computerised system of monitoring and management of police work, comparable to the American model COMPSTAT, which seeks to make chiefs of police accountable for dealing with crimes committed in the areas for which they are responsible. Police work in Pernambuco was territorialised and divided into 26 catchment areas, or *Áreas de Segurança Integrada* (AIS), geographical "areas of integrated security". The PPV management committee meets weekly and monthly to compare, monitor and discuss data gathered in each of these 26 areas of security. Once these meetings are over, the information is not made available to the public (Macedo 2012, 101). A number of police operations[1] are monitored in these meetings, for example: operation *Malhas da Lei*, which monitors the enforcement of arrest warrants in operations by civil and militarised police; operation *Repressão ao Crack*, which monitors the amount of crack cocaine seized and the number of flagrant arrests; operation *Autoria CVLI*, which monitors the degree of resolution of police investigations into intentional lethal crime; operation *CVLI Focos quails*, which monitors the number of police investigations submitted to the justice system in cases of serious crimes where the offenders have been identified; operation *Mandados*, which monitors the number of prison warrants resulting from the integrated work of chiefs of police and the public ministry; operation *Repressão ao Crack 1*, which monitors the number of drug selling points identified by police operations.

The implementation of PPV has also come with increasing use of situational crime prevention methods (Clarke 1997; Clarke and Felson 2004), that is, not only more policing to reduce criminal opportunities, but also closed-circuit television (CCTV) cameras in some locations, electronic monitoring tags for offenders, geo-mapping of hot spots and the placement of ambulances in hot spots to attempt to save the lives of victims of violence. These developments are problematic on a number of levels that are discussed below.

First, three main contested ideologies provide the basis for this model, all of which emerge from the mainstream criminological theories of the Global North. These include (1) deterrence theory (Nagin 2012) through increased policing and incarceration, (2) situational crime prevention theory, as mentioned above, and (3) rational choice theory (Clarke and Felson 2004). The rationale for these theoretical frameworks is that crime is inevitably going to happen – unless the opportunities in the environment are reduced – because it perceives rational individuals as calculating the risks and opportunities of offending. By assuming the inevitability of crime, and adopting an approach that focuses on the management of crime, instead of focusing on addressing the causes of crime, the model neglects the significance of structural, racial, gendered and economic inequalities in motivations to commit interpersonal violent crime. It also marginalises the irrational and emotive aspects of crime, such as bravado, rivalry and jealousy.

The second problem relates to the impacts of this managerial model of control. The model emphasises State definitions of crime, tending to focus on controlling certain crimes, such as drug-related street offenders rather than for instance the violence caused by corporations in environmental disasters or the persecution of drug barons higher up in the hierarchy of the drug trade or even the violence committed by state actors (e.g. the police). The outcome of this is the aggravation of social inequalities by targeting the easier to catch (read poorer) suspects. Remarkably, the impact of the focus on police work is to the detriment of any social measures of security intervention initially proposed by PPV, including social work, training programmes and employment schemes for young people who are likely to become involved with the drug trade and violence.

The policing and targeting of drug-related offenders by arresting them and seizing their drugs assume that targeting drugs equals reducing violence and draws more young people into the youth and criminal justice system. Preventative social measures should take effect before young people become involved in the drug trade, and before they enter the costly, brutalising and inhumane Brazilian criminal justice system (Rosenblatt 2012). Therefore, the programme's emphasis on monitoring, for example, the amount of narcotics apprehended replicates parts of the contested system of security governance of the war on drugs (Simon 2007).

The third problem is that some of PPV's operations were circumstantial and discontinued, raising concerns about the temporality and unsustainability of safety interventions. Fourth, PPV's structure of governance, for the most part, reveals that only data produced by the State or the police are used as indicators for monitoring outputs or "success" and police performance, as illustrated above in the list of some of the police operations and programmes that were put in practice. The absence of adequate means of external control is an important critique raised by members of civil society. This selective use of outputs for monitoring jettisons the importance of relational aspects of policing such as police accountability, citizens' perspectives about police performance and data from victimisation surveys as opposed to police data. The consequences and challenges of this approach are discussed in the remainder of this chapter.

The views of state actors: alleged achievements and challenges

This section examines extracts from in-depth interviews conducted with "experts", including high-ranking state officials involved with the development and implementation of PPV. These include executives and high-ranking members of the police – both the plain clothed investigative civil police (*Polícia Civil* or PC) and the uniformed patrolling militarised police (*Polícia Militar* or PM). High-ranking officials were keen to praise the government's security policy. This is not surprising, given that patronage, hierarchy and political connectedness play important roles in police and government officials' promotions and career prospects in Brazil (cf. Pereira 2008, 199; Denyer Willis 2015, 131–132). Nonetheless, interviewees' narratives enable an analysis of a hegemonic discourse about security interventions and at least illustrate some of the challenges in the field of public security.

According to most high-ranking interviewees, the governor had been brave and ambitious to take on-board the challenge of discussing and addressing the public security problem in Pernambuco, as this was seen as an unsavoury, politically dangerous and difficult topic. Interestingly, it is precisely the image of doing something about law and order that has been attractive to different electorates around the world (Chevigny 2003; Frühling 2009; Malone 2012). In fact, as argued by Uildriks (2009, 16) "all too often police reforms and initiatives to improve the quality of policing are the result of opportunistic and political considerations".

During the ten-year period, that is 2002–2012, lethal violence was on the rise in most states in the northeast region of Brazil – except in Pernambuco,[2] where homicide rates declined between 2008 and 2012 (Nóbrega 2012, 21; Ratton 2014, 11; Waiselfisz 2014, 26). The policy-makers and practitioners who were interviewed offered a series of explanations for this, all of which related to PPV. This is illustrated in the following interview extract with a senior member of the management of the public security secretariat:

> Having the political will is a start. Also, another point is the model of management by results. Third, there is investment; we increased [the security budget] from 20 million [Reais] per year to around 80 million [Reais] per year. It varies from year to year [...] there are plenty of areas of investment that are not included in these 80 million, but they are also important, such as training and recruitment. But this 80 million is mostly structural investment, such as investing in police stations, appropriate cars for the police, appropriate uniforms, guns, bullet-proof vests, handcuffs. [...] we have recruited 10,000 new professionals over the last 10 years. [....] There are cases when you invest in a certain municipality, in all those things, but without achieving a reduction in violence and criminality, so something is missing there. I think it is the model of management by results that we have applied with *Pact* [PPV] that is important.
>
> (23 September 2013)

While experts claimed that the ideas implemented by PPV were innovative, they share many similarities with models of police reform in countries such as the US. For example, PPV emulated performance management systems, such as COMPSTAT, and shared an emphasis on increasing incarceration, just as seen in America's widely contested zero tolerance policing (Dennis 1997; Burke 1998; Young 2011; Silverman and Della-Giustina 2001; Bratton 2005; Dixon 2005; Jones and Newburn 2007; Newburn and Jones 2007).

In fact, measuring police performance is not new in Brazil. For example, the Minas Gerais police went through a number of reforms in partnership with research and academic organisations during the 1990s and 2000s (Ward 2006, 177–179). The idea of territorialising police work by creating new geographical distinctions is not new either. This approach was also adopted in 1999 in Rio de Janeiro in an attempt to better organise and improve public security provision (Husain 2009, 77). It is noticeable that in the opinion of all the government experts interviewed, the results allegedly achieved by PPV were an outcome of investment in *more policing*, including investing in resources; in the *tools* of policing, such as guns and safety equipment; and in investment in the *management* of police work, such as making the police responsible for certain areas and monitoring their targets through the State Planning and Management Secretariat (SEPLAG). This administrative approach raises a number of issues and it assumes that crime can only be prevented through the criminal justice system.

Social measures, by contrast, which can prevent crime, are undermined (e.g. the creation of youth clubs, leisure activities, apprenticeships, quality employment, better education, educational campaigns and substance misuse treatment). Social measures, such as those mentioned, have potential to avoid the long-term impacts of the excessive use of the criminal justice system for criminalised individuals, for society and for the resources of the State.

Despite PPV's managerialism and focus on more policing, its implementers deployed a specific narrative about crime, one that assumed that the responsibility for crime lies beyond the work of the police; a narrative that emphasised shared responsibility among government agencies and society. Once again, this is not a new idea (Garland 1996), not even in the Brazilian context. The federal government had since 2000 launched the National Public Security Plan with comparable principles where responsibility for security is concerned (Mesquita Neto 2011, 391). Macaulay (2007, 645–646) corroborates Garland's (1996) thesis, positing that under high levels of crime, States delegate responsibility to other agencies and social actors, especially where radical criminal justice reforms are unlikely to bring about electoral benefits. An interview with a *Delegada* in the homicide department illustrates the embedment of this narrative of delegating responsibility for crime:

> Many people think safety is a question to be addressed by the police but there's a lot more to it than that. There are issues around education, sanitation, and so on. *Pacto* came to unite all these elements with the objective of reducing criminality in the state of Pernambuco, especially focusing on lethal and intentional violent crime. You will hear a lot about this CVLI (*Crimes Violentos Letais Intencionais* or Intentional Lethal Violent Crimes). The fire-fighters also became involved, there is more planning, and government bodies now have shared targets. So for example, lighting in one area may help reduce criminality so CELPE (an electricity company) may be involved, or closing a bar in another area might help. In summary, we are all [in it] together, with the same objective, which is to reduce lethal crime, which has been happening over the last few years. [...] The state of Pernambuco has been divided into 26 areas, some need more attention than others. For example, [points to a map] this area here, Santo Amaro, was very violent, but now we have about three homicides per month there.
>
> (*Delegada*, civil police, 7 October 2013)

High crime rates have led officials to cast doubts on the ability of the traditional institutions to control crime. Thus, the responsibilisation narrative has emerged in tandem with the acceptance of the limits of the State in crime fighting. This requires multi-agency working, an issue that is further illustrated in an interview with a military police chief (*major*) in Pernambuco:

> We used to think of security as a problem for the police but now it is everyone's responsibility. All the different state agencies are responsible for security. For example, the secretariat of education is responsible too, they need to make sure the schools do not provide opportunities for drug use, they need to make sure the school has appropriate lighting, make sure they engage the students.
>
> (School patrol, military police, 16 October 2013)

The process of expanding the narrative of "security" and widening the responsibility for crime fighting has long been observed in Anglo-Saxon countries, for example in the UK and US (Garland 1996, 2001). This narrative and agenda has been simultaneous with the steady escalation of the size and scope of state agencies of criminal justice and increases in the numbers of cases processed (ibid) in these countries, as well as with continuing international US police assistance, such as the provision of police training (Leeds 2014; Diario de Pernambuco 2015a).

An example of the expansion of the criminal justice system is seen in increasing numbers of investigations being conducted and growing numbers of people being incarcerated. For instance, although homicide investigations may refer to cases committed in previous years, the number of cases investigated in 2007 was equivalent to only 5.4% of the 4,592 homicides committed that year[3] in Pernambuco (Nóbrega 2012, 126). Between September 2008 and July 2009 there was an increase of 430% in the number of police investigations submitted to the criminal justice system in Pernambuco (ibid 156). Despite the tardiness of the Brazilian courts in processing these cases, 21% of them led to imprisonment (ibid). This is a sharp increase in cases brought to justice in comparison to years prior to 2007.

While a growing body of literature has critiqued the consequences of the growth of the penal State (Garland 2001; Wacquant 2009; Cunneen et al. 2013), for the experts interviewed, this new way of working is responsible for the alleged successes of PPV. According to many interviewees, a shift in the way the police would achieve promotions was also an important managerial reform implemented through PPV. Brazilian public office and promotions are notoriously known to be achieved through personal contacts and via a hierarchical structure (cf. Soares 2000), but promotions in PPV would (allegedly) be achieved by results, as argued by the chief of Pernambuco's civil police:

> We began to concentrate on management by results, and we began to have management indicators. In the past, to reach a higher rank in the police one would need around 18 years of experience. But in the new model what mattered were results, so this gave young officers an opportunity and they embraced the changes. [...] This is a change in culture. Before 2007 you had no targets, you worked if you felt like it. [...] In 2009, the bonus system was created, so officers had an incentive to hit targets, for seizing firearms and/or crack cocaine, for example. The culture of private businesses is now implemented inside a public institution – the police.
>
> (24 September 2013)

The idea that there has been a change in police culture, in particular a change towards the "culture of private businesses", as the chief of Pernambuco's civil police claims above, is a crucial tenet of the contested managerial criminology of the Global North (Feeley and Simon 1992; Brownlee 1998; Garland 2001). Under the managerial approach, humanitarian ideals have been misplaced in the move towards business-like and efficiency-oriented policies in which quantitative outputs (e.g. the number of people processed through the criminal justice system) have priority over the ideals of rehabilitation and social crime prevention (e.g. investment in educational programmes and employment and training opportunities for offenders or groups at risk of offending). This approach presents dangers and inherent contradictions to the idea of "efficiency", because, it makes the criminal justice system larger and overburdened, therefore also more expensive and harder to manage (Brownlee 1998).

According to some high-ranking experts, another outcome of PPV was that the investigative police (civil police) began to investigate crimes prior to making arrests. This was an important shift, one that was seen as a new approach in the Brazilian context, which was named *repressão qualificada*, but the idea resembles "intelligence-led" policing. It entails gathering information before making arrests rather than making arrests and subsequently attempting to extract confessions from suspects (often through the use of methods of torture). This is expressed in an interview with the chief of the Pernambuco's civil police:

> Before, the police would go into a favela and kick all the doors down, regardless of whether people were innocent or guilty. People in favelas are poor, that doesn't mean that they're all criminals. Now with this new concept, police intelligence began to have value. In the beginning of Eduardo's government we had 6 people working in intelligence, now we have 200 people. Now the police have a new reality.
>
> (24 September 2013)

This alleged change implies that the police in Pernambuco are now more democratic in the sense that they no longer simply "kick all the doors down" in poor communities to investigate crime. But rather, the police now investigate crimes prior to making arrests with its increased number of intelligence specialists. This is an important point but it significantly contradicts arguments by lower-ranking members of the police and the accounts of community residents that emphasise continuous arbitrary policing and abuse of force. So while politically connected and high-ranking state actors made claims about the innovations, modernisation and democratisation of the police, lower-ranking officials contested these claims and presented further critiques of the public security apparatus. Moreover, the experiences and narratives of community residents and activists challenge any claim that the police have become more democratic, insofar as policing continues to be unequally applied, targeting suspects on the basis of their social status rather than any actual information that has been gathered.

The limits of current modes of control

Although the dominant discourse emerging from government officials and high-ranking members of the public security apparatus is that PPV had reduced homicides in Pernambuco, and is therefore the sole cause for claims of success, more needs to be said about the effects of this programme of state building and about the potential for confounding causal variables. Kahn (2011) argued that the reduction in homicides in Pernambuco, Minas Gerais, Rio de Janeiro and São Paulo was linked to a number of factors, including demographic changes: economic growth after the 2003 crisis, the reduction of social inequality, the issue of the Disarmament Statute in 2003, improved police efficiency in some states, combined with the decrease in the proportion of young population, among other factors, he argued, seem to be stabilising and even reducing violent crime in some states. The drop in homicides can be observed particularly in the big cities of São Paulo, Rio de Janeiro, Minas Gerais and Pernambuco states, to mention only the most important. All these states had in common a large population but a low rate of population growth between 2000 and 2010. Additionally, he argues that the police of these states have undergone extensive reforms with the aim of controlling homicides.

Kahn, in this analysis, has ignored the role of organised crime in some places, such as São Paulo, in monopolising and exerting control over *who* dies and *how many* murders occur (see Denyer Willis 2015 for a broader discussion of this). But he did raise important points such as economic growth and demographic changes – including a decrease in the proportion of the population made up of young males, the group most prone to be involved in violent crimes either as perpetrators or victims. In fact, although state officials claimed accountability for reductions in homicides, recent data show increasing rates of homicide since Brazil's economic downturn in 2014 (Diario de Pernambuco 2015b; Oliveira 2015). This raises questions about the alleged efficacy of securitisation programmes. Moreover, beyond confounding and contributing factors to the reduction in homicides, it is also important to note the effects, sometimes perverse, of methods of state building and control, which raise doubts and questions on the dominant success discourse of securitisation.

Although the overall homicide rate declined in Recife – in 2002 it was 90.5/100,000 and by 2012 it had dropped to 52/100,000, indicating a decline of 42.5% over this ten-year period (Waiselfisz 2014, 39), there remain many challenges in the field of security. The rate of 52/100,000, far from a "success", is well above the national and international average, and it is also above the rate of murders considered to be an "epidemic" (10/100,000). Another challenge is that interpersonal conflicts now affect more women and younger children than in previous years, through their involvement in the drug trade, an issue posed by a *delegada* from the homicide division of the civil police (DHPP):

> In the past, many women died because of domestic violence, today their deaths are often connected to the drug trade [...] Often women in the communities look for the protection that they can get from drug lords. There is a high status associated with being the woman of a criminal. But this woman will spend 24 hours marked to be killed by a rival gang so many of them die in this way. And in other ways too; when there is a dispute or disagreement, people nearby die too. All the structure of the drug trade that you have in different places like Rio, you can find here too but in a smaller scale – there is the person who will deliver the drugs, the one who will split them, the taxi driver who will be involved, the *soldados* (people in charge of "security" and confrontations), the *aviãozinhos* (literally, little airplane, but meaning a child who delivers drugs and messages from the sales point – called *boca* – to the customer). Here *aviãozinhos* are younger: 6 or 7 year olds.
>
> (7 October 2013)

The perceived increase in the involvement of young people in criminal activities, including the drug trade, has intensified debates about reducing the age of criminal responsibility in Brazil (Douglas 2015; Haubert and Cancian 2015). Age and gender, for that matter, have come to the fore in the penal age. The population of incarcerated women has been on the rise. The vast majority of these women are incarcerated due to direct and indirect involvement in, or simply proximity to, the drug trade. For instance, they are the mothers, wives, girlfriends and female relatives of men involved in the drug trade, who are often the ones present at home when the police arrive to search for drugs (Denyer Willis 2015).

Low-income communities in Pernambuco tend to be smaller and accessible by vehicle, facilitating the police's presence. In comparison to Rio, Pernambuco's communities are affected by the drug trade but are not under drug trafficker control. However, the young age of perpetrators and the fact that they trade in small quantities at a time mean that policing and prosecuting them became more difficult. This increases the numbers of street level disputes, due to the multiplication of individual competitors in the trade of small amounts of narcotics. So crime is not as organised as in the southeast of Brazil, and organised brotherhoods, gangs and criminal organisations operate on a smaller scale:

> There were some [organised crime] groups, like Thundercats, Hylanders, but they didn't focus just on the drug trade, they did killings and other criminal activities. They have mostly been dismantled since *Pacto* started.
>
> (Civil police, 26 September 2013)

Thundercats and Hylanders are two of Pernambuco's armed organised criminal groups. They have been associated with multiple offences, such as fraud, drug trafficking, extortion, armed robbery and summary executions, often linked to the *acerto de contas*, that is, an informal type of "justice" or violent punishment to settle debts or punish those who have debts in the underground economy. The *acerto* can also refer to bribe arranged with the police in exchange for freedom (for more details on the dynamics of the *acerto* see Mingardi 2000). However, residents' experiences in the case study communities tell a different story.

In contrast to securitisation programmes in the southeast of Brazil (e.g. UPPs or Pacifying Police Units in Rio), the state apparatus in Pernambuco did not need to reclaim spaces from the control of drug lords. Yet, one similarity between the UPPs and PPV is the expansion of policing in poor communities, as illustrated by the comments of a civil police *delegada*:

> The problems here are different. The drug trade in Rio is far more organised than anywhere else in the country. They are also better armed, with guerrilla firearms. The similarity [in our approach to security] is that here we [also] have the neighbourhood patrol, which *brings the police inside [poor] communities* like the UPPs do in Rio, except that here they come in police cars [not in military tanks or on foot].
>
> (Recife, 24 September 2013)

While in Rio de Janeiro there has been an emphasis on attempting to enforce community policing and the UPP police patrol on foot, the type of policing provided in Pernambuco is more distant. Officers tend to remain in police cars rather than trying to make connections and establish relationships of trust with the communities that they police – a very common complaint in much vehicle-based response policing. Data emerging from interviews with state actors and with community residents reveal that PPV has placed limited (if any) emphasis on the idea of community policing, which is often seen as the antidote to these complaints. The community-policing model, *Policia Amiga* (friendly police) in Pernambuco, was attempted in only 12 communities in all of the state, and ended up being associated with increased police abuse and corruption (Wolff 2014, 176). In the most notoriously violent or feared communities, patrolling on foot increased officers' concerns about possible ambushes (ibid). Yet the alternative – motorised patrols – reinforces the distance between civil society and the State, since officers are unable to interact and establish relationships with community residents. The insufficient number of officers available to work serves only to exacerbate this issue.

Another important regional difference is that while police forces in Rio and São Paulo continue to be responsible for a number of executions and homicides resulting from police action, many expert interviewees praised PPV for achieving one of the lowest rates of police killings in the country.

During 2007–2012, the Pernambucan police killed an average of 31 people per year (Bueno, Cerqueira, and Lima 2013, 124), an average of 0.35 killings per 100,000 inhabitants. However, these figures are actually higher than in the years prior to PPV. In 2004, the Pernambucan police killed 17 civilians, in 2005 they killed 24 and in 2006 the figure was 13 (ibid). Official data on police killings in Pernambuco were not available prior to 2004.

Bueno, Cerqueira and Lima's (2013) data only included cases of police killings of civilians while in confrontation and during working hours. Thus, it did not include off-duty police killings or other police homicides and injuries followed by death – because of the unavailability of these data in many Brazilian states. Bueno, Cerqueira and Lima (2013, 122–123) raised questions about the reliability of this type of data in Brazil, arguing that more effort and investment are needed to produce data that are trustworthy. Nevertheless, in comparison to states such as São Paulo and Rio de Janeiro, Pernambucan police action is apparently less lethal, at least while on duty and according to official statistics. According to Bueno, Cerqueira and Lima (2013), during the same time period (2007–2012), the São Paulo police killed an average of 479 civilians per year (an average rate of 1.16 per 100,000 inhabitants), while the Rio de Janeiro police killed an average of 885 per year (5.55 per 100,000 inhabitants).[4]

One of the effects of Pernambuco's comparatively less lethal policing is that the Pernambucan police have avoided becoming perceived as an enemy to low-income communities (Wolff 2014, 100). The somewhat less lethal application of police force in Recife has allowed them to avoid alienating people in low-income communities to the same extent as in Rio de Janeiro. Security officials interviewed claimed that PPV achieved the "success"[5] of having fewer police killings in comparison to Rio de Janeiro and São Paulo by, on one hand, including police killings in official homicide data. Whereas in most of Brazil, police killings were problematically called *autos de resistência*, which could be interpreted as "acts in self-defence" and not included in intentional homicide rates. And, on the other hand, there was a system of payment by results, that is, bonuses are given to police forces if their area presents low and declining numbers of homicides according to established targets. So, according to high-ranking interviewees, every PM officer and chief of battalion (Major) will receive a bonus for each six-month period in which the area they are responsible for hits targets relating to, for instance, the reduction in the number of homicides by 12% (a figure based on international violence-reduction strategies) and the number of firearms seized. Civil police received their bonuses according to the number of *inquéritos* (police investigations) of homicide cases that they had resolved and sent to the *Ministério Publico* (Public Prosecutor).

Low-ranking interviewees from the military police claimed that they never received their bonus, even if they had achieved their targets. They also claimed that despite declining rates of homicide, it was very difficult to hit the 12% reduction mark. Furthermore, many scholars are suspicious of the accuracy of Brazilian data on police killings, since the "civil police control the state's forensic 'morgues' (*Instituto de Medicina Legal*, or IML), making it possible for civil police officers to hide information that could transform a police shooting into a homicide" (Huggins 2010, 77). Zaverucha (2004) criticises the conflict of interests that can emerge from the work of investigative police with that of what should be the "scientific police" responsible for forensics. For instance, he received complaints that *laudos periciais* (forensic reports) had been altered to hide evidence of torture suffered within police stations. Data about violence thus become compromised at least partly due to the civil police control over forensic information. According to Zaverucha (2004, 113), the morgues remain under the subordination of the Secretariat of Social Defence, which is a police authority, despite their separation from the direction of the civil police. Their full autonomy – functional, administrative and financial – has not been established.

Recurrent examples of military police involvement in *grupos de extermínio* (death squads) as well as in drug and firearm trafficking include the case of *Operação Guararapes* II in Recife's metropolitan region (G1-PE 2012) and the case of three military police officers in another death squad, who killed at least 30 people, in the hinterland of the state of Pernambuco (G1-PE 2015). The cases of police abuse of force are not limited to those connected to death squads, but they also relate to on-duty officers who have not been brought to justice. When police transgressions and brutality are revealed, they do much to maintain the constant erosion of public trust in the State and its institutions.

This section has begun to examine aspects of public security and policing that have not been dealt with by new security interventions. It explored the limits of current models of control and challenges to its claims of success. State actors claimed to have reduced the number of homicides in Pernambuco through the implementation of PPV yet they ignored other potential causal factors and perverse consequences of this phenomenon. The increased focus on deploying the criminal justice system mars state capacity and does not deal with longstanding problems in the police, such as involvement in police violence and death squads. Methods such as community policing, that emphasise the development of relationships with recipient communities, have not been successfully implemented in Pernambuco despite the regional differences highlighted.

Hyper-incarceration

The Brazilian prison system has been described as chaotic, repressive and even a "warehouse wasteland" (Denyer Willis 2015, 56). One of the main challenges for punitive securitisation programmes is prison overcrowding. Nevertheless, police interviewees saw rising rates of incarceration as a desirable effect of their work, given that PPV had focused on policing and imprisoning offenders, growing incarceration meant that they were doing "a better job" at tackling crime. Officials and senior managers at the secretariat for public security in Pernambuco claimed to have no strategy or perceived solution to the issue of overcrowding. Some discussions were taking place with regards to the construction of new prisons, yet no concrete strategy or plan to deal with this issue had been developed. The initial plan of public security, out of which PPV emerged, had mentioned the problem of growing incarceration rates. However, none of its projects proposed a solution to this, even though the plan proposed that the criminal justice system became more effective at "reducing impunity" (PESP-PE 2007, 63). Even the proposed projects that related to the prisons only vaguely refer to improving efficiency and prison management without explaining how these outcomes would be achieved (ibid, 95–96).

Personal email correspondence, dated 24 August 2016, with the Integrated Centre of Communication of the Secretariat of Social Defence in Pernambuco revealed that a number of new prisons are emerging in the state to deal with increasing numbers of prisoners. Those are: the maximum security *Presídio de Tacaimbói*, opened on 8 April 2016 with 676 spaces; the *Presídio de Santa Cruz do Capibaribe*, opened on 10 July 2015 with capacity for 186 inmates; and the *Complexo de Araçoiaba*, which is under construction, with capacity for 2,754 inmates distributed over 7 units. There is also a new institution for young offenders under construction in the city of Arcoverde.

The initial "soft" human-security proposals for community conflict resolution programmes were quickly diluted, not implemented or prioritised. Email correspondences with workers involved in the administration of the public security system indicate that conflict resolution has not been implemented. The views of these workers indicate that there is much resistance and disappointment with the effects of PPV on the prisons, as illustrated by the narrative of a senior lawyer who has worked for nearly two decades in Pernambuco's penitentiaries:

> I am unaware of any planning on the part of the judiciary in the development of PPV. I am also unaware of any conflict resolution interventions or mediation. What we have today are *audiências de custódia* (court hearings prior to custodial sentences), which were a recommendation of the CNJ (National Justice Council). This establishes that the person arrested for a flagrant offence is presented to a judge before a decision is made about whether they will be sent to prison or respond to their trial in liberty. I highlight that this initiative only takes place in the city of Recife due to the shortage of material resources (judges, staff etc.). The decision to provide gratification for officers who hit targets is absurd. Prison overcrowding is unbearable, the state (Pernambuco) has now reached 31,000 incarcerated people, but our capacity is for 11,000. This has led to many recent prison rebellions. Another issue is the insufficient number of

> penitentiary agents. We should have at least 6,200 agents but instead we have 2,000. In response to the deficit of 4,000 agents, some prisoners are given the role of an agent, given a key and the command of a pavilion. That way, any plans to improve the penal system are delayed.
>
> (correspondence 20 August 2016)

There is much to unpack in this extract, not least the absence of conflict resolution, overcrowded understaffed prisons, prisoner rebellions and the issue of prison governance. A significant element of the extract above is the critique of the impact of securitisation methods on prisons and inmates. Yet, according to the Centre of Communication of the Secretariat of Social Defence in Pernambuco (email correspondence 24 August 2016), the court hearings prior to imprisonment implemented since 2015 are leading to increasing liberation of prisoners.

There is much heterogeneity in the data that emerged from the public security system itself. For police interviewees and those involved in the management of the public security system, hyper-incarceration was seen as a sign that the police and the criminal justice system had become more efficient by processing more cases. Nonetheless, the prison population in Pernambuco was increasing before the start of PPV in 2007, which indicates that although PPV may have contributed to the continuing growth of the prison population, it cannot be the sole cause of this phenomenon. For instance, in 1999 there were 7,533 inmates in Pernambuco, and by 2006 this figure had doubled to 15,778 (PESP-PE 2007; Nóbrega 2012, 64).

The prison population in Pernambuco, as well as in the rest of Brazil, has continuously increased since the 1990s (Carvalho 2013). Data from the penitentiary census DEPEN (Ministério da Justiça 2015) show that in 1994 Brazilian prisons housed 129,169 inmates, approximately 88 prisoners for every 100,000 of the country's inhabitants. But by 2011, the prison population had increased to 514,582, approximately 270 inmates per 100,000 inhabitants (Carvalho 2013, 2). In comparison to the national average, which is already high by international standards,[6] the state of Pernambuco has an even higher rate of inmates per overall population: 294/100,000 in 2011 and 327/100,000 in 2012 (see Table 5.1, Figures 5.1 and 5.2 to compare the incarceration rates of all Brazilian states).

It is clear that the rate of incarceration has accelerated during the PPV years. In 2006, there were 185.57 inmates per 100,000 inhabitants and by 2012 this rate had risen to 327.07/100,000. This phenomenon is not unique to Pernambuco or even Brazil. Increasing rates of incarceration have been observed throughout the globe in the last 10–20 years. The Anglo-Saxon literature best captures this development in countries such as the US, the UK since the Thatcher era, Australia, New Zealand and Canada since 2000 (Feeley and Simon 1992; Garland 2001; Wacquant 2009; Cunneen et al. 2013).

Table 5.1 Pernambuco's prison population (2005–2012).

	Total Incarcerated Population	*Prisoners Awaiting Trial*	*Prison Spaces*	*Prison Population Per 100,000 Inhabitants*
2005	17,423	9,437	8,198	220.03
2006	15,778	5,954	8,256	185.57
2007	18,836	10,508	8,298	221.53
2008	19,808	11,243	9,562	226.79
2009	21,041	12,349	9,675	238.82
2010	23,925	13,737	10,135	271.56
2011	25,850	15,177	10,567	293.88
2012	28,769	18,003	11,478	327.07

Source: Ministério da Justiça (2015).

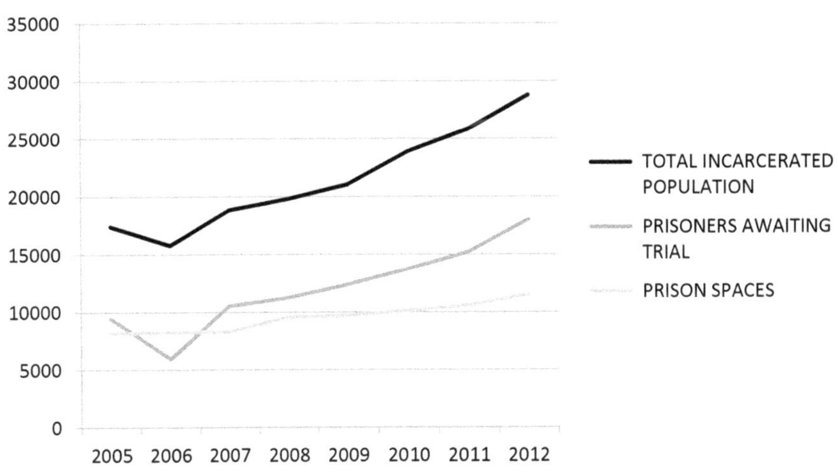

Figure 5.1 Prison population in Pernambuco (2005–2012).
Source: Ministério da Justiça (2015).

This growth in imprisonment is not proportional to growing criminal activity. In some places, crime was dropping while incarceration rates were increasing at disproportionate levels, while in other cases, both reported crime and incarceration rates were expanding. One of the factors that many researchers have associated with the increasing use of imprisonment is the

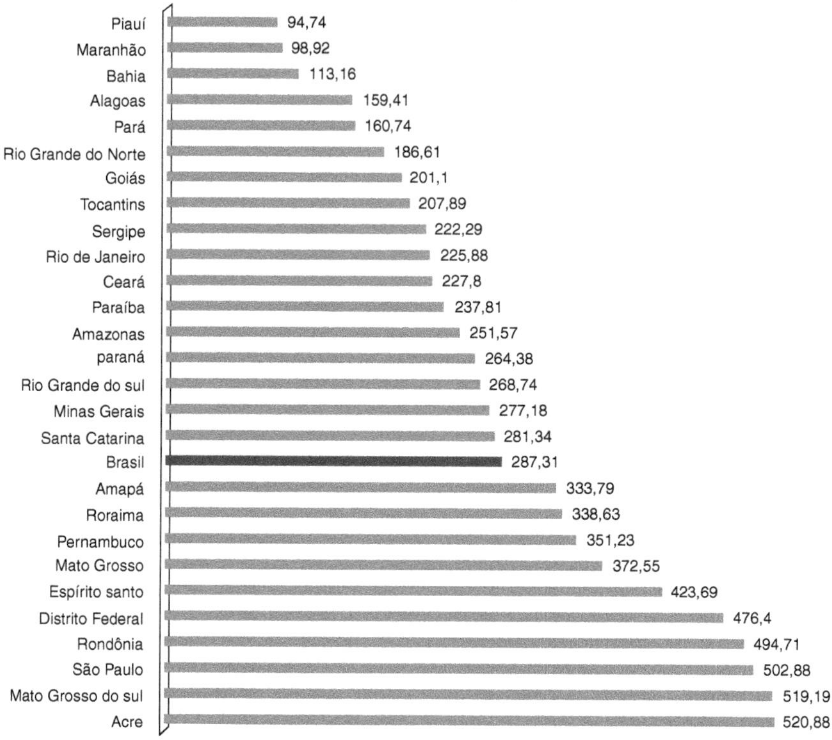

Figure 5.2 Rate of incarceration per state, June 2013 (inmates/100,000 inhabitants). Source: Depen-MJ in Azevedo and Cifali (2015, 115).

growing *social* (rather than *criminal*) insecurity arising from the implementation of free markets and neoliberal policies, for example, the casualisation of wage labour and the commotion of ethnic hierarchies (Wacquant 2012). The rationale behind the neoliberal conceptual framework is that free markets have increased social inequality, while decreasing welfare provision, and that these developments have revived a number of insecurities, not least fear of crime, which contributes to demands for authoritarian crime control of "others", the "have nots", the poor, those perceived as dangerous and subjected to ethnic and racial discrimination (Feeley and Simon 1992; Garland 2001; Wacquant 2009; Cunneen et al. 2013). These authors argue that current social insecurities are therefore coupled with widespread ideologies of individualism and with the increasing commodification of public goods to contribute to a perceived need to police and warehouse the "other", the stigmatised populations seen as criminal and undeserving.

Under this framework, the rehabilitative approach to justice was abandoned and replaced with a focus on the individualisation of responsibility and accountability, and an emphasis on rational choice – all of which dilute the necessity for social and structural responses to crime (e.g. improving education and welfare support, addressing unemployment). According to these authors, the neoliberal philosophy has revived neoclassical concepts such as deterrence and retribution, which have come to be central aspects of current criminal justice.

However, this analysis does not necessarily apply to Brazil, a country that has not followed the traditional neoliberal political economy and instead has expanded overall spending on welfare and education in the 2000s (Neri 2009; Barros et al. 2010; Comin, Barbosa, and Carvalhaes 2012). Furthermore, few would dispute that Brazilian society has been unequal, punitive and racially discriminative towards the poor for centuries before neoliberalism came about. Instead, the expansion of mass incarceration in Brazil may be best explained as an outcome of modifications in sentencing law and practice, the enactment of "tougher" penalties and increasing punitive practices in sentencing. These changes have been driven by popular politics and by mass media influence in triggering punitive reactions to extensively reported events such as high-profile cases (Carvalho 2013; Cunneen et al. 2013; Hall 2014). As argued by Hall (2014), the penal culture refers to "the extent to which social, historical and political ideology coincide in the minds of popular media, government policy and activism" (58–59). Penal ideology or penal culture, as defined below, has played a key role in increasing sentences in the Brazilian case.

Azevedo and Cifali (2015) argue that to understand the paradoxical policies of Brazil, it is important to observe the role of politics at each federative state level. Brazil was politically left-leaning for over a decade (2003–2016), committed to redistributive policies and the reduction of social inequality but at the same time, the country showed increasingly conservative tendencies when it comes to security policies. For instance, while the Worker's Party governed the country (Lula's and Dilma's governments), states such as São Paulo were governed by the PSDB party, which has discursively and in practice enforced a certain style of punitive law-and-order politics, promoting heavy incarceration, in particular for drug-related offences. These are important localised developments with an impact at the national level, since the state of São Paulo's prison population (207,447 inmates in 2013) is disproportionate in accounting for 36% of the country's inmates although the state is home to only 22% of the national population (ibid). Furthermore, Azevedo and Cifali suggest that in recent years many punitive laws have been proposed and rapidly created in contexts of high public demand. Although the number of cases against white-collar criminals has also increased, the demographics of the majority of the Brazilian prison population remain concentrated in low-income and poorly educated individuals who have committed theft or drug-related offences (Carvalho 2013;

Azevedo and Cifali 2015, 119). The criminalisation of activities associated with the poor, or with particular ethnic groups, contributes to the overrepresentation of these populations in prison. If the police and the criminal justice system start to process more cases, clearly more people will be imprisoned. If the police target specific crimes in particular areas, either due to discrimination (by the police, society or policy-makers) or due to actual increased occurrences of these crimes in certain areas, more of these targeted populations will end up receiving some form of punishment. In this way, the emphasis on tackling drug-related offences impacts the growth of the prison population.

Both Macaulay (2012) and Carvalho (2013) explain that Brazilian legislators in the 1990s contributed to the expansion of the prison population with the creation of new crimes (extension of criminalisation), and the limitation of rights in the execution of sentences, which reduced the number of inmates who could leave the prison system. A noteworthy example of this development was the creation of act 8.072/90, which "increased punishment, withdrew progressive sentencing, increased the term for parole and obstructed the commutation and pardon for crimes known as heinous crimes" (Carvalho 2013, 1), including drug trafficking. In 2007, drug trafficking accounted for 15% of the Brazilian male prison population and by 2011 it represented 24.43% of male inmates and 49.65% of female inmates (ibid 3).

Instead of considering the impact of the expansion of the penal system and of the political uses of securitisation, state actors interviewed raised complaints about the efficacy of the Brazilian penal system. They placed the onus of the problem of growing mass incarceration and prison overcrowding simply on the tardiness of the criminal justice system. According to a *delegado* of civil police:

> One of the challenges is that the justice system is very slow. If you go to a prison, you will find that 70% of prisoners are temporary prisoners [prisoners awaiting trial]. They are still awaiting trial. Most should not even be there. This also causes overcrowding in the prisons.
>
> (Interview, 26 September 2013)

Police interviewees argued that many of the people currently incarcerated are not meant to be in prison; they are prisoners awaiting trial for much longer than they are supposed to be in custody. In some cases prisoners await trial for years. The justice system is incapable of dealing with the amount of cases to be processed. According to some interviewees, it is possible to find prisoners in this situation for 5 years, and even 10 years. A number of studies conducted in different parts of Brazil corroborate concerns with this excessive amount of time for cases to be processed in the Brazilian criminal justice system (Pinheiro 1999; Adorno and Pasinato 2007; Ratton, Torres, and Bastos 2011; Ribeiro, Machado, and Silva 2012). The

Brazilian penal code stipulates that the legal duration for processing cases of homicide (*homicidio culposo*) should be approximately 260 days (if the accused is in custody) and up to 310 days (if the accused is not already in prison) between the crime being reported and the first appearance in court (Macedo 2012, 33). However, as shown in Ribeiro et al's (2012) review of studies in this field, the average processing time for cases of homicide varies from 707 days to 2,230 days, which is over 6 years. This situation raises a number of concerns about the disrespect for prisoners and suspects' human rights, and raises questions about the perverse impacts and the sustainability of methods of security that overtly rely on policing and incarceration, exacerbating Brazil's multiple existing injustices and inequalities.

One of the effects of mass incarceration and the brutalising treatment of prisoners has been the emergence, growth and establishment of organised crime groups inside prisons, a topic which has been predominantly studied in the southeast of Brazil (Adorno and Pasinato 2007; Dias 2011; Feltran 2011; Misse 2011; Denyer Willis 2015; Gay 2015). Pernambuco's existing situation indicates that a similar pattern is likely to follow with the expansion of criminal factions such as the *Comando Vermelho* from Rio de Janeiro and the PCC (*Primeiro Comando da Capital*) from São Paulo. Indeed some researchers already predict that the type of prison gang dynamics found in Rio de Janeiro may emerge soon in Pernambuco (Wolff 2014, 96). State capacity will therefore be eroded by the State's own security initiatives which exacerbate the continuing repressiveness and precariousness of the Brazilian criminal justice system.

The activities and power of gangs and organised criminal groups like the PCC are made possible through the prison system, insofar as the prison provides a space to organise, to foster anger against injustice and a justification for joining a criminal organisation that can provide a network of support, governance, rules and survival in the prison (Dias 2011; Feltran 2011; Darke 2013; Denyer Willis 2015). A study by Arruda (2014) conducted in Pernambuco's prisons revealed that groups such as the PCC already have influence over smaller gangs of inmates. Arruda (2014, 186) shows that the prison houses the main leaders of organised crime and functions as the headquarters for drug trafficking. The management of the prison and its inmates is shared between representatives of the State (*poder público*) and the bosses of criminal organisations.

In the narratives of senior members of Pernambuco's secretariat of public security, a loss of hope in rehabilitation was a contributing factor to the increasing use of incarceration:

> This is one of the problems that we face. The prison population has increased a lot. [...] Many crimes are no longer happening because people who are more likely to offend are now in the programme. They offend, the police arrest. We don't have the means to remove people

> from incarceration and stop them from offending, or rehabilitate them. There are [drug rehabilitation] programmes but their efficacy is questionable, sometimes people don't even want to join the programmes [...] We don't have a solution yet, a way to get people off crack.
>
> (23 September 2013)

The apparent solution to crime had rather Americanised connotations. Despite the claims that PPV was exclusively tailored to Pernambuco's context, some experts admitted to having travelled to the US and observed the models of policing that (supposedly) worked – including zero tolerance policing – as shown in an interview with the chief of the Pernambucan civil police:

> Over the years since *Pacto* [*pela vida*] started, the prison population has more than doubled from around 15,000 to 30,000 inmates now. On average, we used to imprison 50 people per month. Now the figure is around 500. Among the *successful* (my emphasis) criminological policies in the world, I had the opportunity to visit New York in 1998 and get to know their *Zero Tolerance* (my emphasis) policing, where they had very high incarceration rate. Here it has not been different. We created Operation *Malhas da Lei*, which consists of the capture of inmates. Today we have this operation in each area, there are 26 *malhas*, I knew it would go well, in six months we went from 50 to 400 captures per month. The secretariat decided this was the secret [to success]. *The secret to success is incarceration. This is our aim* (my emphasis). I don't know any other policy in the world that could revert a situation of violence without incarceration.
>
> (24 September 2013)

So, in the narrative of the chief of the Pernambucan civil police at the time of the research, incarceration is the "aim" of PPV and is perceived as "the secret to success". The question of how success is defined, of course, is important here. The punitive rhetoric on crime, which argues that prison works and that this form of punishment deters crime, is in conflict with the objectives of effectiveness of managerialism and threatens to erode these ideals, since it widens the size of the criminal justice system, increasing the burdens on it and makes it harder to manage.

As Macaulay (2007) puts it, politicians (and the police, it could be added) in Latin America are "deluded in supposing that incarceration is an adequate containment and incapacitation strategy" (638). The very fact that prison gangs have coordinated mass organised criminal acts outside prisons, using their mobile phones and networks, illustrates Macaulay's point. This was made evident when the PCC gang brought chaos to São Paulo by coordinating riots and hostage-taking in 2006 and during the attacks in 2012, which resulted in the deaths of 24 military police, 8 civil police, 7 penitentiary agents, 3 municipal guards and 493 civilians (Cubas 2013, 24). These incidents were not unique. The *Comando Vermelho* (CV) in Rio de Janeiro has also caused major disruption to the city by organising mass criminal acts from within the prison (Penglase 2005). While criminal groups in Pernambuco do not seem as organised and powerful, there is ethnographic evidence that suggests that organised prison groups in Pernambuco are also in control of operations outside the prison. In Brazil, while the prison population has been increasing, overall crime rates, especially homicide rates, have not declined (Dias 2012; Salla 2012; Waiselfisz 2014). This context controverts the mainstream criminological theories of deterrence. The prison has been an unproven method of incapacitation in the Brazilian context. Prisons have instead contributed to increasing criminal organisation. The following section expands on the inherent problems of the ideologies that justify increasing penalisation.

Prioritising managerial reforms

New modes of securitisation (e.g. PPV) are infused with problematic methods and effects. While securitisation programmes improved the capacity of the security system to apprehend more suspects, not a single interviewee said that police training or other crime prevention methods had improved. Lower-ranking officers (e.g. *soldiers* in the military police) complained about the scarcity of training. Likewise, residents in low-income communities believed police brutality and widespread discrimination occurred because the police were not appropriately trained. In the words of one young man from the Tourinho case study, police officers

> come *bulinado* (bullied/harassed) from the academy. In the training of ROCAM [a specialised military police battalion] they get beaten, pepper in their eyes, they get shot with plastic bullets, they have to spend 2–3 days without eating... this creates a monster for the streets.
>
> (Marquinhos, 18 years old community resident, Tourinho, 29 October 2013)

The inadequate training hypothesis seems plausible, but it could also be suggested that beyond inadequate training there are extreme and ingrained social divisions in Brazil that are used as bases on which to attempt to justify disdain, brutality and discrimination. Moreover, factors such as inefficient oversight of police work, inefficient methods of accountability and the lack of trust in the formal justice system's ability to deal with those perceived as criminal all compound the willingness to deploy "rough justice" on the streets and act as a "monster".

For Brazil's key proponents of police reform, managerial reforms are the answer to crime and the ills of the police (Veloso and Ferreira 2008). These authors propose that "increasing police efficacy" (49), "speeding the process of detention" (55) and "repressive and punitive interventions" are "the leading determinants of the reduction of violence" (56–57) in what they considered successful crime reduction initiatives in Brazil and abroad, including the cases of the cities of Boston, New York, Bogotá, Belo Horizonte and São Paulo. Much of this argument is based on the delusion that William Bratton, managerial police reforms and COMPSTAT achieved the "New York miracle" of reduced homicides. Such managerial reforms and modes of securitising the country are visible in the design of PPV, with the monitoring of targets, the use of hot spots and computerised policing systems.

Veloso and Ferreira have also misunderstood the strategies of the Boston Gun Project (known as Operation Ceasefire) by suggesting that a central aspect of Ceasefire was the elevation of rates of imprisonment (51). The Ceasefire evaluation report, which they quote, clearly states that at the heart of the Ceasefire approach was the "pulling levers" framework (Braga et al. 2000, 5). Key to this framework was not increasing *general* rates of incarceration, but rather disseminating a crime prevention message and *targeted* deterrence. One of their central strategies was to "advertise" a speedy response by law enforcement agencies, specifically for cases of violence (not drug offences).

Another important aspect of Ceasefire was the "personalised nature" of the application of its framework (20), which included meetings and forums with gang members and a working group formed of street workers, probation officers, churches and community groups (5). Unlike Veloso and Ferreira, who support the *Broken Windows Theory* proposing targeting low-level crime (see 48), the Ceasefire approach focused on serious violent crime and on targeting illicit firearm traffickers. As the Ceasefire evaluation reports, key to the success of the approach were the efforts of the working group and the circulation of the crime prevention message. These Global North cases of alleged successful violence reduction have been misunderstood and uncritically embraced by Brazilian proponents of managerialism in crime control.

Many Latin American public officials and political leaders, under pressure to show that something is being done about crime and violence, are tempted to try to adopt quick fixes from the US experience,[7] which is "seen to represent something like best practices" (Bailey and Dammert 2006, 2). These ideas are not well understood and may produce unwanted outcomes. They also fail to acknowledge cultural and regional differences. Zero tolerance policing, sometimes referred to as "broken windows", is one such example, taken from New York and imported to countries such as Brazil and Mexico.

Homicide rates in New York dropped from 25.6 per 100,000 inhabitants in 1990 to 8.4 per 100,000 in 1999 and continued dropping thereafter (Young 2011, 120). When Mayor Giuliani and his police commissioner Bratton introduced zero tolerance policing, an aggressive and targeted policing method, supported by a system of computer mapping of high-crime areas, known as COMPSTAT, crime had already been declining (Young 2011, 122). Yet, they claimed that their intervention had led to falling crime and both Giuliani and Bratton received international recognition based on these claims. At the core of their narrative is the idea that the criminal justice system and the police can deter crime. The myth of the New York miracle, as Young (2011) contends, was constructed by the narratives of state actors and social agencies aiming to capitalise on a phenomenon that was disconnected from their interventions.

As Dixon (2005) argued, when New York's crime rates were falling, crime rates were in fact declining all over the US. There is evidence that both high incarceration rates and New York's zero tolerance policing cannot account for declining crime rates in the US in the 1990s and 2000s, since a number of other social factors were at play. Levitt (2004), for instance, presents evidence that the decline in crack cocaine and the legalisation of abortion were important factors in the great American crime drop. Furthermore, as Young (2011) argues this was not an exclusively American phenomenon, crime rates were declining in most of the developed world. Zimring (2007) argues that no single variable, on its own, could account for this phenomenon. He compares the US with Canada, which also saw declining crime rates (albeit without changes in imprisonment).

An over-reliance on policing, repression and punishment as deterrent reinforces social divisions, insofar as this promotes the ideology of "them and us", a criminology of the "other" (Brownlee 1998; Garland 2001), in which offenders and suspects, especially those from socially and economically marginalised backgrounds, are constructed as outcasts, excluded undesirables, whom the rest of us must fear and against whom we require protection. This ideology and discourse of deterrence generate a vicious circle by intensifying the demand for punishment and social control (Brownlee 1998, 326).

Conclusion

This chapter has argued that ideologies informed by mainstream criminological theories emerging in the Global North have penetrated the discourse and practice of police reform in Brazil with perverse consequences for the Brazilian context. It challenged the underlying notions that dominate the methods of security provision in the PPV framework. These ideological foundations are part of a particular field of inquiry: mainstream criminological knowledge. Mainstream, managerial or standard criminology refers to conservative, dominant and traditional schools of thought within the discipline, such as classical, neoclassical and positivist criminology. Focusing on Brazil, this book challenges the practicality of these theories and their ideologies.

Situational crime prevention, hyper-incarceration, broken windows theory and deterrence theory have many limitations, not least that they rely on punishment (through incarceration or the risk of punishment through increased policing and increased barriers to offending) as a deterrent. Punishment is far from guaranteed since an offender may not be caught, or they may come to an informal settlement or agreement – an *acerto* – with corrupt police officers to avoid imprisonment. It is not argued here that there should be no punishment, but that it has not been proven that incarceration is an effective method of crime control. Deterrence is a difficult theory to test, given that only those who have not been deterred come into contact with criminal justice institutions. There is also no evidence that deterrence methods actually reduce reoffending.

In fact, critical criminologists have proposed that removing large numbers of people from certain communities through incarceration – a process which has a notoriously disproportionate impact on the poorest and most ethnically diverse areas – tends to reduce their resources and social capital, therefore making these areas more, not less, prone to crime (Simon 2007). Alongside other scholars, this chapter has also challenged the idea or claim that growing incarceration reduces crime (Dixon 2005; Zimring 2007; Young 2011). Growing incarceration and the application of situational crime prevention against discriminated populations contribute to the extreme inequalities extant in Brazilian society and in the Brazilian criminal justice system, whereby poor blacks end up over-represented, targeted and criminalised.

This chapter discussed some of the regional differences that warrant the study of Recife, including the city's high crime rates, similarities and dissimilarities in methods of policing (e.g. Recife deploys less lethal force and a motorised approach), differences in the drug trade and organised crime (which are smaller in scale and organisation yet more deadly) in comparison to the more studied southeast of Brazil. The chapter drew on the discourses of the powerful to examine how this context and the effects of the informant ideologies of security programmes, as manifested in projects such as PPV, are perceived from the top-down. It drew attention to the increasingly perverse effects of securitisation programmes, such as the high rate of incarceration in overcrowded prisons, and the growth of the deployment of repressive measures of control to the detriment of social measures, providing a critique of the ideologies that make these interventions intelligible in the hegemonic discourses of state actors.

Notes

1 See Macedo (2012) for a detailed description of other police operations, such as: (1) *Contra ameaça*: monitors the number of intimations registered in police stations. (2) *Autoria CVP*: monitors investigations about violent property crime. (3) *Quadrantes de segurança*: monitors the reduction of violent crimes, illegal carrying of weapons and drug-trafficking

offences in each area. (4) *Transporte seguro*: monitors the reduction of crimes against property conducted in means of public transportation. (5) *Autoria IP*: Monitors the number of completed and conclusive police investigations relating to heinous crimes (other than homicide). (6) *Carrossel de Fogo*: monitors the number of firearms apprehended and flagrant arrests relating to intentional lethal crimes in hot spots. (7) *Risco Zero*: monitors the number of firearms apprehended and flagrant arrests relating to intentional lethal crimes in and near bars and nightclubs. (8) *Sossego*: monitors the issuing of police legal terms (*Termos Circunstanciados*) emitted to combat environmental crimes, traffic crimes and sound pollution. (9) *Resgate de vidas*: monitors the work of fire-fighters in partnership with the public health system (*Sistema Único de Saúde*, SUS), considering the speed of the treatment of victims of violent crime with high risk of death in the metropolitan area of Recife, by monitoring the number of rescued survivors.

2 There are some fluctuations in homicide rates (e.g. in the state of Bahia) and there was a mild decline in homicide rates from the year 2011 to 2012 in the states of Paraiba and Alagoas; however, over the entire ten-year period (2002–2012) those states present an upward trend in homicide rates.

3 This was not far from a typical year in terms of numbers of homicides, considering that the average number of homicides from 1998–2007 in Pernambuco was 4,342.

4 Another way of measuring police killings is to compare it as a percentage of the total number of homicides (Bueno, Cerqueira, and Lima 2013, 119). For example, in Pernambuco, in 2012, police killings are 1.54% of the total number of homicides, while in Rio they are 13.53% and in São Paulo 7.71%. The average percentages over the six-year period between 2007 and 2012 would be 1.73% for Pernambuco, 32.13% for Rio and 6.37% for São Paulo. These calculations were made using Bueno's (2013) data.

5 Police killings in the state of Pernambuco are still high in comparison to the US and the UK. Police in the entire US killed 607 civilians in 2011 and the UK police kill on average 2 civilians per year (Wolff 2014, 89).

6 See Carvalho (2013) for a more comprehensive review of these issues and international comparisons of the Brazilian prison population. In South America, Brazil ranks fourth in number of prisoners per 100,000 inhabitants, after French Guiana (316), Suriname (356) and Chile (313). In comparison to European countries, Brazil's rate is also considered high: Spain (160), France (102), England (153) and Germany (88). In absolute numbers, Brazil has the fourth largest prison population, after the US (2,266,832,157), China (1.65 million) and Russia (864,197) (International Centre for Prison Studies 2012).

7 When the implementation of particular "versions" of the ceasefire approach was attempted in other US jurisdictions, it also failed to work.

References

Adorno, S., and W. Pasinato. 2007. "A justiça no tempo, o tempo da justiça." *Tempo Social* 19 (2): 131–155.

Amar, P. 2013. *The Security Archipelago: Human-Security States, Sexuality Politics, and the End of Neoliberalism*. Durham, NC: Duke University Press.

Arruda, R. F. d. 2014. "Geografia do Cárcere: Territorialidades na vida cotidiana carcerária no sistema prisional de Pernambuco." PhD, Universidade de São Paulo, USP, São Paulo.

Azevedo, R. G., and A. C. Cifali. 2015. "Política criminal e encarceramento no Brasil nos governos Lula e Dilma: Elementos para um balanço de uma experiência de governo pós-neoliberal." *Civitas* 15 (1): 105–127.

Bailey, J., and L. Dammert. 2006. "Public Security and Police Reform in the Americas." In *Public Security and Police Reform in the Americas*, edited by J. Bailey and L. Dammert, 1–23. Pittsburgh, PA: University of Pittsburgh Press.

Barros, R., M. d. Carvalho, S. Franco, and R. Mendonça. 2010. "Markets, the State, and the Dynamics of Inequality in Brazil." In *Declining Inequality in Latin America: A Decade of Progress?* edited by L. López-Calva and N. Lustig, 134–174. New York and Washington, DC: UNDP and Brookings University Press.

Braga, A. A., D. M. Kennedy, A. M. Piehl, and E. J. Waring. 2000. *The Boston Gun Project: Impact Evaluation Findings*. Harvard University. www.hks.harvard.edu/urbanpoverty/UrbanSeminars/May2000/BragaBGPReport.pdf.

Bratton, W. 2005. "Crime Is Down in New York City: Blame the Police." In *Policing: Key Readings*, edited by T. Newburn, 472–482. Cullompton: Willan.

Brownlee, I. 1998. "New Labour: New Penology? Punitive Rhetoric and the Limits of Managerialism in Criminal Justice Policy." *Journal of Law and Society* 25 (3): 313–335.

Bueno, S., D. Cerqueira, and R. S. d. Lima. 2013. "Sob fogo cruzado II: letalidade da acao policial." *Anuario Brasileiro de Seguranca Publica*. www.forumseguranca.org.br/storage/download//anuario_2013-corrigido.pdf.

Burke, R. H. 1998. "The Socio Political Context of Zero Tolerance Policing Strategies." *Policing* 21 (4): 666–682.

Carvalho, S. 2013. "Theories of Punishment in the Age of Mass Incarceration: A Closer Look at the Empirical Problem Silenced by Justificationism (The Brazilian Case)." *Open Journal of Social Sciences* 1 (4): 1–12.

Chevigny, P. 1995. *Edge of the Knife: Police Violence in the Americas*. New York: New Press.

Chevigny, P. 2003. "The Populism of Fear: Politics of Crime in the Americas." *Punishment & Society* 5 (1): 77–96. doi:10.1177/1462474503005001293.

Clarke, R. V. G. 1997. *Situational Crime Prevention: Successful Case Studies*. 2nd ed. New York: Harrow and Heston Publishers.

Clarke, R. V. G., and M. Felson. 2004. *Routine Activity and Rational Choice*. New Brunswick, NJ: Transaction Publishers.

Comin, A. A., R. J. Barbosa, and F. O. Carvalhaes. 2012. *Manufacturing Jobs: Economic Cycles, Job Creation and Structural Change*. ESRC Pathfinder Programme on Collaborative Analysis of Microdata Resources, Warwick Institute for Employment Research IER. Accessed 29 July 2013. www2.warwick.ac.uk/fac/soc/ier/research/glmf/heeer/manufacturing_jobs_in_brazil_-_comin_js_pdf.pdf.

Cubas, V. d. O. 2013. "A Ouvidoria e o controle da atividade policial na percepção dos policiais militares." PhD in Sociology, Universidade de São Paulo, USP, São Paulo.

Cunneen, C., J. Cook, E. Baldry, D. Brown, M. Schwartz, A. Steel, and M. Brown. 2013. *Penal Culture and Hyperincarceration: The Revival of the Prison*. Surrey and Burlington: Ashgate.

Darke, S. 2013. "Inmate Governance in Brazilian Prisons." *Howard Journal of Criminal Justice* 52 (3): 272–284.

Dennis, N. 1997. "Editor's Introduction." In *Zero Tolerance: Policing a Free Society*, edited by N. Dennis, 1–28. London: IEA.

Denyer Willis, G. 2015. *The Killing Consensus: Police, Organized Crime, and the Regulation of Life and Death in Urban Brazil*. Oakland: University of California Press.

Diario de Pernambuco. 2015a. "FBI ministra curso para servidores da SDS." March 2. www.diariodepernambuco.com.br/app/noticia/vida-urbana/2015/03/02/interna_vidaurbana,563611/fbi-ministra-curso-para-servidores-da-sds.shtml

Diario de Pernambuco. 2015b. "Homicídios do estado já superam total do ano passado." Accessed 2 December 2015. http://www.diariodepernambuco.com.br/app/noticia/vida-urbana/2015/12/02/interna_vidaurbana,613842/homicidios-do-estado-ja-superam-total-do-ano-passado.shtml#.VmAHdUd-SUo.twitter.

Dias, C. C. N. 2011. "Da pulverização ao monopólio da violência: expansão e consolidação do Primeiro Comando da Capital (PCC) no sistema carcerário paulista." PhD, Universidade de São Paulo (USP), São Paulo.

Dias, C. N., Writer. 2012. "Esecialistas debatem sobre crime organizado." *Globo*, "Entre Aspas".

Dixon, D. 2005. "Beyond Zero Tolerance." In *Policing: Key Readings*, edited by T. Newburn, 483–507. Cullompton: Willan.

Douglas, B. 2015. "Brazil's 'Bullets, Beef and Bible' Caucus Wants to Imprison 16-Year-Olds." *The Guardian*, April 17. www.theguardian.com/world/2015/apr/17/brazil-rightwing-caucus-lower-age-criminal-responsibility?CMP=share_btn_tw

Feeley, M., and J. Simon. 1992. "The New Penology: Notes on the Emerging Strategy of Corrections and Its Implications." *Criminology* 30: 449–474.

Feltran, G. d. S. 2011. *Fronteiras de Tensão: Política e Violência nas Periferias de São Paulo*. São Paulo: Unesp.

Foucault, M. 1979. *Discipline and Punish: The Birth of the Prison*. Translated by A. Sheridan. Harmondsworth: Penguin.

Frühling, H. 2009. "Recent Police Reform in Latin America." In *Policing Insecurity: Police Reform, Security, and Human Rights in Latin America*, edited by N. Uildriks, 21–46. Lanham, MD and Plymouth: Lexington Books.

G1-PE. 2012. "Em PE, tem início julgamento de grupo de extermínio de Jaboatão." *O Globo PE*, October 29. http://g1.globo.com/pernambuco/noticia/2012/10/em-pe-tem-inicio-julgamento-de-grupo-de-exterminio-de-jaboatao.html

G1-PE. 2015. "Três PMs são presos por integrar grupo de extermínio no Sertão de PE." *O Globo PE*. http://g1.globo.com/pernambuco/noticia/2015/05/tres-pms-sao-presos-por-integrar-grupo-de-exterminio-no-sertao-de-pe.html.

Garland, D. 1996. "The Limits of the Sovereign State – Strategies of Crime Control in Contemporary Society." *British Journal of Criminology* 36 (4): 445–471.

Garland, D. 2001. *The Culture of Control: Crime and Social Order in Late Modernity*. Oxford: Clarendon.

Gay, R. 2015. *Bruno: Conversations with a Brazilian Drug Dealer*. Durham, NC and London: Duke University Press.

Hall, S. 2014. "Book Review: Penal Culture and Hyperincarceration: The Revival of the Prison." *Prison Service Journal* (216): 58–59. https://www.crimeandjustice.org.uk/sites/crimeandjustice.org.uk/files/PSJ%20216%20November%202014.pdf.

Haubert, M., and N. Cancian. 2015. "Redução da maioridade penal avança na Câmara após manobra." *Folha de São Paulo*, July 2. www1.folha.uol.com.br/cotidiano/2015/07/1650544-reducao-da-maioridade-avanca-na-camara-apos-manobra.shtml

Huggins, M. K. 2010. "Systemic Police Violence in Brazil." In *Police Use of Force: A Global Perspective*, edited by J. B. Kuhns and J. Knutsson, 73–82. Santa Barbara, CA, Denver, CO, and Oxford: Praeger.

Huggins, M. K., M. Haritos-Fatouros, and P. G. Zimbardo. 2002. *Violence Workers: Police Torturers and Murderers Reconstruct Brazilian Atrocities*. Berkeley, Los Angeles, and London: University of California Press.

Husain, S. 2009. "On the Road to Demilitarization and Professionalization of the Police in Brazil." In *Policing Insecurity: Police Reform, Security, and Human Rights in Latin America*, edited by N. Uildriks, 47–78. Lanham, MD and Plymouth: Lexington Books.

Jones, T., and T. Newburn. 2007. *Policy Transfer and Criminal Justice*. Maidenhead: Open University Press/McGraw Hill.

Kahn, Tulio. 2011. "Exploring the Relationship between Crime and Economic Performance in Brazil after 1994 Using Time Series Econometric Technique." Workshop, Pathfinder PBR5 Network Project.

Leeds, E. 2014. "Police Militarization: Similarities between Ferguson and Brazil." September 29. www.wola.org/commentary/police_militarization_similarities_between_ferguson_and_brazil.

Levitt, S. 2004. "Understanding Why Crime Fell in the 1990s: Four Factors that Explain the Decline and Six that Do Not." *Journal of Economic Perspectives* 18 (1): 163–190.

Macaulay, F. 2007. "Knowledge Production, Framing and Criminal Justice Reform in Latin America." *Journal of Latin American Studies* 39 (3): 627–651. doi:10.2307/40056546.

Macaulay, F. 2012. "Deepening the Federative Pact? The Dilma Government's Approach to Crime, Justice and Policing." *Critical Sociology* 38 (6): 823–834.

Macedo, A. d. O. 2012. "'Policia, quando quer, faz!' Analise da Estrutura de Governanca do 'Pacto pela Vida' de Pernambuco." Masters, Universidade de Brasilia.

Maciel, A. 2015. "Aumento da violência se deve à não implantação de todas as ações do Pacto pela Vida." *JC Online*, April 17. http://jconline.ne10.uol.com.br/canal/politica/pernambuco/noticia/2015/04/17/aumento-da-violencia-se-deve-a-nao-implantacao-de-todas-as-acoes-do-pacto-pela-vida-177151.php.

Malone, M. F. T. 2012. *The Rule of Law in Central America: Citizens' Reactions to Crime and Punishment*. New York: Continuum International Pub. Group.

Mesquita Neto, P. d. M. 2006. "Paths toward Police and Judicial Reform in Latin America." In *Toward a Society under Law: Citizens and Their Police in Latin America*, edited by J. S. Tulchin and M. Ruthenburg, 153–170. Washington, DC: Woodrow Wilson Center Press.

Mesquita Neto, P. d. M. 2011. *Ensaios sobre segurança cidadã*. São Paulo: Quartier Latin, Fapesp.

Mingardi, G. 2000. *Tiras, gansos e trutas: segurança pública e polícia civil em São Paulo (1983–1990)*. Porto Alegre: CORAG.

Ministério da Justiça. 2015. *Relatórios Estatísticos/Analíticos do Sistema Prisional do Estado do Pernambuco*. Accessed 30 March 2015. www.novo.justica.gov.br/

Misse, M. 2011. "Crime organizado e crime comum no Rio de Janeiro: diferenças e afinidades." *Revista de Sociologia e Política* 19 (40): 13–25.

Nagin, D. S. 2012. "Deterrence: Scaring Offenders Straight." In *Correctional Theory: Context and Consequences*, edited by F. T. Cullen and C. L. Jonson, xiii, 244 p. Thousand Oaks, CA: SAGE.

Neri, M. 2009. "Income Policies, Income Distribution, and the Distribution of Opportunities in Brazil." In *Brazil as an Economic Superpower?* edited by L. Brainard and L. Martínez-Diaz, 221–269. Washington, DC: Brookings Institution Press.

Newburn, T., and T. Jones. 2007. "Symbolizing Crime Control: Reflections on Zero Tolerance." *Theoretical Criminology* 11 (2): 221–243.

Nóbrega, J. M. J. 2012. *Homicídios no Nordeste: Dinamica. Relações causais e desmistificação da violência homicida*. Campina Grande: EDUFCG.

Oliveira, W. 2015. "Pacto pela Vida da sinais de fracasso." *Diário de Pernambuco*, March 2. http://blogs.diariodepernambuco.com.br/segurancapublica/?p=8014

Penglase, B. 2005. "The Shutdown of Rio de Janeiro: The Poetics of Drug Trafficker Violence." *Anthropology Today* 21 (5): 3–6.

Pereira, A. W. 2008. "Public Security, Private Interests, and Police Reform in Brazil." In *Democratic Brazil Revisited*, edited by P. R. Kingstone and T. J. Power, 185–208. Pittsburgh, PA: University of Pittsburgh Press.

PESP-PE. 2007. *Plano Estadual de Seguranca Publica: PACTO PELA VIDA*. Recife: Cultura. www.seres.pe.gov.br/index/pacto_pela_vida.pdf.

Pinheiro, P. S. 1999. "O passado não está morto: nem passado ainda é." In *Continuidade autoritária e construção da democracia*, edited by P. S. Pinheiro, 39–72. São Paulo: NEV/USP.

Ratton, J. L., C. Galvão, and M. Fernandez. 2014. "Pact for Life and the Reduction of Homicides in the State of Pernambuco." *Stability: International Journal of Security & Development* 3 (1): 1–15. doi:10.5334/sta.dq.

Ratton, J. L., et al. 2014. Pact for Life and the Reduction of Homicides in the State of Pernambuco. *Stability: International Journal of Security & Development* 3 (1): 18, 1–15. doi:10.5334/sta.dq.

Ratton, J. L., V. Torres, and C. Bastos. 2011. "Inquérito policial, Sistema de Justiça Criminal e políticas públicas de segurança: dilemas e limites da Governança." *Revista Sociedade e Estado* 26 (1): 29–58.

Ribeiro, L., I. Machado, and K. Silva. 2012. "Tempo na ou da justiça criminal brasileira: uma discussão metodológica." *Opinião Pública* 18 (2): 355–382.

Rosenblatt, F. F. 2012. "A Youth Justice Approach to the Street Children Phenomenon in Brazil: A Critical Review." *Youth Justice* 12 (3): 229–244.

Salla, F. 2012. *Sistema Prisional no Brasil: Balanço de uma Década*. São Paulo: NEV/USP. 5° Relatório Nacional sobre os Direitos Humanos no Brasil 2001–2010. http://www.usp.br/imprensa/wp-content/uploads/5%C2%BA-Relat%C3%B3rio-Nacional-sobre-os-Direitos-Humanos-no-Brasil-2001-2010.pdf.

Silverman, E. B., and J.-A. Della-Giustina. 2001. "Urban Policing and the Fear of Crime." *Urban Studies* 38 (5/6): 941–957.

Simon, J. 2007. *Governing through Crime: How the War on Crime Transformed American Democracy and Created a Culture of Fear*. Oxford and New York: Oxford University Press.

Soares, L. E. 2000. *Meu casaco de general: 500 dias no front da segurança pública do Rio de Janeiro*. São Paulo: Companhia das Letras.

Tulchin, J. S., and M. Ruthenburg. 2006. *Toward a Society under Law: Citizens and Their Police in Latin America*. Washington, DC: Woodrow Wilson Center Press.

Uildriks, N. 2009. *Policing Insecurity: Police Reform, Security, and Human Rights in Latin America*. Lanham, MD and Plymouth: Lexington Books.

Veloso, F., and S. G. Ferreira. 2008. "Mecanismos de Gestão na Segurança Pública." In *É Possível: Gestão sa Segurança Pública e Redução da Violência*, edited by F. Veloso and S. G. Ferreira, 25–77. Rio de Janeiro: Contra Capa/Instituto de Estudos de política Econômica (IEPE).

Wacquant, L. C. 2012. "The Wedding of Workfare and Prisonfare in the 21st Century: Responses to Critics and Commentators." In *Criminalisation and Advanced Marginality: Critically Exploring the Work of Loïc Wacquant*, edited by P. Squires and J. Lea, 243–258. Bristol: The Policy Press.

Wacquant, L. c. J. D. 2009. *Prisons of Poverty*. Vol. 23. Minneapolis and London: University of Minnesota Press.

Waiselfisz, J. J. 2014. *Mapa da Violencia 2014: Os jovens do Brasil*. www.mapadaviolencia.org.br/pdf2014/Mapa2014_JovensBrasil_Preliminar.pdf

Ward, H. H. 2006. "Police Reform in Latin America: Brazil, Argentina, and Chile." In *Toward a Society under Law: Citizens and Their Police in Latin America*, edited by J. S. Tulchin and M. Ruthenburg, 171–205. Washington, DC: Woodrow Wilson Center Press.

Wolff, Michael J. 2014. "Criminal Authorities and the State: Gangs, Organized Crime, and Police in Brazil". PhD Thesis in Political Science, University of New Mexico, USA.

Young, J. 2011. *The Criminological Imagination*. Cambridge and Malden, MA: Polity.

Zaverucha, J. 2004. *Policia Civil de Pernambuco: O Desafio da Reforma*. Recife: Editora Universitaria UFPE.

Zimring, F. 2007. *The Great American Crime Decline*. Oxford: Oxford University Press.

Chapter 6

Life, crack and violence in the favelas

This chapter draws on the lived experiences and ethnographic accounts of residents and activists living with insecurity in poor communities in Recife. Studies focusing on the Anglo-Saxon experience have argued that young people's frequent use of public space has made them more available as a population to be policed, and that safety interventions and methods of policing have increasingly criminalised, excessively policed (often on the basis of their socio-economic status) and yet also under-protected those young people (Loader 1996; McAra and McVie 2005; Squires and Goldsmith 2010). But to date, few academic studies have focused on young people's experience of policing in the context of the new securitisation initiatives and state-building exercises in Brazil. There is insufficient work that provides insight into how young people in low-income communities respond to new securitisation interventions in Brazil. This chapter asks what shifts, continuities and silences can be observed in the field of public safety from the perspective of youth in Recife's *periferias*. How do the subjects of new modes of securitisation perceive these programmes? What impact has *Pacto pela Vida* (PPV) had on lived experiences of security and on the type of security that is on offer in low-income communities? This chapter critically examines the impact of managerialist criminological ideologies on the quality of policing, police accountability and on the relationship between marginalised community residents, young people and the police in Brazil.

This chapter provides a glimpse of the world and perceptions of Brazilian non-elites that are poorly understood and rarely examined. The data were gathered in two low-income communities in Recife's metropolitan region. Both communities faced similar problems associated with securitisation. After months of fieldwork in the communities, the findings revealed that young people perceive the police as brutal and distant. Negative experiences of policing and of life at the edge of the city in communities where drug trafficking and extermination groups torment the life of residents became recurring themes. Young people's experiences of criminalisation are revealed in their narratives about the imposition of disrespectful policing on poor residents perceived as deserving (*trabalhadores* or workers) and the treatment of residents as *bandidos* (criminals).

Criminal justice reforms did not reach these communities in any meaningfully positive way. Resident's voices reveal the continuous operation of death squads, police killings and unfair treatment at the hands of state authorities. Interviews with residents, and observations in the communities, conducted in 2013, 2014 and 2016 show the effects of early death and the problematic spread of firearms and crack cocaine. Moreover, in contrast to the discourses of success presented by officials and examined in previous chapters, ethnographic data from these communities reveal rather bleak and perverse consequences of new security interventions. Sexual violence, rape and child abuse have been completely overlooked by managerial violence-reduction programmes, leaving large proportions of the female and young population disproportionately affected by and under-protected from non-lethal violence. Residents of poor communities were excessively targeted, monitored, criminalised and simultaneously under-protected. Space has become increasingly deeply divided along class, racial and gender lines.

I argue that the continuing conflation of poverty and criminality and the racialisation of punitive crime control are reproduced in militarised interventions in poor communities despite efforts to modernise or implement new security agendas. As such, this chapter provides a counter-narrative from below, a critique of the hegemonic technocratic discourse of "success" in public security intervention that was deployed by state actors. Managerial reforms have exacerbated some of the ills of the Brazilian criminal justice system. For example, police in Brazil adopt illegal practices to reach quantitative targets, the model of policing has remained practically unchanged, and protection rackets and organised criminals continue to operate from within prisons.

Tourinho

> The ROCAM[1] (militarised police patrol on motorbikes) gave him a *baculejo* (a forceful and violent stop and search). They looked at his ID card, took 40 reais (equivalent to approximately £13 at the time) from his wallet and called him a shameless cripple. He wasn't disabled or anything, he might have smoked [marijuana] and he had a broken leg.
>
> (Luther, community resident and activist, September 2013)

Young people's experiences of stop and search in Tourinho were traumatic. Their friends' experiences were also distressing and resonated known problems of coercive and militarised policing (Huggins 1998). Securitisation programmes had increased sporadic policing in the community, by increasing motorised police patrols and police crackdown operations, but it had not improved policing practices, neither the quality of the interactions and dialogue between the police and community residents nor the level of police accountability. Policing methods did not attempt to abide by the principles of consensual community policing. The *baculejo* illustrates the continuity of inadequate, violent and adversarial policing. The term *baculejo* is used locally to describe a violent or coercive stop and search where the police may, for instance, apply pressure to the suspect's interlaced fingers while his/her hands are on his/her head, punch the suspect or kick his/her legs to spread them open. This approach provoked much disdain for the police in the community.

Young people argued that although cases of homicide might have decreased, other forms of violence continue in the community. They argued that this violence was different from what they saw on TV in Rio de Janeiro, where they often heard reports of police entering communities shooting. In Pernambuco, instead, the police entered the community *dando lapada* (giving out beatings). Young people referred to the police as the *capitão do mato*, a historical character from the time of slavery, who was responsible for capturing fugitive slaves and punishing those who caused disorder or who disobeyed their masters. The analogy said much about the type of policing available for poor black communities. The analogy of the *capitão do mato dando lapada* has parallels to the general state approach to these communities, insofar as the access to general public services beyond policing is also inadequate and socially unjust.

Lourdes, one of my key informants, although initially reluctant to talk about security or topics that risked associating marginalised people in the peripheries with crime, explained that the social distance between the community and the roles of the police was one of the problems with securitisation. Since the police were there to target residents as suspects, acting with violent and oppressive measures, they were unable to develop relationships in the community that would facilitate their work. In her words

> If *Pacto pela Vida* is something that should get to us, they should have contact with the community and know what happens here. But they don't know the reality of the community. *É eles lá e nós aqui* (they are over there and we are here).

Another young female activist in the community elaborated that the problem was not solely that the police had little contact with residents, but also that the contact they had tended to be brutal and lacked dialogue:

> They [the police] don't arrive chatting; it is all done on the base of violence. I watched them stop a group of four guys the other day and ask for their ID cards. The boys didn't have their IDs. The police ordered them to put their hands on their heads. One guy was a bit slow so the officer gave him a *bufetada* [a slap] that sent him into a wall

> and then to the ground. It is better to trust a thief than the police. One side is insecurity, the other is fear.
>
> (Estrela, 17 years old, 29 October 2013)

Having to face threatening behaviour by the police was the norm for the young people in this study. Numerous accounts of police misconduct emerged in our conversations, from minor to severe verbal and physical abuse. Just as Brinks (2008) argued, the communities that were least patrolled were the recipients of the most acute forms of police brutality. Marquinhos, a young black male resident, was picked up by the police for no particular reason and taken to the police station with three friends. This is how he described this negative encounter:

> The officer sat next to his partner, with his gun pointed at us. We asked him: "could you not point your pistol at us? None of us is a bandit", [to what] he replied: "do you want me to point it at my partner? Do you?". So I said [sarcastically] "but in our direction it's ok, is it?" He got up, went towards a guy who he'd arrested, and stepped on his hands like this [demonstrates]. Then he started asking the boy where the *boca* (drug-selling point) was. After 30 minutes of *massagem* (literally "massage", but meaning beating/torture), the boy was *pianinho-pianinho* (docile/withdrawn).

Such methods of policing and governing the young and the marginalised are reminiscent of practices described in Foucault's (1979) work, insofar as they act on and intend to discipline the body of the excluded. But Foucault did not claim to speak for the colonies and ex-colonies. In Brazilian poor communities, governing the marginalised continues to entail physical brutality against the bodies of young poor black males, visibly in public spaces well beyond medieval times. The European Foucauldian framework does not enable an understanding of the continuing issues of visible physical violence against the marginalised in ex-colonies, such as Brazil. These issues can only be understood in the historical and socio-economic context of Brazil.

Existing policing practices caused fear and anger in the community. But fear emerged from other sources too, beyond local criminals and the police, the local prison and its guards were another part of the State that caused distress and carried negative connotations for residents. As I walked around Tourinho with Lourdes, around one of the largest prisons in Latin America, I was told that there were regular shootouts by the prison wall. "Guards shoot at people trying to throw parcels over the wall", she said, "only last week I was on my phone walking down this street when I heard the shots and run [to avoid a stray bullet]. The community lives with these dangers on a daily basis".

Proximity to the prison meant that many participants were in tune with the dynamics of prison–community relations and aware of the ways in which the prison meshes with the *periferias*. The intensification of policing that came with PPV, the increasing targeting of drug offenders and incarceration of members of extermination groups had caused important changes in the landscape where organised criminal groups operate. Although a recent study by Wolff (2014) claims that criminal behaviour in Recife's low-income communities remains "unconstrained by the organisational and socialization dynamics of prison gangs" (97), according to residents of low-income communities[2] surrounding the prison, criminals in Recife's prisons do indeed have an impact in the community even from within the prison's walls.

According to residents, Recife's prison inmates have control over drug shipments and coerce residents to hiding inmates in their homes when there is a prison escape. Organised criminal groups coerce young people in the community to throw parcels containing weapons and drugs over the prison wall. A study conducted by Arruda (2014), which was conducted with ex- and current inmates inside Pernambucan prisons, revealed that well-connected prisoners have control over and involvement with criminal organisations operating inside and outside the prison. This is supported by data emerging through conversations with residents in Tourinho.

For local residents, PPV's methods had done little to reduce fear and insecurity. The increasing use of inadequate and chaotic prisons and local young offenders' institutions aggravated residents' anxieties. These institutions were the sources of multiple examples of corruption, firearm and drug trafficking, affecting the community and other state institutions, such as the school. Lourdes had arranged an interview with a local teacher Samuel, who was 25 years old at the time we discussed these anxieties:

ROXANA: "What are the main problems faced by young people in your neighbourhood?"

SAMUEL: "I think the lack of space, lack of activities, drugs, violence and fear. This is the society of fear. Some of my students are armed in the classroom selling drugs. I leave my home and I don't know whether I will come back again. About ten years ago my neighbours could sit outdoors till late playing dominos. Now by 8pm everyone is indoors. I was in a music gig [in the community] the other day but it had to be interrupted because two people were murdered. I see children working as *aviãozinhos* [delivering drugs or messages for drug dealers]. Just this week 100 young offenders escaped from the FUNASE (a young people's detention centre). All that? How? Did anybody see it happen? How do they get hold of guns? Through the police themselves. It costs R$40 reais (about £13 at the time) for a little gun, R$300 (about £100 pounds at the time) for a [model] 38".

ROXANA: "Really?"

> SAMUEL: "It's very easy to buy guns. The police themselves sell guns to bandits. Unfortunately, we have to live as if we were in prison. In my house I use 8 locks, but it has to be like that, there are armed men constantly walking by. There's no security for us. But [pauses sarcastically, and sighs] they have built the arena. (the football stadium for the 2014 World Cup)".

Residents saw that the State had funds to make certain investments, such as spending on the preparations for large sporting events, but public money was hardly ever invested in the communities most at need. These communities bore the brunt of the availability of firearms, police corruption and violence and drug trafficking, all of which became familiar themes in interviews with community residents. In this context, for many young men, access to firearms and involvement in the drug trade offered an artificial form of safety, a level of income that occasionally available, often temporary, minimum wage jobs could not afford them (see also Goldstein 2003). In the words of Samuel:

> *O tráfico* (drug trafficking) is everywhere. Today a rock [of crack cocaine] is R$5 (under £2). It is easy money, easier than sweating to build a home. But there is no territorial dispute like you see in other places, because each community has its "dono" (owner/drug lord) and the *bandidos* (ordinary criminals rather than bandits) are more united than the community as a whole.

Top-down attempts at securitisation had not improved feelings of security on the ground level. Residents provided ample evidence of the systematic violation of their civil rights – not least the right to safety. According to residents, the police was not concerned with providing safety but rather with attending to their own private interests:

> Most of the time the police car is carrying a *novinha* (attractive young 16–17 year-old female). Most of us have no contact with the police. They are just there in their cars … We never talk. People with money wet [bribe] the hands of the police and get their attention. The police work for the government but really they act like a private service. Those who can't wet their hands don't receive any attention. The police don't know how to approach us, they have poor training and go straight to the *tapa* (slap/violence).
>
> (Samuel)

These are familiar complaints throughout Brazil: police violence; the lack of dialogue in police–community interactions; and ineffective, distant policing – "the police are just there in their cars … we never talk". When residents did encounter the police they were stereotyped, considered to be criminals on the basis of their appearance and where they live, and were subjected to repression:

> There are many minors (young people aged under 18) being killed in brutal ways here. The impact of crime is large. The community has not mobilised about this. The police are violent and don't work properly and they judge by appearance.
>
> (Najha, male, 18 years old, mixed ethnic background)

> The government have invested a lot in repression, little in education and little social assistance, they have reduced the number of homicides, [but] increased the prison population.
>
> (Baque forte, male, 33 years old, black)

Another key informant and co-researcher, Luther, commended this critique. Luther, an activist and arts teacher from the community, teaches graffiti to schoolchildren, on a temporary "verbal" contract with the local municipality. He doesn't have *carteira assinada* (signed employment contract and official employment documentation). He says that the municipality doesn't want any commitment with employees like him. And he will get a little extra cash being on a verbal contract since his taxes are not being paid. The following is an extract of a conversation we had while he showed me around the neighbourhood, explaining that repressive policing and the prison could not resolve drug-related offences in the community:

LUTHER: "We live right where the drug trafficking occurs. It is up to you if you want to go up or not. That is where they stay waiting for people coming to buy".

ROXANA: "Are the customers coming from outside the community or from within the community?"

LUTHER: "Most are from the community. For the young people it's like a job. Sometimes they get into trouble with the police but a couple of weeks later someone else will take on that job. So it's this circle of things, the drugs are always around. [...] That big derelict house was a FEBEM (young offender's institution). Then it was mostly used as a base for drug sales and it has also been used for prostitution. A girl was killed selling drugs here, during the night. Don't worry, we are OK [safe] here in the daytime. We think a group of guys came to take her stash and killed her. But art has power to change things, we did some work here to reclaim the building, we got a donation and used the money to buy tins of spray paint to do our [graffiti] work here. These two girls over there, they are selling drugs, they hide it in the bushes until they get a customer with cash. Some people have been caught here by undercover police. People who sell need guns to defend themselves, if someone comes to take their stash. [...] That *quadra* (cement football pitch) over there is also another 'point' for drugs. That area over there is a favela invasion. Over that hill is where the drugs are being sold now. We can go up if you want, it is safe to go up with me now. They know me around here".

[We go up a steep alleyway].

LUTHER: "*Dá-le* Edson [greets a friend walking pass]. This is the reality here, those small kids are selling drugs, some as young as 9 or 11 years old".

ROXANA: "Are there many people out at night here?"

LUTHER: "Most people selling drugs are out at night, that is when the money is there to be made, the rest of the residents are usually indoors, unless they study or work at night. So some of those guys sitting on that wall over there are lookouts, if the police come over they'll use their mobile phones to let the *patrão* know that *sujou* (they inform the boss). Some of these young men have orders to retaliate and shoot at police, they have position of respect with the boss so they are given a gun to carry around their waist. Others will run into the *mata* [woods] where in the dark it'll be very hard to see them. You don't need to go far to see children involved in the drug trade.

[…]

Many politicians come around promising bricks and cement. Asking for a vote. But don't actually do anything for the community. The houses here are mostly rented; they are expensive 300–350 reais a month (£100–116 at the time). People who work here try to save to build a house and rent it. […] Some of these guys are working in the trade to send money to other guys who got caught and are in prison. There is this aspect of power in the drug trade. The trade is so 'banal', people from the community walk pass and don't even look. On this street here, the guys throw bags of drugs over the walls of the prison wall, sometimes it has been arranged even with the security man in the prison or arranged by mobile phone with the guys inside".

Luther's account reveals many similarities to the experiences of cities like Rio de Janeiro, insofar as very young children become involved in the drug trade, sometimes as lookouts and eventually as armed guards for the trade. His narrative retells well-known problems of clientelism and state neglect for living conditions in the neighbourhood. When residents were asked what could be done to resolve the issue of insecurity and drug-related violence, most participants pointed to the government and the State as responsible for these tasks. They explained that they had already done their share of the work by paying taxes, so they expected better policing and more state investment in spaces for leisure in the community, activities and better training opportunities for the young, as well as more investment in the creation of good quality well-paid jobs and less corruption in the police and the State more generally. Community residents explained that these were some of the reasons why they had joined the 2013 street protests. Luther angrily summarised the community's security demands and the racial and social inequalities experienced in the community (and in most of the country):

> There is some policing here because the prison is inside the community. It is bad with the police and worse without them. What the community needs is more professionals, educators, psychologists, social workers and so on. But because of the police's culture, they suspect anyone that walks by with a plastic bag in their hand; they stop and search because in poor communities the police see everyone as a bandit. I've seen this with my own eyes. It is normal here. If you live near the *boca de fumo* (drug sales point) they are immediately rude to you. For them, any citizen out on the streets at 11pm is involved [in the drug trade]. If a rich kid gets caught, they are labelled chemically dependent [on illicit drugs] and taken to rehab, if a poor guy is caught, he's thrown in the prison. What is the use of the Brazilian prison? It just jails the mind 24 hours a day. You never hear of a young person who left a Brazilian prison and started university. The carceral system doesn't regenerate anyone.

Luther's views about the prison were not unique in the communities studied. Other residents supported the critical view that the prison has few functions other than to exclude certain groups in society since, as Luther put it, the prison does not stop crime or rehabilitate offenders: it "doesn't regenerate anyone". Luther and three other community activists had spent time in youth penal institutions providing arts workshops to young offenders, and reported the horrors of the conditions in which young people were incarcerated in these institutions. These included common cases of torture, risk of losing one's life in recurrent rebellions and disputes, overcrowding and insufficient socio-educative programmes. These issues warrant further research.[3]

Vitoria

It was eleven thirty in the morning. Approximately 30 children were lying on the concrete floor, in a space of about 12m2; then they would start moving around, working out. There is plenty of loud talking and screaming on the background. An adult monitors what they do. This is their physical exercise class. The school's amenities are very small and there are no green spaces or recreational areas, other than this concrete floor where the young people are exercising. The security guard opens the door and lets me in. The admin staff are running around trying to attend to all the requests and answer all the questions posed by young people who come into the small air-conditioned office area. The atmosphere is tense and the staff seem stressed. The students, who are coming in, want to know whether they will have any classes or any teaching. Some of the teachers have not turned up for work. One of them called to say she had childcare issues that day. Another teacher had been sporadically coming to work due to health problems. There was no one to substitute them. The admin staff are trying to operate a miracle with the timetable. They explain this is a daily occurrence because, the state government hires most teachers on temporary contracts, and according to the admin staff, temporary workers often have little regard for the school or the children. I sit down to wait for my interviewee, Gustavo. I am nearly five months pregnant and my bump is already visible, giving rise to a lot of interest and questions from the young people. They ask about the gender of the baby, if my son will have an English name, and where he will be born. I try to steer the conversation to learn more about the young people. Gustavo is late. More young people come into the office, they ask for new rucksacks. The school's deputy director tells me that the children sell the rucksacks that they are given at school for R$10 (roughly £3 at the time). The young people claim that the last rucksack they were given was damaged, or ended up stolen or lost. A small child walks in the office with no uniform. He looks about ten years old. He is delivering food for the staff from a local business. He receives some change for his work. Since Gustavo has not arrived and I cannot get hold of him on the phone, I agree to provide cover for the absent teachers and deliver an English class. The students are thrilled, they ask if I can stay and teach them every day. Gustavo arrives after my class. He is tall, ethnically mixed and quiet. He is sixteen years old and has recently committed some offences in the community. The staff at the school were keen to warn me about this. His latest known infraction was the theft of a motorbike in front of the school. He gives me short answers to most of my initial questions but when we start talking about police-community relations he decides to tell me about one of his encounters with the police in the neighbourhood. "I was out at midnight with four friends, we were coming back from a football match in the stadium. We watched Sport (local team) against Náutico (local team). The police stopped us and asked what we were doing out at that time. We said we're coming back from the football. Then they started beating us to the ground, kicking and punching us. A neighbour woke up and called two of his brothers who work for the civil police to stop them. We went to the police station the next day but nothing was done about it". Despite reporting the crime, and despite nothing being done about it by the police, Gustavo says he would like more policing in the neighbourhood to feel safer. He explains that not all the police are violent and corrupt (Field note, 2 October 2013).

The field note above highlights the most evident issues in Vitoria: the inadequate provision of state services, poverty and brutal policing. Access to the Vitoria was facilitated through a contact in the local school. Most of the participants at the school were students aged between 16 and 18. However, some were mature students who also lived in the community or had returned to education to attend evening classes. Some of the staff that lived in the community were also interviewed, like Zefinha, the school chef, a resident of Vitoria since the 1970s. Zefinha explained that when she first moved to Vitoria, there were few houses; there were many trees and green spaces. Over the years more and more houses were self-built by residents and their growing families, so now there is barely any unoccupied space in the area and hardly any leisure spaces for young people. Almost every space is needed for housing and every space is used. She explained that there was plenty of work around in the past, but in the last decade, the community saw the establishment of the drug trade, in particular the crack-cocaine business, so drug dealers became the main "employers" in the community. According to residents, like Zefinha, in the drug trade, young people can earn better wages, but this business has brought a rise in drug-related disputes and homicides. Many students, she explained, are drug users and drug dealers. This was not immediately noticeable.

The differential treatment that the police provide often depends on one's social class, ethnicity, age and gender, generating hostility in community–police relations. This was the case in both case-study communities. Paradoxically, despite being exposed to inappropriate safety provision and differential policing, people in low-income communities demand more policing.

The local *escola estadual* (state-funded school) where most of the research was conducted in Vitoria, like the remainder of the neighbourhood, occupies a particular space in the city, an area seen as undesirable and peripheral (*periferia*), a working-class neighbourhood, spatially segregated from the predominantly white middle and upper class parts of Recife and yet interconnected to the city through the workers, voters and people that live in Vitoria. The neighbourhood is densely populated with small self-built brick houses, with some narrow pavement on some streets, most of which have open sewers, no green spaces such as parks or gardens, and hardly any public spaces where residents could gather, except for the *quadrinha* (a cement football field) where young people gather to socialise and where some drug dealers conduct their business.

Young people frequently wanted to be interviewed to occupy their time during the daily *aulas vagas* (free time with no lessons due to the routine absence of schoolteachers). Many interviews brought out very similar themes to those raised in Tourinho, such as concerns about inappropriate distant policing, police corruption, drug trafficking and routine homicides. Participants repeatedly complained that there was no dialogue between residents and the police and that officers were seen in the neighbourhood only after a crime or traffic accident happened.

One of the disparities between the communities was that in Vitoria, young people seemed even more under-protected, isolated and entrapped at home due to fear of violence. Just as Caldeira (2000) demonstrated in *City of Walls*, in relation to upper- and middle-class people, people in the low-income communities studied also put up metal bars on the doors and windows of their homes to feel safer, they had high levels of suspicion and their habits were changing to avoid interactions in public. In his ethnographic study in a different Recife community, in the early 2000s, Koster (2009, 283–284) referred to an informal curfew placed on residents by drug traffickers, particularly at night. Residents would be told to stay indoors, for instance, when traffickers were executing other gang members at night. Bystanders would also be killed to avoid incriminating evidence. Vitoria and Tourinho's residents also made references to similar situations, and adapted to these occurrences of violence by staying indoors in the evenings, sometimes as early as 8:00 p.m.

Inappropriate security provision can deteriorate public life in many ways, including by leading fearful citizens to withdraw from public spaces (Frühling 2009; Perlman 2010; Saunders-Hastings 2013; González 2014) or from participating in political and community life (e.g. participation in public debates, or through associations, protests and community organisations). The police, as the most visible institution of the State in charge of citizens' protection, also fulfil many political functions. All policing is in this sense political but not necessarily egalitarian or conducive to democratic participation. The police can be used as a political tool to protect *some* citizens from *other* citizens. They can also enable politicians to achieve political ends, either by gathering votes through their associations or through the services that they provide to certain citizens, or even simply by being visible in some areas and appearing to be protecting some citizens. As such the corporation is a politicised institution with potential to either improve or deteriorate public life and the conditions in which democratic ideals can be fostered.

Residents feared crime, lack of protection from it, but also feared being mistaken for a criminal or *bandido* by police. In a deeply unequal society such as Brazil, to be constructed as a *bandido* or criminal has profound consequences for the chances of life or death of poor black people. Whether imagined or real, the *bandido* category can also impact their chances of employment, of being free to use public spaces or simply of having freedom from time in prison. At first, this fear of being thought to be a criminal might seem unwarranted, but a closer look into local relations provides the rationale for the worker versus *bandido* division.

One afternoon, a friendly elderly resident who owns the local bakery, Dona Lalá, asked what I was doing in the community. I explained that I was researching and writing about injustice in Recife. She advised me to speak to Seu Antonio; she said "a great injustice had happened to him", which would show me how the Brazilian State treats the poor. She arranged a meeting for me to meet Seu Antonio at her house one afternoon when he would be around to fix her sink. While Dona Lalá went off to the housework at the back of the house, I talked to Seu Antonio on the porch behind the metal fence where we could catch a breeze and some shade from the scorching sun.

Seu Antonio was a short, frail-looking man, slim and dark-skinned, his face and hands had many wrinkles. I imagined he was in his early 60s but in fact he was only 48. His appearance resulted from years of hard labour and suffering. Despite the relative power asymmetry between researcher and informant (Spivak 1988), Seu Antonio was very receptive and keen to tell me his story, which emphasised his identity as a worker rather than a *bandido*. Seu Antonio explained that he was arrested in *Alto do Pinhal* – an even less affluent part of the neighbourhood – where he had met Dona Lalá and her family before they moved. During his youth, he had been a close friend of one of Dona Lalá's ten children. Prior to our meeting, he was unfairly sentenced and incarcerated for 3 years and had been to five different prisons. The following excerpt retells Seu Antonio's story:

ROXANA: "Can you tell me more about how the arrest happened?"

SEU ANTONIO: "At that time, I was in the habit of drinking [alcohol] with a friend in Alto do Pinhal. He invited me for a beer at his house. I was sitting in the living room and he went to the kitchen to get something. I didn't know, but he was rolling marijuana. I never smoked that stuff. I didn't know he smoked. He was selling it too". [He pauses, waiting for a reaction or for more questions]

ROXANA: "So what happened after your friend was in the kitchen?"

SEU ANTONIO: "Some police entered the house, with guns and arrested everyone. Me too. I couldn't understand what was going on. They took me, didn't want to know that I had nothing to do with the drugs. In court, the *safado* (shameless, dishonest person) [his friend] incriminated me. He said I was involved too. I had no money to pay the lawyer, who wanted R$2,000 (£700 at the time) to free me but I couldn't pay. In prison, people with money don't stay more than 2–3 days. The son of a shop owner I met inside left in 2 days because his father paid".

This type of heavy-handed raid or occasional policing is common in Brazil's most marginalised communities and slums. Seu Antonio finds it necessary to assert his innocence by explaining he "had nothing to do with the drugs" and "never smoked", emphasising that he stayed in prison only because "he could not pay" the lawyer, while "the son of a shop owner" paid and became free. For Seu Antonio this was not an option. Having migrated from the countryside's dry lands with his mother and siblings to Recife, he had to leave school at age 10 to work and support the household. Seu Antonio's case is one of many stories in which the poor (and often black people) are criminalised and receive differential treatment from all the institutions of the criminal justice system because of their socio-economic circumstances.

When asked what prison was like, Seu Antonio said he was respected by inmates and was never beaten because his recorded offence was not seen as serious enough. He said that for the most part, prisoners only persecuted people who committed sexual offences, or those who had hit their mothers. For these inmates, seen as undeserving, the only perceived solution was death by beating. Here lies another telling episode of the blurred boundaries of injustice. Seu Antonio had seen some of these offenders get murdered in jail. To obtain protection, many inmates join gangs in prison, an issue already documented by ethnographers (Penglase 2008). But because Seu Antonio "minded his own business", and was not seen as undeserving, he was offered a role of respect, that of the *chaveiro* (translates as keyholder).

The *chaveiro* is responsible for maintaining order inside the prison. Other prisoners elect him and the informal rule is that the group will do as he says. The *chaveiro* makes the decisions and can also offer protection to prisoners under threat by inmates. This form of self-governance in Brazilian prisons is a consequence of increasing incarceration, precarious physical conditions and overcrowding (Darke 2013; Arruda 2014). In this context, the *chaveiro*'s role becomes necessary, to provide order and informal justice. *Chaveiros* in Pernambucan prisons manage prison wings as if they were a market (Arruda 2014). This includes the management of all transactions that occur informally among prisoners and between prisoners and outsiders, including food, clothing and drug sales.

Zaverucha (2004, 42–43) argues that prison authorities are complacent[4] with this practice, since they are aware of it and either authorise, fail to eliminate it and even incentivise the election of a *chaveiro*. The *chaveiro* has a similar role to the *preso de ordem* (ordering inmate). Until the early 2000s, prisoners used to be kept captive in overcrowded cells in police stations in Pernambuco. The *preso de ordem* would accomplish the tasks that police officers did not want to get involved with in these cells, not only because police wanted to avoid the foul odour from overcrowded cells but also because they wanted to avoid contamination with common diseases and ailments caused by unhygienic conditions in cells (Zaverucha 2004). The *preso de ordem* would, for example, provide water in buckets for prisoners to drink, resolve conflicts between prisoners, collect laundry and so on, in exchange for an early release.

Seu Antonio's story is telling of the practice of informal governance in prisons through the role of *chaveiros*. He explained that those who stole from inmates would receive a severe beating with a piece of wire, wood or the shaft of a wooden broom. He argued that thieves should not be mixed with *matadores* (hit-man), because thieves would get together to kill *matadores*. This seemed contradictory, the line drawn between being a thief and a murderer being rather blurred if thieves also kill. Seu Antonio explained that *matadores* were hired on the outside to kill thieves in cold blood, but in prison thieves made up the vast majority of inmates, so together they could get revenge.[5] While in prison, Seu Antonio had no idea when he was going to be released. But one day, after three years of incarceration, a prison warden asked him if he wanted some work in the prison. It was some labouring work in exchange for a couple of days on the outside. Allowing prisoners a "day-off" on the outside has been sanctioned by law in Brazil (McCann 2008, 64). The possibility of going out made him accept the work.

It was then, in 2011, that he went to Dona Lalá's house, looking to talk to her son Seu Zé to tell his story and ask for work. The type of work he did was often temporary, informal and low-paid, what is known colloquially in Brazil as *bico*; the nearest equivalent Anglo-Saxon academic term is sub-employment. He explained that his *bicos* were in the local construction industry. He has known Dona Lalá since he was 15 years old; he worked with two of her sons and has been a family friend since. So a few days after he told Seu Zé about the injustice that happened, a lawyer went to the prison and he was released. Seu Antonio was keen to show me some paperwork that he carried around with him, with numbers that I could use to look up his files and see official reports about his innocence. Only by making alliances with a family that had a somewhat higher-class status and available cash, Seu Antonio was able to access the formal justice system.

This excerpt illustrates why people in low-income communities fear associating with criminals or being mistaken as a *bandido*. It also shows how, for the majority of Brazilian citizens, the post-democratic Brazilian state continues to govern in undemocratic and unjust ways. Seu Antonio had a number of his human rights violated, including the right to life, liberty and security (Article 3 Universal Declaration of Human Rights [UDHR] and Article 6 of the International Covenant on Civil and Political Rights [ICCPR]), the right not to be subjected to torture or to cruel, inhuman or degrading treatment or punishment (Article 5 UDHR and Article 7 ICCPR), the right to equality before the law and equal protection by the law (Article 7 UDHR and Article 26 of the ICCPR) and the right not to be subject to arbitrary arrest, detention or exile (Article 9 UDHR and Article 9 ICCPR).

It is commonly heard in Brazil that there is no justice for the poor, and indeed, this is well founded in the everyday experiences of the poor. It emerges from a society where social inequality is intertwined with institutions that need reform, such as the prison and the police, and can only be understood in the context of existing power relations. Brazilians have constitutional rights to justice but in practice access to justice is deeply unequal (Holston and Caldeira 1998; Zaluar 2010). Seu Antonio's case is one example of the multiple forms of abuse, violence and violations that have become routine and occur in a large scale in Latin American countries. These violations are not necessarily a deliberate part of state policy, which was the case during previous Latin American military dictatorships (Engstrom and Hurrell 2010).

Seu Antonio's case exemplifies one of the perverse outcomes of increased policing without the democratisation of police values. Poor black males are arrested, simply for being in the wrong place at the wrong time, without having necessarily committed an offence. A number of violations of his rights, as argued above, followed his arbitrary arrest. He became simply another number to be measured by police performance statistics, mistakenly assumed to be a "success" arrest of a member of an armed and drug-related criminal group. This type of police arbitrariness generates resentment towards State institutions and reinforces the authority of organised criminals that claim to provide security in these communities.

Gendered inequalities

Gender studies have pointed to the importance of acknowledging and understanding the effects of the performance of gender roles (Butler 1988; Drybread 2014), the ways in which patriarchal relations or the dominance of masculine values over feminine values perpetuate gender inequalities and the manifestations and effects of certain forms of masculinities centred on the ethos of violence and bravado (Bourgois 2003; Connell 2005; Zaluar 2010). Feminist studies have also argued for the importance of understanding the silences (Ryan-Flood and Gill 2010) that expose patriarchal relations and gender inequalities. What is not said can say much about how gender inequalities manifest. For instance, while policing and new modes of securitisation have allegedly aimed to reduce homicides – a type of violence that victimises men far more than women – interventions have been silent about the ways in which non-lethal violence against women might be addressed. Sexual and non-lethal violence – the types of violence most often committed against women and girls – have been neglected. Key limitations of new modes of securitisation are made visible through the intersections of gender, race, age and class inequalities in Brazilian society.

Here I adopt the definition of patriarchy as a "gender system in which men dominate women and what is considered masculine is more highly valued than what is considered feminine" (Chesney-Lind 2006, 9). Symbols, values, representations and the performance of femininity, and even the lives of feminine bodies, are less valued. Few would deny the existence of multiple forms of gendered violence and the repression of women in multiple spheres of social life in Brazil, such as the family, work, religion, in communities, politics and in the criminal justice system (Hautzinger 2007; Gregori 2010). However, the role and place of women in patriarchal societies is often under-theorised or left unaddressed. Patriarchal dominance can take many forms, including through high levels of violence against women, rape, inadequate access to justice, the neglect of women's needs in policies of crime control and the ways in which crime control affects gendered bodies differently. Patriarchal and sexist ideologies demarcate gendered power relations and portray women's bodies as the property or object of desire and dominance by men.

Wilding (2010) suggests that in Latin America women are consistently missing from mainstream debates about violence, whether as victims or perpetrators of violence. In Vitoria, three out of every ten participants, male and female, expressed concerns about rape or violence against women. This is likely to be an underestimate, considering the stigma and shame associated with these topics and the reluctance to associate oneself with the role of victim of sexual or gender-related crime. Nonetheless, these concerns were based on common knowledge about unreported sexual and violent crimes against women. These themes are demonstrated in an interview with Alice, a 16-year-old student:

> I don't spend much time out on the streets so I don't know much about the neighbourhood. I know that we have problems with sanitation [...]. There are also mudslides in the community during the rainy season so people can lose their homes. There is plenty of drug trafficking and drug use, especially crack cocaine [...] now and then you hear of a young person who was killed [...] Well, like a friend of my cousin's, he was killed because of drug debt. That is quite common. There are also cases of men killing their women. Recently a guy shot, killed and cut up the body of his woman, because of jealousy. She was very pretty and polite, she was 21 years old.

Neither the police nor drug traffickers were able or willing to control violence against women. Traffickers were not as organised or in control of the community and social order in the community as in Rio de Janeiro (Arias 2006). Cerqueira and Coelho (2014, 6) estimate that there are 527,000 cases of rape in Brazil every year and, of those cases, only 10% are reported to the police. Their study, drawing on data from the Brazilian National Health System database (SINAN, *Sistema de Informações de Agravo de Notificação do Ministério da Saúde*), reveals that 89% of victims of rape are female and 70% are children and adolescents (ibid, 26).

Many young women, like Alice, were concerned about being raped and avoided public spaces because of a rational fear based on known cases of rape and violence against women in the community. While new modes of militarised securitisation, such as PPV, focus on curbing levels of homicide, such interventions fail to address serious cases of violence against women. This is not to say that women are not affected when men in the community, their sons, partners and male friends are killed or when they are the recipients of police solutions to crime (such as incarceration). Both homicides and male-centred modes of securitisation have a multitude of impacts on communities and women, such as loss of income, bereavement and family breakdown. But by being silent and marginalising the importance of the variety of crimes in the city, PPV provides a very partial form of public safety provision. The policy is, in this sense, made by men and for men.

By being androcentric, focusing on repressing crimes that mostly affect men, such as homicide, criminal justice interventions based on orthodox criminological theories have left out gender issues. As argued by Young (2011, 189) "the lens of orthodox criminology not only distorts, it leaves out". The data that are measured, monitored and emphasised in police targets – such as the amount of drugs apprehended and the number of cases of homicide – have nothing to say about rape or victims of serious non-lethal violence. The security apparatus has disregarded the provision of women's safety in at least two ways: (1) by failing to include women in any significant or genuinely proportionate and representative form in the running of the system and (2) by failing to consider and monitor violent crimes that affect women in the performance outputs that are measured.

The government of Pernambuco created a Secretariat for Women, but it is still unclear what impacts this has had at street level or for people's daily lives. This new and small secretariat for women promotes a number of programmes focusing on gendered violence, including campaigns against violence against women and the training of public sector professionals who deal with victims of domestic violence (Portella and Nascimento 2014, 53). It also runs four shelters for victims and their children. None of these projects produce performance indicators and neither are their outputs monitored by PPV, a critique already made by sociologists involved with the initial design (albeit not the implementation) of the PPV (ibid). Moreover, data from interviews with members of the Secretariat for Women reveal that these are small-scale projects that are unable to deal with the scale of gendered violence in the area. Certainly some improvements or moves in the right direction have started at national level, prior to PPV, such as the creation of women-only police station (*delegacias da mulher*). However, with the creation of PPV, Pernambuco has seen increasing rates of incarceration of women rather than increasing security for women. In an interview with a senior member of staff of Recife's Secretariat for Women (28 January 2016), I was told that with increased policing and growing incarceration of men involved in the drug trade, more women in low-income communities have been pushed into the drug trade, sometimes due to lack of alternative economic means or coerced by their imprisoned partners, leading to sky-rocketing rates of incarceration of women too.

Alice's narrative has parallels with the case of two sisters from her community, Vera and Simone. Vera had been in an abusive relationship for nearly 25 years with Fernando, and her extended family had had enough of seeing her hiding her bruises. Vera was withdrawn, ashamed and depressed. She relied on her abuser as a source of income. According to Simone, Fernando was an "alcoholic and schizophrenic" and in one of his crises he had threatened to kill the entire family. His daughters were so scared of him that one fled to Rio de Janeiro in search of a better life and the other started sleeping with a knife concealed under her pillow. Simone explained how her family had decided that it was time to do something about Fernando. He was a threat for the entire family and they knew that the formal justice system could not deal with him efficiently enough to ensure the safety of Vera and her daughters. At the time, the family, which included Vera and Simone's siblings, was debating whether to hire a *matador* (a hit-man), to exterminate Fernando. In their view this was the only solution to Vera's and the family's suffering at the hands of Fernando. Fernando is still alive and Vera continues to live with him. The family's decision was swayed by one of the evangelical siblings who argued against the killing. Both of their daughters have now moved to Rio de Janeiro but many members of the family still think that they need to take justice in their own hands. This gap in public safety service provision to women and surviving victims of violence, beyond fostering inequalities, has potential to erode the capacity of PPV by generating more work related to homicides inflicted by militias, *matadores*, illegal security groups and death squads that are keen to fill the security gap, or to "employ violence (e.g. vigilantism) as a means of creating their own extra-legal forms of security" (Arias and Goldstein 2010, 4).

The inadequate and unequal provision of access to justice in programmes such as PPV compound and contribute to the status quo by neglecting and being silent about gender violence. Although at the national level Brazil has implemented some innovative gender-focused initiatives, local public security policies such as PPV have generally failed to focus on women's needs and to address the social and power inequalities that engender gender violence. On the national scale, Brazil started to criminalise domestic and family violence in 2006 with the creation of the Maria da Penha law. The country's women-only police stations were first established in 1985, and access to them has been expanded with the opening of 475 units (Hautzinger 2007; UN Women 2011). Evaluations from the United Nations suggest that women-only police stations have increased access to services such as counselling, legal and social support (UN Women 2011, 1). However, women-only police stations are not open overnight or at weekends when cases of rape and violence are more likely to occur (Mendonça 2015) and large numbers of complaints brought to women's police stations never enter the legal system (Gregori 2010). Neither the police nor mediators available in low-income communities are able to establish dialogue with residents to prevent these crimes from happening. The public need to trust the police to report these crimes, and the police needs to be responsive and present so that community–police relations can be developed and trust can be built. Furthermore, criminalising approaches cannot address the economic and gender inequalities (Hautzinger 2002, 2007) that force abused women to stay in these relationships.

Youth crime

If the neglect of women and gender inequalities are weaknesses of new modes of securitisation, another issue is the lack of attention to the age of victims and perpetrators of crime. The roots of youth crime and victimisation cannot be resolved through policing and incarceration. Despite not having reached the level of organisation present in Rio de Janeiro, the drug trade has become so widespread in Recife that most young people interviewed had friends or family who had become involved with the trade, often at a very young age:

GEORGE (18 YEARS OLD, MALE): "The main problem here is drugs. Lots of my old school friends are in this life in drugs".

ROXANA: "Are they using drugs or selling them?"

GEORGE: "Both. They are selling and smoking crack and marijuana".

ROXANA: "When did they get involved with this 'life in drugs'?"

GEORGE: "When they were 11 or 12 years old. Many are dead already".

ROXANA: "Really?"

GEORGE: "Yes, because of drug debt. They end up in fights. Young people killing young people. Sometimes it's rivalry, or because one took the selling spot of the other. Or they have a misunderstanding over how they split the product between them [...] sometimes I hear them arguing about it".

ROXANA: "So, do they have a boss?"

GEORGE: "Yes, they do [...] but no one talks about this. The police came and did a clean-up last month. Sometimes the police take their guns and drugs. There were others bosses who were arrested but this guy came to take their place".

George seemed aware of police action in the community; however, repressive action did not suffice to resolve the cycle of violence in the drug trade. Neither did it stop ever-younger children from engaging in the drug trade. The perception that the police are unable to succeed in the war on crime and drugs because people aged under 18 cannot be prosecuted and penalised in the same way as adults is one of the rationales for demands to reduce the age of criminal responsibility in Brazil. So far the move towards reducing the age of criminal responsibility has been one of the main successes of conservative (and sometimes evangelical Christian/protestant) groups such as the so-called *Bancada Bala, Boi e Biblia* (also known as the *bancada BBB* or "Bullets, Beef and Bible" caucus) and the *Bancada da Bala* (the bullet lobby) formed largely by politicians that are linked to the armaments industry and ex- or current members of the police that have turned to politics to propose increasingly punitive agendas (Douglas 2015). However, repressing this kind of crime (drug related) through policing does not stop it from happening, as the data here and international studies reveal (Shiner 2016). There were new candidates and recruits willing to re-establish business as usual once arrests had been made. Moreover, there is incontestable evidence that incarcerating younger people neither reduces crime nor rehabilitates young offenders, but that it does lead to negative life-outcomes (Squires and Stephen 2005; MacDonald 2006, 2010; Gomes 2015). Residents' experiences suggest that the police presence on its own might deter some crimes, but cannot address the various forms of violence and drug-related crimes in the community:

> The problem is mostly drugs and fights between couples. It's not safe here. After 8pm you can't really sit outdoors. Like, there was a guy sitting near my neighbours' that got hit by a stray bullet [...] There's no dialogue between the police and the residents. I don't think people fear them, but they don't trust the police. [...] They take bribes and even drugs, without arresting.
>
> (George)

Nearly all participants mentioned police corruption in the neighbourhood, including accepting payments instead of arresting suspects. The drug trade, in particular the growing trade in crack cocaine, has increased illicit cash exchanges and provides more opportunities for corrupt police to extort drug dealers and traffickers. Despite police corruption, improving and increasing "dialogue between the police and residents" was a key demand by residents.

Police discrimination, mistrust and criminalisation

In Tourinho and in Vitoria, the drug trade provided an alternative source of income and lifestyle to some young men with few qualifications and few well-paid employment prospects, just as in Bourgois' (2003) study of crack dealers in East Harlem, USA. Involvement in the drug trade and access to firearms provided some status, power, visibility and the possibility of enacting a certain form of masculine identity and bravado, even if their life expectancy would be cut short. Older residents and young people themselves were aware that what they called a *vida no mundo das drogas* (life in the world of drugs) would likely lead to either early death or trouble with the law. But easy access to firearms and the lack of opportunities and meaningful activities led many young people towards the drug trade and a vicious circle of unregulated violence.

Unlike in southeast Brazil (e.g. Rio de Janeiro), traffickers did not interfere with the day-to-day opening and closing of schools and local businesses. But the drug trade and firearms were present within schools, thus interfering with some aspects of services in the local community. Residents argued that an increase in policing was not enough to ensure safety and address drug-related violence in the neighbourhood. As explained by one young female student:

> My best friend had to move to the interior of the state because her cousin, and neighbour, killed two *chefes de boca* (bosses of a drug selling point). The entire family was under threat so she had to leave.
>
> (Karine, 16 years old, female)

As in Tourinho, in Vitoria most participants wanted more policing, despite complaining about multiple police ills and brutality. It was possible to code the interview data from 116 participants into four categories about their perception of the police presence in their neighbourhoods. Only nine participants (8%) responded that they thought the police were sufficiently present in their community. Sixty-five respondents (56%) said that the amount of policing in their neighbourhood was inadequate. Thirty participants (26%) did not want to comment on this topic and seven (6%) said that the police was sometimes sufficiently present in the area. What was more disturbing is that seventy-two participants (62%) responded that they feared and mistrusted the police, while only fifteen (13%) responded that they did not fear or mistrust the police and twenty-nine respondents (25%) refused to comment. People felt distant to the police, there being no dialogue or positive interaction with them. Residents would occasionally call the police and report a crime anonymously over the phone. However, most people were unlikely to provide information to the police during investigations, partly this was because the police were hardly present in the community, while the people that they may be "snitching" or informing on, were there most of the time. The *lei do silêncio* (literally "law of silence") remains strong.

People feared revenge but in some cases they simply did not trust the police, given that when residents and young people did talk face-to-face to the police, their encounters were rather unpleasant. Police officers interviewed claimed to be attempting to do their work and follow orders, but in some cases, this work entailed arbitrary stop and searches to meet targets. The arbitrariness of stop-and-search operations deteriorated community–police relations and led to conflict between officers and residents. Most young males interviewed explained that if they were outdoors after 9:00 p.m. they were immediately seen as criminals. Some of these young men claimed that the police would "plant" drugs in their pockets to arrest them. Some had also seen friends being arrested in this way. Young males also reported that the police extort cash from residents under threat of arrest. Many had been victims of police violence, as illustrated by Gustavo's experience. The dominant discourse about violence reduction and managerial police reform – which focuses on targets such as drugs and firearms apprehensions, numbers of arrests and number of people processed through the criminal justice system – obscures the multitude of ways in which arriving at these targets or acclaimed results affect and generate costs to the marginalised. The data presented here provide a challenge to the narratives of "success" of state interventions.

Experiences of police brutality were common, in much the same way that Garmany (2014, 1242) suggests, on the basis of his research in a favela community in a different northeastern Brazilian state, that "hostility and disrespect toward the poor have become institutionalised procedure". Bernardo, 16, from an indigenous background, had been a victim of arbitrary brutal tactics during a stop and search carried out by a special militarised police force called GATI (*Grupo de Apoio Tatico Itinerante – Policia Militar de Pernambuco*, GATI-PMPE). Bernardo explained that during recurrent stop-and-search operations, police officers had punched and kicked him (and other young people in the community), and ordered him to interlace his fingers while physically compressing them, causing intense pain. Specialist militarised shock troops, such as GATI, or ROTA in São Paulo or BOPE in Rio de Janeiro, formed by heavily armed military police were created to combat threats of a "terrorist" nature, armed banked robberies and serious armed conflict. ROTA for example, was created during the last military dictatorship in Brazil (1964–1985), specialising in armed conflict and political repression. Yet, when armed conflict was no longer a motive for this type of policing, these troops turned to the combat of ordinary crime without abdicating the methods developed during periods of military arbitrariness (Pinheiro 1982, 60). The current research shows that GATI, just like ROTA, continues to arbitrarily deploy militarised repression methods on ordinary civilians perceived as suspects.

Physical punishment and extra-legal methods of social control were commonly imposed on the bodies – particularly the young, indigenous or Afro-Brazilian bodies – of people who live and utilise public space in particular territories, in the criminalised slums and territorially peripheral communities, the spaces perceived as dangerous, criminal, undeserving and undesirable to inhabit. Both violence and the repression emerging through the public security apparatus are unevenly distributed in the city. Residents of the *periferias* are the population most exposed to violence emerging from the drug trade and from the most repressive methods of policing, as demonstrated in several studies (Cano 1997; Zaluar 2004; Feltran 2008, 2011; Garmany 2011; Fernandes 2013). In both case-study communities, non-lethal police violence, such as the *baculejo* (forceful stop and search, often involving a physical beating) had been common. But there were also cases of police killings. One young man had seen his brother being shot by the police in 2013, he explained:

> My brother was coming back from a gig at night when one of his mates stole his silver chain, so he decided to call the police. When the police came, instead of treating him as a victim, they accused him of theft and of carrying a firearm. He didn't have a firearm. They shot him but he survived [...] My other brother was involved in drug trafficking and he was shot and killed by the police in 2012. My mother was devastated. The officer who shot him was disciplined and lost his uniform [lost his job].
>
> (João, 17, Vitoria)

Despite being the most victimised group in the community, young indigenous and black people were also the most targeted, criminalised, punished and executed group by the police. Young black males were the focus of police surveillance, just like in other parts of Brazil (cf. Adorno 1995) and the world (Wacquant 2008; Cavadino, Dignan and Mair 2013, 291). Inevitably, the more a group is targeted by penal and repressive institutions, the more likely it is that they will become over represented in crime statistics (as offenders) and in penal institutions, such as the prison. Systematic institutional racism generates a vicious circle of criminalisation – the more black people are over-represented in the penal system as offenders, the more they are the subjects of surveillance and the targets of police work.

Conclusion

Drawing on data from two case-study communities in the peripheries of Recife, this chapter has presented a critique of securitisation, based on the voices of people in marginalised communities. These communities are in the epicentre of multiple social inequalities. Interviews with residents, mostly (albeit not all) young (aged 16–29), revealed the current state of policing, the gaps in security provision and the consequences thereof, such as the continuity in neglectful, criminalising and violent methods of control. Residents felt distant from the police but when they interacted, those encounters were adversarial and reflected enduring problems of disrespect for the rights of poor, indigenous and Afro-descendant citizens.

While securitisation programmes focused on targeting homicides, a crime that affects more men than women, they did not address wider forms of violence, including structural, symbolic and non-lethal violence. Female victims of abuse and rape were left neglected and unprotected, leading some residents to seek alternative forms of security provision from *matadores* (hired killers) and extermination groups. Furthermore, since female victims of serious non-lethal violence were uncounted and unrepresented in the dominant framework that focuses on monitoring quantitative targets, there was no observable attempt to deal with their victimisation in any meaningful way. While claims of reduced numbers of homicides were good for political campaigns, modes of securitising the city did little to resolve insecurity in marginalised communities, which saw ever-younger children join the drug trade and ordinary residents criminalised by racist, sexist and classist policing and public security interventions. As such, the chapter provided a critique of the dominant technocratic discourse of "successful" securitisation presented in the media, in the narratives of state actors (especially high-ranking government actors) and even in the discourse of some academics (Ratton, Galvão and Fernandez 2014).

Notes

1 ROCAM-PMPE or *Rondas Ostensivas com Apoio de Motocicletas*.
2 Author interviews with Lourdes and Luther, Tourinho, 4 August 2013.
3 To read more about the youth justice system in Pernambuco consult Amorim, Melo, and César (2016), Nolasco (2010) and Schuler (2015).
4 A police investigation document (Oficio 052/2001-DIR, of 23 January 2001) about the death of Helio Jose Muniz on 14 January 2001 in the Prison Anibal Bruno revealed that the directors of the prison were fully aware and supported Helio's role as *chaveiro*. His case and death were highly publicised in the media as he was known for admittedly killing over sixty people in Camaragibe, a municipality in the outskirts of Recife's metropolitan region, including thirteen members of the police and an ex-mayor. Helio became a central character in a documentary entitled "O Rap do Pequeno Principe contra as Almas Sebosas", translates as "The Little Prince's Rap Against the Wicked Souls" (Caldas and Luna 2000).
5 I asked how he knew whether someone was a thief or a matador. He said, they could tell by the prison number, but sometimes they could tell by a piece of paper on their cell which states what crimes the inmate has been convicted for.

References

Adorno, S. 1995. "Discriminação racial e justica criminal em São Paulo." *Novos Estudos Cebrap* 43: 45–63.

Amorim, A., R. d. A. Melo, and I. d. A. César. 2016. "As unidades socioeducativas na Região Metropolitana do Recife (2011–2012): considerações sobre problemas estruturais, funcionamento e proposta pedagógica." *ARACÊ – Direitos Humanos em Revista* 3 (4): 177–195.

Arias, E. D. 2006. *Drugs & Democracy in Rio de Janeiro: Trafficking, Social Networks, & Public Security*. Chapel Hill: University of North Carolina Press.

Arias, E. D., and D. M. Goldstein. 2010. "Violent Pluralism: Understanding the New Democracies of Latin America." In *Violent Democracies in Latin America*, edited by E. D. Arias and D. M. Goldstein, 1–34. Durham, NC and London: Duke University Press.

Arruda, R. F. d. 2014. "Geografia do Cárcere: Territorialidades na vida cotidiana carcerária no sistema prisional de Pernambuco." PhD, Universidade de São Paulo, USP, São Paulo.

Bourgois, P. I. 2003. *In Search of Respect: Selling Crack in El Barrio*. 2nd ed. Cambridge: Cambridge University Press.

Brinks, D. M. 2008. *The Judicial Response to Police Killings in Latin America*. Cambridge and New York: Cambridge University Press.

Butler, J. 1988. "Performative Acts and Gender Constitution: An Essay in Phenomenology and Feminist Theory." *Theatre Journal* 40 (4): 519–531. doi:10.2307/3207893.

Caldas, P., and M. Luna. (Directors). 2000. *O Rap do Pequeno Principe contra as Almas Sebosas*. Brasil, 31 August 2001. Production Companies: Luni Producoes; Raccord Produções; Rec Produtores; Cinematografica; Superfilmes Distributors: Europa Filmes (Brazil) and Riofilme (all media).

Caldeira, T. P. d. R. 2000. *City of Walls: Crime, Segregation, and Citizenship in São Paulo*. Berkeley: University of California Press.

Cano, I. 1997. *Letalidade da ação policial no Rio de Janeiro*. Rio de Janeiro: ISER.

Cavadino, M., J. Dignan, and G. Mair. 2013. *The Penal System: An Introduction*. 5th ed. London: SAGE.

Cerqueira, D., and D. d. S. C. Coelho. 2014. "Estupro no Brasil: Uma radiografia segundo os dados da Saúde (versão preliminar)." Online, IPEA.

Chesney-Lind, M. 2006. "Patriarchy, Crime, and Justice: Feminist Criminology in an Era of Backlash." *Feminist Criminology* 1 (1): 6–26. doi:10.1177/1557085105282893.

Connell, R. W. 2005. *Masculinities.* 2nd ed. Berkeley: University of California Press.

Darke, S. 2013. "Inmate Governance in Brazilian Prisons." *Howard Journal of Criminal Justice* 52 (3): 272–284.

Douglas, B. 2015. "Brazil's 'Bullets, Beef and Bible' Caucus Wants to Imprison 16-Year-Olds." *The Guardian*, April 17. www.theguardian.com/world/2015/apr/17/brazil-rightwing-caucus-lower-age-criminal-responsibility?CMP=share_btn_tw.

Drybread, K. 2014. "Murder and the Making of Man-Subjects in a Brazilian Juvenile Prison." *American Anthropologist* 116 (4): 752–764. doi:10.1111/aman.12147.

Engstrom, P., and A. Hurrell. 2010. "Why the Human Rights Regime in the Americas Matters." In *The Human Rights Regime in the Americas: Theory and Reality*, edited by M. Serrano and V. Popovski, 29–55. Tokyo: United Nations University Press.

Feltran, G. d. S. 2008. "O legítimo em disputa: As fronteiras do "mundo do crime" nas periferias de São Paulo." *Dilemas* 1 (1): 93–126.

Feltran, G. d. S. 2011. *Fronteiras de Tensão: Política e Violência nas Periferias de São Paulo.* São Paulo: Unesp.

Fernandes, F. L. 2013. "Youth Gang Members in Rio de Janeiro: The Face of a 'Lost Generation' in an Age of Fear and Mistrust." *Bulletin of Latin American Research* 32 (2): 210–223. doi:10.1111/blar.12030.

Frühling, H. 2009. "Recent Police Reform in Latin America." In *Policing Insecurity: Police Reform, Security, and Human Rights in Latin America*, edited by N. Uildriks, 21–46. Lanham, MD and Plymouth: Lexington Books.

Foucault, M. 1979. *Discipline and Punish: The Birth of the Prison.* Translated by A. Sheridan. Harmondsworth: Penguin.

Garmany, J. 2011. "Drugs, Violence, Fear, and Death: The Necro- and Narco-Geographies of Contemporary Urban Space." *Urban Geography* 32 (8): 1148–1166.

Garmany, J. 2014. "Space for the State? Police, Violence, and Urban Poverty in Brazil." *Annals of the Association of American Geographers* 104 (6): 1239–1255.

Goldstein, D. M. 2003. *Laughter Out of Place: Race, Class, Violence, and Sexuality in a Rio Shantytown.* Berkeley and London: University of California Press.

Gomes, K. 2015. "Brasil vai na contramão mundial ao debater redução da idade penal." *Carta Capital*, April 29.

González, Y. M. 2014. "State Building on the Ground: Police Reform and Participatory Security in Latin America". PhD thesis, Political Science, Princeton University.

Gregori, M. F. 2010. "Violence and Gender: Political Paradoxes, Conceptual Shifts." *Vibrant – Virtual Brazilian Anthropology* 7 (2): 216–235.

Hautzinger, S. 2002. "Criminalising Male Violence in Brazil's Women's Police Stations: From Flawed Essentialism to Imagined Communities." *Journal of Gender Studies* 11 (3): 243–251. doi:10.1080/0958923022000021278.

Hautzinger, S. J. 2007. *Violence in the City of Women: Police and Batterers in Bahia, Brazil.* Berkeley: University of California Press.

Holston, J., and T. P. r. Caldeira. 1998. "Democracy, Law, and Violence: Disjunctions of Brazilian Citizenship." In *Fault Lines of Democracy in Post-Transition Latin America*, edited by

F. Aguero and J. Stark, 263–296. Coral Gables, FL: North South Centre Press, University of Miami.

Huggins, M. K. 1998. *Political Policing: The United States and Latin America*. Durham, NC: Duke University Press.

Koster, M. 2009. "In Fear of Abandonment: Slum Life, Community Leaders and Politics in Recife, Brazil." PhD, Wageningen University, Netherlands.

Loader, I. 1996. *Youth, Policing, and Democracy*. London: MacMillan.

MacDonald, R. 2006. "Social Exclusion, Youth Transitions and Criminal Careers: Five Critical Reflections on 'Risk'." *The Australian and New Zealand Journal of Criminology* 39 (3): 371–383.

MacDonald, R. 2010. "Paths of Exclusion, Inclusion and Desistance: Understanding Marginalized Young People's Criminal Careers." In *Escape Routes: Contemporary Perspectives on Life after Punishment*, edited by S. Farrall, S. Richard, S. Maruna, and M. Hough, 34–57. London: Routledge.

McAra, L., and S. McVie. 2005. "The Usual Suspects? Street-Life, Young People and the Police." *Criminology and Criminal Justice* 5 (1): 5–36.

McCann, B. 2008. *The Throes of Democracy: Brazil since 1989*. Halifax, NS and London: Fernwood and Zed Books.

Mendonça, R. 2015. "Violência doméstica: 5 obstáculos que mulheres enfrentam para denunciar." *BBC Brasil*. www.bbc.com/portuguese/noticias/2015/12/151209_obstaculos_violencia_mulher_rm.

Nolasco, A. G. P. 2010. "Adolescentes em cárceres contemporâneos invisíveis, quem se interessa? Um estudo da FUNASE – Unidade Jaboatão dos Guararapes-PE." Mestrado Profissional em Gestão Pública para o Desenvolvimento do Nordeste (MA in Public Management to the Development of the Northeast), Universidade Federal de Pernambuco (UFPE), Recife-PE.

Penglase, B. 2008. "The Bastard Child of the Dictatorship: The Comando Vermelho and the Birth of "Narco-Culture" in Rio de Janeiro." *Luso-Brazilian Review* 45 (1): 118–145.

Perlman, J. E. 2010. *Favela: Four Decades of Living on the Edge in Rio de Janeiro*. Oxford and New York: Oxford University Press.

Pinheiro, P. S. 1982. "Policia e Crise Politica: O Caso das Policias Militares." In *Violencia Brasileira*, edited by R. e. a. DaMatta, 57–92. São Paulo: Brasiliense.

Portella, A. P., and M. G. d. Nascimento. 2014. "Impactos de Gênero na Redução da Mortalidade Violenta: Reflexões sobre of Pacto pela Vida em Pernambuco." *Revista Brasileira de Segurança Pública* 8 (1): 48–68.

Ratton, J. L., C. Galvão, and M. Fernandez. 2014. "Pact for Life and the Reduction of Homicides in the State of Pernambuco." *Stability: International Journal of Security & Development* 3 (1): 1–15.

Ryan-Flood, R., and R. Gill. 2010. *Secrecy and Silence in the Research Process: Feminist Reflections*. London: Routledge.

Saunders-Hastings, K. 2013. *"Los códigos de antes": Insecurity, Nostalgia and Community Experience in Mara territory*. Washington, DC: LASA, 2013 Congress of the Latin American Studies Association, 29th May–1st June 2013. P. 1–25.

Schuler, F. R. 2015. "Entre of proposto e o executado: Uma análise da execução do plano de reordenamento do sistema socioeducativo do estado de Pernambuco nas unidades de intervenção da FUNASE/PE nos anos de 2012 a 2014." Masters in Human Rights, Universidade Federal de Pernambuco (UFPE), Recife-PE.

Shiner, M. 2016. *Drug Policing: What Is It Good for?* After the Drug Wars: Report of the LSE Expert Group on the Economics of Drug Policy. www.lse.ac.uk/IDEAS/publications/reports/pdf/LSE-IDEAS-After-the-Drug-Wars.pdf.

Spivak, G. C. 1988. Can the Subaltern Speak? In *Marxism and the Interpretation of Culture*. edited by C. Nelson and L. Grossberg, 271–313. Urbana and Chicago: University of Illinois Press.

Squires, P., and C. Goldsmith. 2010. "Bullets, Blades and Mean Streets: Youth Justice and Criminal Justice Failure." In *Children Behaving Badly? Peer Violence between Children and Young People*, edited by C. Barter and D. Berridge, 197–215 . Chichester: Wiley-Blackwell.

Squires, P., and D. E. Stephen. 2005. *Rougher Justice: Anti-Social Behaviour and Young People*. Devon: Willan.

UN Women. 2011. "Women's Police Stations in Latin America Case Study: An Entry Point for Stopping Violence and Gaining Access to Justice (Brazil, Peru, Ecuador and Nicaragua)". www.endvawnow.org/uploads/browser/files/security_wps_case_study.pdf

Wacquant, L. c. J. D. 2008. *Urban Outcasts: A Comparative Sociology of Advanced Marginality*. Cambridge and Malden, MA: Polity.

Wilding, P. 2010. "'New Violence': Silencing Women's Experiences in the Favelas of Brazil." *Journal of Latin American Studies* 42 (4): 719–747. doi:10.1017/S0022216X10001343.

Wolff, M. J. 2014. "Criminal Authorities and the State: Gangs, Organized Crime, and Police in Brazil." PhD, University of New Mexico, USA.

Young, J. 2011. *The Criminological Imagination*. Cambridge and Malden, MA: Polity.

Zaluar, A. 2004. *Integração Perversa: Pobreza e Tráfico de drogas*. Rio de Janeiro: FGV.

Zaluar, A. 2010. "Youth, Drug Traffic and Hypermasculinity in Rio de Janeiro." *Vibrant – Virtual Brazilian Anthropology* 7 (2): 7–27.

Zaverucha, J. 2004. *Policia Civil de Pernambuco: O Desafio da Reforma*. Recife: Editora Universitaria UFPE.

Chapter 7

Policy and practice

What is to be done?

So far, this book has brought to light conflicting constructions of securitisation programmes, and revealed significant challenges in the implementation of safety measures. This chapter moves from the microanalysis of ethnographic data and beyond the macro analysis of structural conditions to consider ways in which police and state practice may be more productively guided to promote the public good and a peaceful society. Such discussions are centred on the challenges of demilitarising the police in Brazil, changing public perceptions of offenders and reducing high levels of inequality.

This chapter examines some further challenges to the democratisation of Brazilian policing, drawing on reflections, observations and interviews emerging from the two case study communities and from politically active members of civil society, including activists and members of non-governmental organisations (NGOs) concerned with the issues of public safety and justice. The chapter argues that securitisation had been fabricated as a success based on the measurement of certain quantitative outputs – such as the temporary reduction of homicide rates, the increasing numbers of people processed through the criminal justice system, increasing apprehension of drugs and firearms – while neglecting the limits of this type of measurement and disregarding the importance of qualitative aspects of security interventions. Drawing on the Brazilian case, and expanding on long-standing quantitative/qualitative debates in the social sciences (Westmarland 2001; Silverman 2010; Young 2011), this chapter examines some of the epistemological problems in the prioritisation of quantitative measures over qualitative ones. Overlooked qualitative aspects include citizens' perspectives, police accountability and external independent policing oversight, the hidden and under-studied impacts of security interventions, such as the continuation of organised criminals and death squads operating from within overcrowded prisons.

Recent studies focusing on Brazil have begun to theorise issues around the monopoly of violence in Brazil (Arias and Goldstein 2010; Denyer Willis 2015). The data presented in this chapter suggest the need for social theory that does not emanate from a hegemonic Euro-American (Global North) unidirectional point of view, and for theory that does not exclude large sections of humanity in the Global South. Part of this debate is based on the need for a post-colonial perspective, an approach that does not unthinkingly align itself with theories from the Global North. For instance, state theories about the monopoly of violence, often originating from the European context (Tilly 1992), are frequently deployed in debates relating to the Brazilian case. Although there is credit in considering who, how and whether violent relations take place, the monopoly of violence may not be the best framework to understand the State or violence in Brazil, since arguably neither the State nor organised criminal groups (at least outside São Paulo) have ever had a monopoly of violence.

This chapter debates (i) the limits of the ways in which progress or success in public security interventions are measured, (ii) the effects of undemocratic, distant and brutal policing, such as the coexistence of the police with violent organised crime and death squads, (iii) the inadequacy of means of civil participation in the establishment and monitoring of public security interventions and (iv) the extent of the state presence in low-income communities or State-civil society engagement. Finally, the chapter offers a reflection on the debate around measures that may promote democratic – which is to say transparent, accountable and respectful – policing. These include the demilitarisation of the police and the security apparatus, structural changes to this system and the creation of a permanent means of dialogue between civil society and the police.

The manipulation of quantitative data

Community activists and residents were highly suspicious of the accuracy of government statistics. They argued that in most low-income communities, residents had not noticed a drop in violent crime. In fact, levels of lethal violence fluctuate and it may be difficult for residents in poor communities to notice declining crime rates at street level. In comparison, statistical figures are more easily observed. However, even where statistics can be observed, there are multiple confounding issues at stake and numerous classifications that can impact statistical data. As elaborated by Denyer Willis (2015, 38), a potentially violent death can be classified in various different ways:

> found bones (ossadas), found bodies (corpo achado), suicide (suicídios), suspicious death (morte supeita), death to be clarified (morte a esclarecer), robbery followed by death (roubo seguido de morte, or latrocínio), manslaughter (homicídio culposo), resisting arrest followed by death (resistência seguida de morte), multiple homicide (chacina), and intentional homicide (homicídio doloso).

Eight of these categories are possible in Pernambuco, with the exception of the notoriously contested "resisting arrest followed by death", which was used throughout Brazil to justify police killings, but has been abolished as a category for labelling violent deaths in Pernambuco with the creation of PPV (*Pacto pela Vida*). Nonetheless, such diversity in classifying a violent death reveals the ways in which crime data can be manipulated, used and misused.

Crime data are also frequently hidden or disguised in Brazil. In an interview with a senior member of the statistics team (Gerência de Análise Criminal e Estatística or GACE) of the secretariat for public defence of Pernambuco, I was told that although the State gathers data on all recorded crimes, including serious violence that does not necessarily lead to death, for instance, rape and violence against women; however, the data are not used to monitor performance, unlike data on homicides and drug apprehensions. These crime records are not available to the public; they are classified allegedly to avoid causing panic and increasing fear associated with certain areas.

The Associação dos Delegados de Pernambuco (ADEPPE or association of chiefs of civil police of Pernambuco), dissatisfied with working conditions and low pay, started a campaign in August 2015 to pressure government officials to negotiate these issues. As part of the campaign, the ADEPPE published crime rates that are significantly higher than those released by Pernambuco's secretariat of social defence (SDS). For instance, according to the SDS, there were 3,785 cases of car theft in Pernambuco from 1 January to 31 July 2015, while according to ADEPPE, there were 7,955 (Oliveira 2015a). According to the SDS, there were 380 robberies on public transport from 1 January to 31 July 2015, but according to ADEPPE there were 971 (ibid).

The potential for manipulation of data is a key concern in the Brazilian context, since the police control the morgues (IML) and there are no effective independent institutions of oversight, as the latter section of this chapter reveals. Moreover, much of the work that the police do is not easily quantifiable in the same way that arrests, gun apprehensions and numbers of deaths are. What residents are clearly able to judge is the quality of policing and their relationship with the police. In residents' views, the police's relative absence (sporadic presence), brutality, indifference, corruption and prejudice have not changed with PPV – these characteristics of policing were not easily addressed by PPV's system of monitoring quantifiable performance targets.

Death squads

The type of policing available made many residents feel unsafe and sometimes led them to rely on the work of illegal private security groups and death squads. Many residents were victims of extortion from these groups, who charged them fees for security. In these circumstances, community residents felt that the police were, in effect, protecting the rich and criminalising the poor. In the words of a key informant in Tourinho:

> We don't feel safe. We ask ourselves: who's worse, the bandits or the police? Because the police are meant to protect us but they sometimes kill. We live in a violent society that values having, not being. The police force was created to protect the rich, not the poor.
>
> (teacher, artist, activist, October 2013)

Revenge, whether fuelled by interpersonal conflicts or by disputes relating to the drug trade, was used in place of a dysfunctional and slow criminal justice system, or where formal avenues of justice could not be utilised (e.g. to settle disputes in the underground economy). Since citizens are unable to access justice through state institutions, they are increasingly likely to seek extra-legal forms of security (Arias and Goldstein 2010; Davis 2010).

The context of high insecurity made private security options appealing to residents, so that the efforts to improve personal safety go beyond the middle- and upper-class gated community. Low-income community residents also tried to increase their safety using gates, locks and avoiding being outdoors in the evenings, due to fear of crime and violence. Many paid small fees, such as R$3 per week, for illicit private security in the community, which was sometimes delivered by ex-police officers, deploying violence as a means of conflict resolution.

The infrequent presence of on-duty police was another factor in compelling residents to piece together alternative security solutions. Hired killers manage and systematise illicit security companies in poor communities, extort residents for the service provided, even after they have been imprisoned. These illegal groups continue to manage their business and earn an income from within the prison, operating inside the community even while they remain incarcerated:

> Most people here pay R$3 per week for security. On Saturdays a man comes to collect the money from each household. If you are not in, he will come again on Sunday. The leader of the gang, Marcos Cabeça Afundada ("Sunken-Head Marcos") is in prison but his guys still work for him. Many hit-man, who used to look after a street each, are in prison but the money continues going to them. From inside prison they can order a killing [of a local thief]. I can't tell you exactly what happens if a resident refuses to pay [the fees]. Sometimes their house will get burgled. But the *matador* assures you that if anything is taken from you, he will reimburse you for what was taken. It's bad with him, and worse without him.
>
> (Luther, 29 October 2013)

Illicit security and extermination groups formed by ex-policemen operated by extorting money from residents in return for their services while also working as an insurance company, promising to reimburse residents for potential losses, as long as the fees of R$3 per week (R$13 per month) were paid (the equivalent of around £2.50 per month or 4 hours of labour paid at the minimum wage in Brazil). However, residents were coerced into paying these fees since they were aware that they would be victimised if they did not, potentially by the same group that provides this form of security. Extermination groups were responsible for informal justice in the community, killing petty criminals, people who owed money or even drug dealers and users. According to numerous residents of Tourinho, since the leader Marcos had been imprisoned, the number of drug dealers in the community had increased:

> Some people miss the time when Marcos was out because the community did not have problems with drugs. The drugs problem started here in the last 7 or 10 years. But you know he was not arrested because of the community. No one here would have spoken about him (reported him to the police). But his friends are also ex-police officers and they are all being investigated for being part of an extermination group. When he was investigated they found 60 fighting cocks in his house and an imported pistol, apparently worth R$20,000 (£6,670 at the time), which could shoot even under water. He got done for that. Now everything here is run down, there is crack cocaine everywhere. The public market is full of zombie addicts – kids, women and men. When Marcos was out, the problem in the community was just homicides between rival security groups. People died because of the competition between extermination groups. One group would start terrorising the community to damage the reputation of the other group, because they wanted to take over the security business, it caused all sorts of fights.

The parasitic nature of the security business escalated levels of violence in the community. Dellasoppa (2010) argued that militias and informal security groups, usually backed by policeman living in poor communities, have presented themselves as the security solution for these areas while simultaneously "breaking down" the State's monopoly on legitimate force. But discussing the issue as a "breakdown" of the monopoly of violence suggests that such a monopoly has in fact existed at some point in the history of Brazil. What is observable is that these groups have multiplied the sources of violence in communities in the peripheries of the city.

Even where the State has attempted to monopolise violence through state building programmes and securitisation interventions, these attempts have proven inadequate. That is because, even though the police carried out a number of operations to arrest members of death squads in Pernambuco (Alston 2010) and the main leaders of these groups had been imprisoned, they were still able to maintain their power and coercion in the community, operating from within the chaos of the Brazilian prisons, through their networks. In this context, Luther explained that nobody in the community would want to be seen talking to the police:

> If you are seen talking to the police and then they seize some stuff [e.g. firearms] from one of the [extermination] groups, later your house could be burgled because they think you grassed them up [informed on them]. It is not worth the risk. Some people might do it but only anonymously.

Criminal groups in the community needed and wanted to avoid any contact with the police or with police informants, as this could increase the costs of their operations. For this reason, they were concerned with the identity of their clientele. Transparent, non-sporadic, demilitarised (in practice, dress-code and equipment) and accountable policing could go some way to increasing trust and proximity between citizens and the police, and to reducing the demand for death squads.

Civil society and police oversight

Community activists and members of NGOs are labelled as "civil society experts" because as a group they have insight into both the perceptions of state officials and the perceptions of people in recipient communities, given that their work bridges these two worlds. This group voiced the core critiques of new modes of securitisation, which related to the focus on repression as opposed to social prevention of crime, as well as to the amount of money invested in these aspects of crime control, and the impacts of escalating incarceration and overcrowding in prisons. According to activists, PPV reinforced a traditional conservative approach to public security policies, emphasising repressive policing. They were dissatisfied with the level of police oversight, with the lack of police accountability and demanded independent monitoring of PPV as a programme through councils, a request which was not met seemingly due to lack of political will.

Between May 2007 and September 2010, a group of Pernambucan journalists financed by the Associação do Ministério Público de Pernambuco (Association of the Public Prosecutor Ministry of Pernambuco, AMPPE) organised a blog – PE Body Count – that consulted public security institutions about the numbers of cases of homicide on a daily basis. While the blog existed, information of about 14,000 homicides – including time, name of victim, location and other details – was made publicly available. A digital counter of homicides was placed in the centre of Recife and on the web for one year. The blog and the counter worked to pressure the government for reforms and as a method of independent monitoring of the conditions of public insecurity. According to interviews conducted by Macedo (2012) with members of the team who ran the blog, cases of violence were often under-reported in official statistics and sometimes registered as deaths from falls, electric shocks or traffic accidents, instead of as homicides.

But when the blog's funding was no longer available and with the employment of some leaders of social movements in government jobs, independent methods of monitoring this public security apparatus were no longer available (ibid).

Latin America is known to have insufficient mechanisms for police or state agencies to consult and engage with citizens about what they want from police, except for rare public consultations (Ward 2006, 199). As argued by Ward (2006), when police reforms are attempted without the participation of civil society (NGOs, community groups, individual citizens and research organisations), they can generate suspicion about the extent of commitment and transformation, especially in places where citizens have high levels of distrust for the police. Madalena, a sociologist who had been involved with the public security department, summarises the main critiques made by civil society activists and debates them with members of the public:

MADALENA (23RD JULY 2013): "Pacto pela Vida is very expensive [...] Pacto [pela Vida] led to improved targets but the public prosecutor (Ministério Público) says that 90% of police investigations received are poor and lack information. Another issue is that it is common for the police to be involved in death squads, such as *os justiceiros*. So one of the objectives was to tackle death squads. [...] There has been some reduction in homicides but an increase in violent property crime. Crime is migrating. Some targeted areas, like Santo Amaro, have improved but criminality has increased in other areas. Unfortunately, the only method of crime prevention implemented has been repressive: increasing policing, there has not been any increase in social interventions".

FEMALE RESIDENT: "We need vocational courses and apprenticeships to occupy the young people here. They used to queue for any opportunity of training. We asked for two training schools and instead we received an academia da cidade (a program for physical activity/exercise)".

MADALENA: "Pacto is only 10% about prevention and 90% about repressive policing. There has been some reduction in homicide statistics since it has been prioritised and even the fire service is involved in trying to save victims of violence before they pass away. So, if someone has been run over and at the same time there is a call about someone who has been a victim of attempted homicide, the second will be prioritised because the person who was run over may die but this won't affect the homicide rates. We need an independent conselho (council) to monitor this public security policy and to press for improvements but there is resistance and a lack support and interest from the government to have this established". (Madalena – Sociologist – July 2013)

Community activists made a number of criticisms in relation to PPV: the policy is expensive, focused on repressive crime control and lacks organised official external supervision. One of the main critiques was that to some extent the provision of emergency health care and the practice of rescuing people who had already been victims of violence had enabled a decline in homicides. While this practice had an impact in homicide rates, it did not stop violence. As Madalena exemplifies above, the fire service is now more active in rescuing and prioritising victims of homicide and people who have been shot, but this does not stop members of the community being shot or victimised in the first place. The strategy of stationing ambulances in and around areas considered hot spots for violence during high-crime periods (e.g. weekends) has "substantially increased the survival rate of gunshot victims without necessarily affecting the overall number of violent incidents" (Wolff 2014, 176). This approach has not reduced the fear of crime and scepticism by residents in the poorest and most affected communities.

Civil society activists argued that the focus on increased policing sidelines the need for a broader and systemic approach to security, one that includes more methods of social crime prevention. Residents demanded programmes devoted to addressing social inequalities and preventing crime, such as increasing opportunities for vocational training and education, recreation, family welfare, employment and routine police patrol on foot. As argued by Bailey and Dammert (2006, 19), simply relying on increased police presence and more crime repression can produce more convictions (including of non-guilty persons), stretch the criminal justice system (which then becomes more vulnerable to inefficiency and injustice) and overcrowd the prison system (where advanced criminal skills can be developed). The political unwillingness to systematically and recurrently engage with the public in the long term, and the failure to support an external oversight council for PPV, were important shortcomings of the programme. If the purpose of the police is solely coercive, without negotiation or consultation, they are effectively an authoritarian and undemocratic institution. A lack in oversight limits the ways in which the police can be subjected to democratic standards of accountability.

The Pernambucan constitution (Article 101) created the Conselho de Defesa Social (Council of social defence) to coordinate public security interventions (Alepe 2015), but the government has not put this into practice (Zaverucha 2000). As Engstrom and Hurrell (2010, 3) put it, the democratic regime in Latin America remains State-centred, operating with relatively minimal civil society participation. Institutions such as the National Public Security Council (Conselho Nacional de Segurança Pública, CONASP) have a limited consultative role instead of a deliberative role and its members are appointed by government officials rather than elected (Leeds 2013), limiting their impartiality.

The government officials interviewed argued that there were already other institutions in place to monitor the police, such as the *corregedorias de polícia* (the police internal affairs and complaints office). However, it is common knowledge that those institutions are not independent from the police, neither are they run by civil society, so they are unable to provide effective and independent police oversight. Police themselves staff the *corregedorias*. State officials argued that PPV had weekly meetings to monitor the police. However, this was an internal, and therefore not independent, method of control and oversight.

Chevigny argues for a combination of internal and external oversight of the police, suggesting that "real accountability will have to combine internal and external controls" (1995, 267). He explains that when monitoring comes exclusively from outside, it leads to resistance and a lack of cooperation on the part of the police, therefore making it very difficult for outsiders to investigate. As a result, recommendations made by outsiders are easily ignored. If monitoring comes exclusively from internal structures, it becomes ineffective and existing habits are liable simply to become normalised.

In Pernambuco, mechanisms of external oversight directed at monitoring PPV have not been developed. PPV suffers from low levels of information transparency, and engagement with civil society only occurred sporadically and infrequently at the beginning of the governor's mandate (Ribeiro 2014, 5 and 20). There were no systematic mechanisms – such as an external council, an external committee or even regular community meetings with state actors – to ensure that the state was responsive to citizens' demands and to complaints about PPV, policing and safety. The council of public safety or CONSEGs (Conselhos de Segurança Pública) that had existed in some locales in the previous government of Jarbas Vasconcellos were not present in the territories of the case studies. To summarise, in Recife (and in many other parts of Brazil), there exist few formal opportunities for public deliberation about policing and public safety interventions.

There are some institutions that can enforce external control over police activities, but they do not have this oversight as their main task. As Cubas (2013) notes, some examples are Comissões de Assembleias Legislativas (Committees of Legislative Councils), Comissões das Ordens de Advogados (committees of barristers associations), Ministérios Públicos Estaduais (state public ministries), committees by religious groups, national and regional human rights councils, international organisations, civil society organisations and the press. Few mechanisms of external oversight have focused on the control of police abuse of force and police violations of citizens' human rights. Some exceptions are the police ombudsmen (ouvidoria), an institution directed by a representative from civil society and with the autonomy to denounce cases brought to its attention, and therefore with some power to monitor police abuses.

The state public ministry and some international organisations can also monitor the police. However, few people in low-income communities are aware of these institutional resources and their roles. Most residents (albeit not all) interviewed were very distrustful of the state and its institutions and are unlikely to report crimes, especially crimes committed by the police.

Even the police themselves are unlikely to report their colleagues in cases of abuse of force and inappropriate treatment of citizens, leaving those problems to be dealt with by internal oversight institutions, as illustrated in a study about the Brazilian police ombudsmen (Cubas 2013). Furthermore, the extent to which complaints against the police lead to any outcome, or punishment, beyond the initial denúncia (complaint communication) is unclear. Brazilians commonly say that such complaints *acabam em pizza* (end in pizza), meaning that nothing is done about them. There was no independent organisation or member of civil society present at PPV's weekly meetings to discuss or monitor the intervention. New equipment, flashy PowerPoint presentations, meetings at the SEPLAG with men in suits and police, PPV adverts on television and headlines in local newspapers, all served to convey a certain image of the security apparatus which was in stark contrast to the reality experienced at ground level in poor communities.

Building state presence through security interventions

PPV, just like the UPPS (Unidade de Policia Pacificadora, or Pacification police units) in Rio de Janeiro, is an exercise of state-building insofar as the State is rhetorically, figuratively and physically increasing presence in poor communities, under the banner of securitisation, regardless of the motivations or intentions of this development (such as to cater "security" for large sporting events, to look to be doing something about crime, and to support a political campaign). This type of state-building has not yet dissipated old habits of clientelism, old forms of state engagement and methods of political bargaining in poor communities. It illustrates that the State is not absent, but rather inadequately engaged with these spaces and their residents. Residents in poor communities complained about the selective type of state presence that is available to them. During election year, there was more opportunity to engage with state officials and politicians, especially those asking for votes and arranging vote buying. But for residents, the quality of the provision of basic services, such as health care was inadequate. They often experienced water shortages, poor schooling, precarious lighting, open sewers running through the community; as well as a violent state presence experienced through brutal encounters with the police. Many residents, despite wanting increased and better-quality policing, thought that the best way to resolve the problem of safety was to invest in better-quality education for the young, opportunities and provide spaces for leisure and culture as well as well-paid job opportunities. These social measures, in their view, had been sidelined by security measures focusing on more policing and more surveillance (e.g. the installation of closed-circuit television cameras). While most participants from low-income communities claimed to have heard of PPV, most had no idea what the government or the police were doing differently. Young people expressed disaffection with the police and feelings of disconnection from public institutions and public policies:

> The secretariat of public defence only represses and controls the population. Pacto pela Vida is a mechanism of control, full of racism, homophobia and awful stop and searches. Repression is the tactics of the police and it is directed at the poor and black people from the periphery.
>
> (Maria, 26 years old, black, Tourinho)

In fact, residents' perception that little had changed in practical terms at street level may be supported by recent increases in homicide rates. Media reports reveal that from March 2014 the number of homicides in Pernambuco rose again (Oliveira 2015b) and government data confirm this trend. This raises questions about the sustainability of PPV's crime control methods. An interview with Delegado Ramon (PC) published on the Diário de Pernambuco (20 June 2014) indicates that police in the state are dissatisfied with their working conditions, overworked (some police work up to 64 hours per week), under pressure to meet targets and paid the second worst salary among all Brazilian state police forces. These were some of the concerns that led police officers to strike, impacting the recent negative results of PPV (Oliveira 2014). The dissonance between what communities and activists view as important measures of an efficient public safety system and what the State itself claims as a successful and efficient system, suggest the need to debate democratic demilitarised public safety interventions.

Democratic public security?

> I took part in the initial process of the program but there was no space to debate youth and human rights, there was only repression and spread sheets with numbers and statistics. There was no room for social movements. The result is simply more police cars, with their attention turned to commercial locations and evangelical churches.
>
> (Baque Forte, 33 years old, activist, Tourinho)

Community activists and those who became involved with social movements felt disheartened about PPV. They explained that there was no room to debate the intervention and no real public participation in the day-to-day running of the programme. PPV had come from above and was being implemented from above, regardless of what people thought at ground level. Young people, particularly those most politicised and involved in the student mobilisations and protests of 2013, argued that PPV was a tool of oppression by the State, used against the poor and indigenous population:

> In practice Pacto is a program of repression towards the poor. The police are poorly trained, they instil fear in residents of peripheral neighbourhoods.
>
> (Malungo, 22 years old, Tourinho)

It was common knowledge that police practice and the way they approach suspects differed according to social class. The problem of officers "knocking down the doors of shacks" in favelas, invading them without a warrant, was especially noticeable during the night, when fewer witnesses are present. The practice of operating at night was instituted at least as far back as during the military regime (1964–1985), according to Huggins (1998, 136), as it enables the police to hide their activities while also inculcating fear in the targeted population. Disrespect, discrimination and police violence towards low-income residents remain common. Goldstein's (2003, 177) research in the 1990s in Rio de Janeiro shows that "the forms and levels of daily violence and suffering in the city are experienced differently according to class, race, gender, and location". Just as Anthony Pereira (2000) argued, in this context, democracy is rendered inoperative. Where the practices of formal institutions, such as the police, are enacted through such an extremely unequal social order, and the rule of law is differentially experienced according to social status, access to citizenship rights and democracy are at best limited and inadequate. The differential treatment and disparities in the way security and repression are distributed are perennial examples of social inequalities in Brazil.

Holston and Caldeira (1998, 263) argued that one of the paradoxes in Brazilian democracy is that while political institutions have been democratised, citizenship is compromised as citizens suffer continuous violations of their civil rights, and violence and impunity are standard. On the one hand, the State is responsible for violent and corrupt policing, while on the other hand, police violence is tolerated due to popular "support for illegal and/or authoritarian measures of control" (Holston and Caldeira 1998, 265). It could be argued that this paradoxical aspect of a "disjunctive democracy" (ibid, 264) – tolerance of violent policing – is not applicable in this study, according to data emerging from the residents of Tourinho and Vitoria. Residents wanted less repressive and discriminatory policing; paradoxically, they wanted more police patrolling the streets on foot (not staying in their cars). One young male summarised it well:

> We need the demilitarisation of the police. The way it is now, they don't make us feel safer, they don't protect the community, their impact is negative. They don't respect residents – and if you're poor, you're treated like a bandit.
>
> (Jose Claudio, 17 years old, Tourinho)

Contradicting Holston and Caldeira's (1998) point, the residents of Tourinho and Vitoria did not favour military and violent police practices. As argued by Goldstein (2003, 199), questions about democracy and citizenship must be connected to the experiences of the poor. The lived experiences of the poor are under-described, under-analysed and simplified as homogenous responses to politics and policies that go against their interests. However, insofar as the debate on militarised policing goes, in the two Pernambucan case studies, residents' responses to issues of policing and security did not seem to conflict with their interests. Community residents repetitively talked about their wish for the demilitarisation of the police. Many viewed the police force as a repressive agency of the State, particularly towards the poor. They wanted and needed policing, but they demanded a model of policing that respected them and viewed them as citizens instead of enemies and suspects.

Clearly, declining homicide rates benefit the population as a whole, poor or otherwise. However, it is unclear whether it was the implementation of PPV that led to this temporary decline in murder rates. The adequacy – in terms of model, quality, quantity and distribution – of public security provision remains questionable. PPV is founded on what Young (2011, 191) would call a "cosmetic criminology", insofar as it treats crime as a mere blemish, addressing it through superficial administrative measures while ignoring processes of stigmatisation, prejudice and power inequalities inherent in the policy, in the security apparatus and in the criminal justice system. One key reform that localised and managerial interventions such as PPV were not able to achieve is the democratisation of the police, which – as suggested above – is a key demand on the part of residents of low-income communities. Essential to this is the demilitarisation of the police and public security apparatus as the section below suggests.

Demilitarisation

More than three decades after the end of Brazil's military dictatorship, the demilitarisation of the police has not yet occurred. The violent police response to the 2013 protests against rising bus fares and the famous case of the disappearance of the builder Amarildo after being captured by the military police in Rio de Janeiro also in 2013 revived the debate about demilitarisation (Bonis 2013; Kawaguti 2013; Araújo 2014; Welle 2014). One year later, the Truth Commission that investigated crimes committed by the last military dictatorship (1964–1985) stated its support for the demilitarisation of the police, among other recommendations (Folha de Sao Paulo 2014). The UN's Human Rights council had recommended demilitarisation in May 2012 to reduce the amount of extra-judicial killings by the police in Brazil (Bonis 2013) and a study by the Fórum Brasileiro de Segurança Pública (N = 21,101) found majority support for demilitarisation among members of the Brazilian military police (Welle 2014).

The demilitarisation debate is complex and contested for a number of reasons.[1] By law, the Brazilian 1988 constitution established the existence of a military police, required to be an auxiliary force to the army if the country is for instance at war. This has implications for the structure of the police and their training, which is essentially military and centred around combatting enemies, rather than focused on service to civilians. So first, demilitarisation would require at a minimum, an amendment to the constitution, which is a lengthy process, requiring political will and majority approval on a series of voting sessions at the legislative. It is highly unlikely that Brazil's current far-right, ex-military president Bolsonaro (2019–date) and his cabinet, formed mostly of military hard-liners, would embrace demilitarisation.

Second, the distinctive possible ways to demilitarise and re-establish the police are contested (Kawaguti 2013). There are questions around, for instance, whether the military police would be integrated to the civil police, or whether an entirely new force would be created. Another question hangs over which branch of the State would be in charge of policing, the municipalities or each federative state. There are also questions around the salary, pensions and job benefits of existing members of the military police after they become inoperative. Finally, although as illustrated above, many Brazilian scholars[2] support the demilitarisation and agree that it could lead to positive outcomes, demilitarisation on its own is unlikely to eradicate police violence. This argument is reinforced by the common knowledge that civil police are also notoriously violent and corrupt, with a reputation for torturing suspects rather than killing them at the rate of the military police. It could be argued that although demilitarisation would not guarantee the end of police violence, it is at least possible to suggest that it has the potential to reduce it, and to promote better policing through the unification of the police. This does not mean that Brazil needs one single police force or a centralised police. Rather, the country could benefit from having police forces responsible for completing the full cycle of policing, trained through coordinated groups of institutions founded on democratic principles rather than militarised and separate institutions (as is the case currently for military and civil police).

At least four proposals[3] have been presented by politicians to demilitarise the police, all of which recommend the unification of the main police forces – the civil and the military police – so that one force would be responsible for the full cycle of policing (Kawaguti 2013; Welle 2014). This measure would eliminate the current division of functions, between investigative police (PC) and patrolling police (PM) and reduce the existing competition, conflict and lack of collaboration between the different police organisations. The specialist in public security Ignacio Cano makes an important point, arguing that although demilitarising the police would be beneficial, demilitarising the entire public security apparatus and its policies is essential to reduce police violence (Araújo 2014). This could entail for instance, less involvement of military personnel in policy-making and implementation, signalling the end of army involvement in public security matters, the end of military training, hierarchy and the end of a military justice system.

Overall, the findings of this research strongly suggest that there is public support for demilitarisation in the communities studied and that demilitarisation would be a step towards improved public safety. As argued by the previous coordinator of the Secretariat of Security, Justice and Human Rights of the estate of Rio de Janeiro Jacqueline Muniz (2006), democratising police practices and improving police–citizen interactions need not wait for constitutional amendment. Willing public leaders, estate governors, secretaries of public security and chiefs of police could take measures to democratise policing. These would stress the importance of transparency in policing in order to limit opportunities for police deviance. Thorough explanations of police procedures must take place, enforcing systems of rewards and punishments for, respectively, democratic and deviant policing practices. Once demilitarisation is achieved, more profound and lasting transformations are possible, including changes to the structure of the police and types of police training, ultimately aiming to change police culture.

Conclusion

This chapter has argued that securitisation in Pernambuco had been deemed a success based on a narrow set of quantitative measurement indicators, to the neglect of qualitative indicators, such as the voices and experiences of indigenous and marginalised peoples. The problems of quantitative measurement, including the manipulation of data, reinforced a clear dissonance between the experiences and demands of civil society and claims made by the State. Community residents generally took the view that although there had been noticeable increases in the amount of policing, the model of policing remained the same – militarised, violent, disrespectful of citizens' human rights, sporadic and distant. Paradoxically, in spite of these issues, residents demanded more policing, just as they also demanded better policing. Residents were fully aware of the need for organised security provision. Inadequate policing had led to the formation of alternative security groups, informal extermination groups and death squads formed (although not exclusively) by off-duty or ex-police officers who extorted money from residents in return for protection, even when members of these groups had already been incarcerated. There was awareness among residents that simply incarcerating members of organised criminal groups was insufficient, since criminals continue to run their business from inside overcrowded and chaotic prisons, through networks involving corrupt prison staff, police and visitors. Criminals diversified into various activities beyond extortion and informal security provision, and the community witnessed sprawling crack-cocaine drug and firearm trafficking as well as armed robberies. Moreover, new groups of organised criminals emerged when previous ones had been dismantled. Although there is no single solution for these problems – which are entrenched in structural material inequalities and discriminatory social relations – some measures explored in this chapter may have potential to moderate these issues, including the democratisation and demilitarisation of public safety interventions.

Notes

1 See Mesquita Neto (2011, 241–268) for a discussion of previous attempts to demilitarise public security in Brazil.
2 Many scholars have made their views public, through the media, on the topic of demilitarisation, for instance, Ignacio Cano, Luis Eduardo Soares, Fabio Gomes França, among others.
3 The first three proposals – by politician Chico Lopes (from Brazil's communist party, PC do B), senator Blairo Maggi (from the PR party) and Celso Russomano (PRB party) – divert in some aspects, see Kawaguti (2013). There is a further demilitarisation proposal to amend the constitution (PEC 51/2013) by senador Lindbergh Farias (from the worker's party, PT-RJ), which essentially proposes the unification of the police forces and the autonomy for each federative state to establish their force's structure (see Welle, 2014).

References

Alepe. 2015. *Constituição do Estado de Pernambuco*. Accessed 20 January 2020. https://legis.alepe.pe.gov.br/Paginas/texto.aspx?tiponorma=12&numero=1989&complemento=0&ano=1989&tipo=&url.

Alston, P. 2010. "Follow-Up to Country Recommendations – Brazil". Report of the Special Rapporteur on extrajudicial, summary or arbitrary executions, Philip Alston. www2.ohchr.org/english/bodies/hrcouncil/docs/14session/A.HRC.14.24.Add4.pdf.

Araújo, T. 2014. "Desmilitarização da PM é só parte da mudança necessária na segurança no Brasil, dizem especialistas." *Brasil Post*, May 13. www.brasilpost.com.br/2014/05/13/desmilitarizacao-seguranca_n_5229091.html.

Arias, E. D., and D. M. Goldstein. 2010. "Violent Pluralism: Understanding the New Democracies of Latin America." In *Violent Democracies in Latin America*, edited by E. D. Arias and D. M. Goldstein, 1–34. Durham, NC and London: Duke University Press.

Bailey, J. and L. Dammert. 2006. *Public Security and Police Reform in the Americas*. Edited by J. Bailey, and L. Dammert, 1–23. Pittsburgh, PA: University of Pittsburgh Press.

Bonis, G. 2013. "É possível desmilitarizar a polícia brasileira?" *Carta Capital*, August 21.

Chevigny, P. 1995. *Edge of the Knife: Police Violence in the Americas*. New York: New Press.

Cubas, V. d. O. 2013. "A Ouvidoria e o controle da atividade policial na percepção dos policiais militares." PhD in Sociology, Universidade de São Paulo, USP, São Paulo.

Davis, D. E. 2010. "The Political and Economic Origins of Violence and Insecurity in Contemporary Latin America: Past Trajectories and Future Prospects." In *Violent Democracies in Latin America*, edited by E. D. Arias and D. M. Goldstein, 35–62. Durham, NC and London: Duke University Press.

Dellasoppa, E. 2010. "Urbanization, the State, and the Privatization of Policing." In *Police Practices in Global Perspective*, edited by J. Eterno and D. K. Das, 103–130. Plymouth: Rowman & Littlefield.

Denyer Willis, G. 2015. *The Killing Consensus: Police, Organized Crime, and the Regulation of Life and Death in Urban Brazil*. Oakland, CA: University of California Press.

Engstrom, P., and A. Hurrell. 2010. "Why the Human Rights Regime in the Americas Matters." In *The Human Rights Regime in the Americas: Theory and Reality*, edited by M. Serrano and V. Popovski, 29–55. Tokyo: United Nations University Press.

Folha de S.Paulo. 2014. "Comissão Nacional da Verdade propõe desmilitarização da polícia." *Folha*, December 10. www1.folha.uol.com.br/poder/2014/12/1560275-comissao-nacional-da-verdade-propoe-desmilitarizacao-da-policia.shtml.

Goldstein, D. 2003. *Laughter out of Place: Race, Class, Violence, and Sexuality in a Rio Shanty-Town*. Berkeley and London: University of California Press.

Holston, J., and T. P. r. Caldeira. 1998. "Democracy, Law, and Violence: Disjunctions of Brazilian Citizenship." In *Fault Lines of Democracy in Post-Transition Latin America*, edited by F. Aguero and J. Stark, 263–296. FL: North South Centre Press, University of Miami.

Huggins, M. K. 1998. *Political Policing: The United States and Latin America*. Durham, NC: Duke University Press.

Kawaguti, L. 2013. "Como desmilitarizar a polícia no Brasil?" *BBC Brasil*, August 22. www.bbc.com/portuguese/noticias/2013/08/130813_sub_desmilitarizacao_lk.

Leeds, E. 2013. "Civil Society and Citizen Security in Brazil: A Fragile but Evolving Relationship". www.wola.org/sites/default/files/downloadable/WOLACivilSocietyandCitizenSecurityinBrazil.pdf.

Macedo, A. d. O. 2012. "'Policia, quando quer, faz!' Analise da Estrutura de Governanca do 'Pacto pela Vida' de Pernambuco." Masters, Universidade de Brasilia.

Mesquita Neto, P. de M. 2011. *Ensaios sobre segurança cidadã*. São Paulo: Quartier Latin; Fapesp.

Muniz, J. and D. Proença Júnior. 2006. "Os rumos da construção da polícia democrática." *Boletim IBCCRIM* 14 (164): 1–4.

Oliveira, W. 2014. "O outro lado do Pacto pela Vida." *Blog Segurança pública*. Accessed 20 January 2020. https://blogs.diariodepernambuco.com.br/segurancapublica/?p=7115.

Oliveira, W. 2015a. "Pacto pela Vida da sinais de fracasso." *Diário de Pernambuco*, March 2. http://blogs.diariodepernambuco.com.br/segurancapublica/?p=8014.

Oliveira, W. 2015b. "Trinta e oito carros são roubados por dia em Pernambuco *Segurança Pública*." *Diário de Pernambuco*. Accessed 12 August 2015. http://blogs.diariodepernambuco.com.br/segurancapublica/?p=8790.

Pereira, A. W. 2000. "An Ugly Democracy?: State Violence and the Rule of Law in Post-Authoritarian Brazil." In *Democratic Brazil: Actors, Institutons, and Processes*, edited by P. Kingstone and T. J. Power, 217–235. Pittsburgh, PA: University of Pittsburgh Press.

Ribeiro, L. M. L. 2014. *Modelo de Gestão por Resultados do programa Pacto pela Vida, Pernambuco, Brasil*. GobernArte: Categoria Governo Seguro. http://publications.iadb.org/bitstream/handle/11319/6564/GobernArte, Categoria governo seguro (Version en Portugues).pdf?sequence=4.

Silverman, D. 2010. *Doing Qualitative Research: A Practical Handbook*. 3rd ed. London: Sage.

Tilly, C. 1992. *Coercion, Capital and European States: AD 990–1992*. Oxford: Wiley-Blackwell.

Ward, H. 2006. Police Reform in Latin America: Brazil, Argentina, and Chile. In *Toward a Society under Law: Citizens and Their Police in Latin America*, edited by J. S. Tulchin and M. Ruthenburg, 171–205. Washington, DC: Woodrow Wilson Center Press.

Welle, D. 2014. "Cresce o debate sobre desmilitarização da PM." *Carta Capital*, August 6.

Westmarland, N. 2001. "The Quantitative/Qualitative Debate and Feminist Research: A Subjective View of Objectivity." *Forum Qualitative Sozialforschung/Forum: Qualitative Social Research* 2 (1), art 13.

Wolff, M. J. 2014. "Criminal Authorities and the State: Gangs, Organized Crime, and Police in Brazil." PhD, University of New Mexico, USA.

Young, J. 2011. *The Criminological Imagination*. Cambridge and Malden, MA: Polity.

Zaverucha, J. 2000. "Fragile Democracy and the Militarization of Public Safety in Brazil." *Latin American Perspectives* 27 (3, Violence, Coercion, and Rights in the Americas): 8–31.

Chapter 8

Conclusion

The legacy of undemocratic rule occurs through multiple state institutions, including militaries, judiciary and, not least, the police and security apparatus. Brazil is a young democracy, but democratic transition and the reinstatement of elections do not necessarily imply the democratisation of state institutions or the reduction of violence.[1] As Pereira (2005, 200) argued, "Transitions to democracy very rarely wipe out – in one dramatic reform – the accretion of years and sometimes decades of authoritarian practices and mentalities". Nonetheless, the continuity of an authoritarian legacy does not mean that there has been no change. What are the impacts of reforms and new public security policies on those most in need of protection? How do residents of Brazil's low-income communities perceive security agencies and the new approaches to security? How do they relate to the police in contemporary Brazil? What differences are there between the security needs of the understudied northeast of Brazil and the southeast? What difference does this make for the types of policies and practices necessary to exert a monopoly of violence, or at least to control violence?

This book contributes to existing debates around these questions. It sits at the intersections of critical criminology, state crime, international/transnational crime and security. In offering an analysis that combines first-hand ethnographic data, critical criminological literature on governance and crime control, with the Brazilian sociology of crime and violence and considering the role of state and civil society actors in relation to the continuation of and resistance to urban violence, this project fills an important gap in knowledge. By examining the marginalised voices of people in poor communities in the northeast of Brazil and exposing the fallacies inherent in the dominant narratives of powerful state actors it challenges the way in which notions of crime control are constructed. Drawing on extensive periods of research undertaken in Brazil, this work provides a unique opportunity for an English-speaking audience to develop their understanding of criminological theory in global perspective. The research challenges current policy, practice and thinking associated with crime, criminals and criminal justice in the Global South.

The central argument of this book is that managerial police reforms and new security programmes, namely PPV (*Pacto pela Vida*) in Pernambuco, have not been the panacea to criminological problems. These reforms have not addressed long-standing issues of discriminatory policing. They have also failed to tackle brutalising, militarised police training and practices. The overall model and style of policing, in spite of the implementation of new security interventions, remains unchanged ("old wine in new bottles"). New security interventions had no effect in making the police adopt democratic principles such as accountability and equality before the law, especially when the police interacted with marginalised people in low-income communities. Neither were these new programmes sufficient to inhibit diverse forms of violence and the continuing operation of organised criminals in these communities. Instead, increasing use of policing and incarceration as methods of crime control exacerbated existing inequalities, with the most vulnerable populations being worst affected. The book contributes new insights to the criminological and public security literature in Brazil, which had, first, both largely marginalised the stories and lived experiences of the poorest communities in the northeast of Brazil and second, failed to challenge the narrative of "success" about new methods of crime control deployed in this region of the world.

While this book has challenged new modes of securitisation in Brazil, and considered some of their effects, this does not mean that all the changes produced so far have been negative. For example, proposals to control firearms and monitor the confiscation of firearms have the potential to reduce violence. The same effect could not be expected from monitoring drug-related arrests and confiscation of drugs. What this book argues is that it is important to consider the wider cumulative effects of securitisation and managerialism, which have profound implications for police-community relations, criminal justice institutions (e.g. the prison) and the exacerbation of social inequalities.

Here I synthesize the material presented in preceding chapters to elicit new understandings of what it means to live in the context of high violence or work in the Brazilian criminal justice system in this context. I pose new questions and areas for future research. First, I consider inequalities in knowledge production that warrant the work of this book. I emphasise the importance of developing research methods that privilege co-producing knowledge with residents of low-income communities and prioritising engagement with theories and knowledge that emerge in other parts of the world, beyond the Global North. Second, I examine the *lessons* that can be learned from the experience of a Brazilian state that emulated a violence reduction programme founded in criminological theories of the Global North. Finally, I caution readers of the dangers identified with exporting criminal justice practices without critically investigating local conditions and challenges to policy implementation.

Inequalities in knowledge production

While the criminological literature has largely been produced in the Global North and in Anglo-Saxon countries, Brazilian literature on public security has for the most part focused on the southeast of the country. Both, therefore, have tended to neglect the northeast of Brazil, and cannot fully account for all regions of a continent-sized country such as Brazil. Significant regional differences render dominant theories and public policies inadequate to some contexts. Explaining and addressing regional problems needs to account for diversity – for example, criminals are exceptionally well organised in the southeast of Brazil yet rates of violence measured by homicide incidents are much higher in the northeast, an issue illustrated in earlier chapters. Public security or safety provision, crime and violence rank as some of the most important and contested topics for Brazilian people. Yet, much literature in Brazil focuses on the experiences of the southeast region, where drug traffickers in poor communities have been so powerfully organised that they have been described as "parallel states" (Leeds 1996). In these cases, traffickers have assumed control over entire communities, taking the law into their own hands, controlling the flow of who is allowed in and out of communities and making it difficult for the police to interact with local people. In some cases, traffickers also assume the role of welfare provider, dispensing loans, jobs and medication, yet at the same time they coerce residents into turning a blind eye to trafficking or hiding drugs and firearms in their homes.

The case studies in Recife provide evidence that criminal groups there have not been organised or powerful enough to be considered "parallel states" within poor communities. And yet both the southeast and the northeast regions face similar problems when it comes to the need to be able to walk the streets safely, or to co-produce policing through consensual practices rather than having it imposed on citizens without respect for their human rights and needs. The police, in all of Brazil, do not operate according to democratic principles (transparency, accountability, equality before the law). Instead, the police function in ways that reproduce deep-seated social inequalities among the population.

Whether in the southeast or the northeast of Brazil, the State is not as absent as one might initially think in poor communities. The development of the public safety programme *Pacto pela Vida* (PPV) is one example of state building and illustrates the interactions of the State with people in poor communities. While some studies have argued that the implementation of the PPV programme has been a success (Ratton, Galvão, and Fernandez 2014), these existing enquiries have not elicited the voices of marginalised groups subjected to these interventions. The cases of Tourinho and Vitoria have much to reveal about the impact of the new security agenda. This investigation is particularly important given that PPV had gained enough positive publicity to receive international awards and to potentially influence national policy, as stated in interviews with government agents[2]; with Brazil's national secretariat for public security (SENASP) proposing in 2016 to implement PPV at the national level. It is therefore essential to understand what implications this could have for Brazil and the Global South.

Lessons from securitisation

The states of Rio de Janeiro, São Paulo, Minas Gerais and Pernambuco have, since the 2000s, seen overall declining homicide rates (with some upward fluctuations). The literature theorising this phenomenon is becoming polarised. On one side are the scholars who argue that a number of factors related to government interventions are responsible for this decline. Among these, we have former advisor and head analyst of the São Paulo State Secretariat for Public Security, Tulio Kahn, who argued that improved policing was a key factor in declining homicides (Goertzel and Kahn 2009; Kahn 2011); Beatriz Magaloni (2015), supporting the UPPs in Rio; and, former advisor in the field of Public Security to the deceased ex-governor of Pernambuco Eduardo Campos, Ratton (2012) in Pernambuco.

On the other side are a minority of researchers conducting qualitative and ethnographic research who argue that evidence from the ground up can enrich this debate, provide alternative explanations and raise important questions about public safety and public security provision. Among these are Feltran (2008, 2011), Dias (2011), Wolff (2014) and Denyer Willis (2015). Feltran, Dias and Denyer Willis all argue that policing and hyper-incarceration in the state of São Paulo have not caused the decline in homicides, but rather that they have enabled or facilitated the monopoly of violence by one criminal group, the PCC (*Primeiro Comando da Capital*). In their view, the State's public security provision has had perverse impacts and has not contributed to reducing crime in the ways it claims. In fact, recent evidence from ethnographic research reveals that the expansion of mass incarceration in Brazil and the practice of dispersing key members of organised groups to prisons in different parts of the country have facilitated the expansion of factions and criminal brotherhoods to other regions and neighbouring countries (Manso and Dias 2018). As a result, Brazil now has the third largest prison population and has experienced recurring deadly riots in prisons in the north and northeast of the country where organised groups are in conflict over the monopoly of profitable drug businesses.

Securitisation has therefore had diverse effects throughout the country. Depending on where the questions to evaluate public security provision, and interventions such as PPV, are asked and on who is asked those questions, an entirely different discourse emerges. Evidence from poor communities (Chapter 6) provides a critique of the dominant discourse of successful intervention and successful policing. The statistical reduction of homicides in Pernambuco, whether accurate or not, did not speak to people in these communities. For these communities, the mainstream criminological literature (as labelled by Taylor, Walton, and Young 2013), the theories on crime prevention, policing and reform (Clarke 1997; Clarke and Felson 2004; Bratton 2005) emerging from the Global North and deployed in the development of security policies in the Global South do not address the developments at the micro level in the peripheries of Recife.

Theories such as "Broken Windows" (Bratton 2005; Wilson and Kelling 2013) and situational crime prevention[3] (Hirschi and Gottfredson 1988; Clarke 1997; De Souza and Miller 2012) have been used to promote managerial criminology around the globe, from COMPSTAT in New York to PPV in Recife, regardless of their applicability or of their perverse outcomes. Brazil's proponents of managerialism have often misread and misunderstood homicide reduction programmes from the Global North, such as Operation Ceasefire, as illustrated in previous chapters. These authors incorrectly interpreted the central element of Ceasefire as the increase in rates of incarceration (Veloso and Ferreira 2008), and some seem to believe that COMPSTAT and crime management technologies could make the Brazilian police more accountable and reduce crime (Soares 2008, 12–15), showing little awareness of the established critiques of managerialism, COMPSTAT and the New York miracle. The fact that academics from the Brazilian left – who are proponents of police demilitarisation and supporters of the human rights agendas, such as Luiz Eduardo Soares – support contested managerial crime control measures that risk exacerbating social inequalities suggests another paradox that warrants further research.

The dominant managerial success discourse is disconnected from the voices of people in low-income communities. The overall feedback from people in the case-study communities revealed dissatisfaction with the State and with the type of security and policing that is provided. While technocrats may argue that the only type of data that can truly convey results are statistics about actual crime rates, this dismisses the importance of police-community relations. Statistical reductions in homicide may look good on paper but they do not mean that the police are less violent and brutal in these communities. Neither do they truly represent reductions in violence. Residents had numerous complaints about cases of disrespect and abuse of their human rights on the part of the police. Homicide data do not reflect the cases of non-lethal violence, when the victim survives, such as rape and gender violence or police abuse of force. Statistical counts are also manipulated in the classification of deaths or in the manoeuvring of evidence collected at the morgues (IML), which are controlled by the police.

This book started by outlining the development of a body of literature on youth crime and marginality around the globe. It addresses the need for research that engages with the perceptions of young people and research that deploys ethnographic methods in the field of public security in the northeast of Brazil. It contributes to the emerging body of literature that is developing southern theories, and a southern criminological approach, through an engagement with knowledge produced by academics in Brazil and an engagement with the perceptions of under-represented groups in civil society, namely young people and residents from low-income neighbourhoods. As such, this book ultimately develops a critique of mainstream criminological theories developed in the Global North and emulated or inadequately applied in the Global South.

The main themes emerging from interviews with public officials, high-ranking members of the civil and military police in Pernambuco, and civil society representatives were presented first, not because there is any superiority over the data emerging from poor communities, but because this approach helps to contrast the stark differences between the dominant discourse of success about government interventions and the narratives of people who are subjected to these interventions and state practices. An analysis of the high-profile program of public security *Pacto pela Vida* (PPV) in Pernambuco and arguments that the police managerial reform had reduced homicides, revealed the transplantation of Americanised crime control methods and criminology, developed in an atypical context – that of advanced industrial countries in the Global North – to societies such as Brazil.

Continuing with the emerging critique of the new security agenda, Chapter 4 outlined some of the contradictions emerging in high-ranking officials' and police narratives, such as examples of class, gender and ethnic discrimination and acknowledgements of police corruption. It suggested that managerial police reforms have not targeted or addressed the endurance of these problems, which hinder the development of policing that is respectful of citizens' human rights. The chapter also shows some of participants' views about the increasing use of policing as an alleged solution to structural and social problems in poor communities. The narratives that emerged from interviews with low-ranking members of the police, who live in low-income communities, were critical of PPV's methods – including the continuation of brutal street policing orders from superiors, and even the extent to which the hard data presented by the government was reliable.

Chapter 6 focused on the perceptions of residents and young people in the two case study communities. The two communities, defined by their socio-economic context and territorial boundaries on the peripheries of the city, are not usually visited, but rather are more frequently avoided because they frighten and vex the middle- and upper-class public. For residents in both communities, the type of policing that they received was distant, sporadic and counterproductive. Residents feared local organised criminal groups in charge of informal security, extermination groups but also feared speaking with the police, who were hardly present in their neighbourhoods, except during the occasional motorised patrol. Moreover, when residents did have contact with the police, they were also subjected to brutal policing methods and were treated as criminals instead of being protected. This generated hostility and resentment but did not reduce demands for more and better policing.

The chapter also illustrated some of the main gaps in security provision in the PPV program, such as its lack of focus on gender issues and its silences on the issues of non-lethal violence against women. Drugs, violence and a lack of decent job opportunities were mentioned as key problems in the community in almost every interview. Residents also complained about other problems such as rubbish collection and general infrastructure (public transport networks, local health care, water shortage), yet concerns about safety always ranked first for residents. Some of the reasons for their concerns were personal experiences of victimisation, including being victims of theft and armed robbery or seeing friends and family victimised. In fact, most residents were concerned about armed robbery on the streets, a crime, which does not necessarily affect homicide statistics, since many victims survive. Many participants in the two communities had experienced numerous cases of bereavement among family and peer groups, because of crime and violence in their neighbourhoods. This increased their fear, their feelings of being under-protected and their withdrawal from public spaces. It also contributed to the power and influence of extortion groups selling security in the neighbourhoods.

Chapter 7 discussed some of the epistemological problems of focusing exclusively on quantitative outputs to measure success in crime control, not least because all data, even quantitative data, can be manipulated. Moreover, the chapter shows that despite increasing managerialism in crime control, increased policing and incarceration, organised criminals still exert influence outside prisons, from within them by operating over, under and through the walls. The chapter reviewed PPV as a state-building exercise and the type of state presence that it provides, contrasting the discourse of success with the counter-narratives of people in the case study communities. It engaged with the views of civil society representatives from non-governmental organisations and social movements, who were both more critical of PPV's methods, especially its dominant focus on repressive policing, and more in-tune with the views of people in low-income communities. It also examined the difficulties of achieving the demilitarisation of policing and security in Brazil.

Lessons from this book can be learned and applied beyond Brazil, since other countries face similar issues – including countries attempting to make their institutions more democratic, or transitioning from authoritarian rule (e.g. Iraq, other Latin American countries), or suffering high crime and inequality rates, growing vigilantism and similar security issues (see Arias and Goldstein 2010, 6–10 for a discussion of this). That said there is a caveat to the effect that – for reasons discussed in this book regarding the danger of importing frameworks from elsewhere – this would need to be done with care. Mainstream proposed solutions, or those that become implemented such as managerial reforms, can be understood as part of broader shifts in social control with comparable developments found in many other countries (Loader 1996; Brownlee 1998; Maguire 2000, 316). The effects of these developments and the risks they pose vary according to the socio-economic context and history of each locale. They impact on populations differently through: the exacerbation of social inequalities; the deterioration of police-community relations; the development of problematic prison complexes; the further organisation of criminal groups; and the additional erosion of public spaces, safety and human rights, all of which become permissible in the agenda of securitising through particular forms of crime control.

This book makes, at the very least, a twofold contribution to the academic literature on youth, policing and security. First, few qualitative studies deploying ethnographic methods have looked at how young people respond to violence and security issues in Brazil. With the exception of some of the research conducted in São Paulo (MNMMR, IBASE, and USP-NEV 1991) and Rio de Janeiro (Goldstein 2003; Zaluar 2004), few studies have focused on the effects of institutions and methods of crime control through the lens and experiences of young people or marginalised people in the northeast of Brazil, with some exceptions (see, e.g. Drybread 2014; Moore 2015).

For the most part, the literature in this field, in Recife, has emerged from public health quantitative studies concerned with identifying and connecting causal variables to dead bodies (Falbo, Buzzetti, and Cattaneo 2001). Studies focusing on the profiling of victims of homicide in Recife (Arnold, Falbo, and Figueiroa 2002) do not provide in-depth qualitative data about young people's lives and perceptions, neither do they allow for any agency from the part of the researched. Although some analytical academic work has briefly mentioned the Recifense case (Mesquita 1993; Huggins and Mesquita 2000), this work has not allowed for the voices of the marginalised to emerge. This leads to an insufficient consideration of the humanistic and spontaneous aspects of social phenomena and social action. The first overarching contribution of this book was to address this gap in the literature. Nonetheless, it must be acknowledged that there is a growing body of research about the effects, dynamics and intersections between prisons and communities outside prison in Brazil (Silvestre 2008a, 2008b, 2016; Moore 2015) and relating to youth justice institutions in the northeast of Brazil (Nolasco 2010; Drybread 2014; Schuler 2015; Amorim, Melo, and César 2016).

The second main contribution was to address the gap in relation to the emergence of new security agendas. In particular this focused on the impacts of the securitisation programme PPV (2007–date) in Pernambuco. Few studies have focused on PPV, and the ones that have tended to emulate or even generate the State's dominant technocratic discourse of success (Ratton, Galvão, and Fernandez 2014), or to look at PPV's system of governance (Macedo 2012), without engaging with the recipient populations, which is to say the people most affected by security programmes. By engaging with the everyday lives of the marginalised, this book enabled a comparison between the discourses of the governing and the governed. It allowed for responses to emerge from below and exposed the realities of the field of security and policing in some of Brazil's most neglected populations.

Securitisation and policing in Brazil penalise people on the basis of their appearance, social background and perceived deservedness. Citizens who do not appear to be *trabalhadores* (workers) – by not using a uniform, or by being unemployed, or by not having the reputation of a worker – and those poor indigenous and afro-descendant citizens who use public space are criminalised or considered *bandidos* (criminal), even when they have not committed a crime. Those who have a criminal record are forever considered undeserving *bandidos* and expendables. They are exposed to unlimited violations that are not constructed as crimes. They are treated, disciplined and handled as disposable bodies, the bodies that can be tortured, punished, incarcerated and disrespected during forceful militarised police stop-and-searches. Improved police training and increased opportunities to generate dialogue between these populations and the police are essential to amend thin and impoverished youth-police relations and community-police relations. Although residents complained that the police were distant and often disrespectful, they perceived a need for policing and public rather than private forms of security. Regular community public security forums that are inclusive of all residents, rather than available to small vocal minorities, open to dialogue and feedback between the police and the community; and an external and independent civil society council to monitor public security policies could go some way in addressing the problems and consequences of distant policing and arbitrary security policies.

Although research on policing in Latin America has been growing since the 1990s, few studies have examined the impacts of security interventions and police reform in Latin American cities from the perspective of recipient communities. Studies also face difficulties in measuring the success of reforms and identifying factors that are useful for comparison before and after reform (Ward 2006). This book provided an inquiry into the impacts of a particular public security intervention – PPV – in Recife, from the perspective of state actors (police and government officials), civil society (activists, NGOs) and residents of low-income communities. It revealed that there are a number of conflicting narratives between groups of research participants, and that their perceptions about the outcomes of securitisation are rather conflicting. On one hand, there has been a step forward in the state of Pernambuco with the development, at state level, of the idea that "security" cannot be simply a commodity for the rich (e.g. private security) and that it needs to be universally provided (public security) in order for all citizens, regardless of their social class, to be safer. On the other, public security policies have evolved but remain discriminatory and repressive. Access to public services, including security (but also beyond, e.g. education) is still inadequate, hindering wider progress to reduce crime and make citizens' safe. The level of violence against youth, class and ethnic discrimination and inequalities remain high in Brazilian society and within state institutions such as the police.

The data presented above reveals that by focusing on homicide reduction and increasing levels of incarceration, PPV has side-lined other important crimes in poor communities, including rape, non-lethal violence, violence against women, extortion and crimes committed by state actors, such as police abuses of force and abuses of human rights in prisons and young offender institutions. Women have been overlooked by the policy and so have the needs of young people. PPV defined and over-enforced the idea of security as the reduction of homicides; this has taken precedence over the overall protection of human rights. Respect and fairness towards people in low-income communities should go hand-in-hand with legitimate policing or democratic police reform. Most residents in the low-income communities studied did not notice the effects of public security interventions at ground level. In sum, the protection of the rule of law has not been the emphasis of programs such as PPV. Changing the focus and methods of security programs is fundamental to promoting more democratic, just and accountable policing. This needs to start from the training and structure of the policing but cannot be exclusively centred in criminal justice approaches.

Data from the case study communities revealed that simply incarcerating members of organised criminal groups did not, according to residents, dismantle extermination groups in charge of the sale of security in these communities. From inside the prison, members of these groups continued to manage and profit from a parasitic business, which, in the context of only sporadic policing, extorts money from residents in forcibly selling an alternative form of security. Despite attempts at state-building such as PPV, the monopoly of violence in these communities continues to be fragmented and the marginalised continue to be treated as expendable nonentities victimised both by violent police and by illegal security groups which are themselves often made up of ex-police officers.

Key local demands were social and preventative interventions such as investment in (1) vocational training for the young, (2) better-quality education, (3) access to leisure spaces and cultural activities, (4) improved work opportunities, (5) the demilitarisation and enhanced training for the police to develop dialogue and respect for human rights in their interactions with the public. Residents viewed these as essential to reducing violence. Instead, PPV focuses on more policing (albeit unsatisfactorily), on imprisoning offenders and on measuring and monitoring targets.

Ultimately, this approach is leading to the escalation of the prison population in an unsustainable manner. At the time of the research, there was no sustainable strategy for addressing the overcrowding in prisons, the prison-breaks, the rehabilitating offenders, or for dealing with the burden on the criminal justice system and courts. Nevertheless, there has been an overall statistical reduction in the number of homicides in the state of Pernambuco and in Recife (with recent fluctuations upwards[4]). It is difficult, and perhaps impossible, to assess whether this is a direct impact of *Pacto pela Vida* or whether there may be other influencing factors. Kahn (2011), for instance, also included in his analysis of declining homicides in the main cities of São Paulo, Rio de Janeiro, Minas Gerais and Pernambuco, the decrease in the proportion of young people in the population, the influence of an improved economy since 2003 and the degree of success of measures of gun control. It is possible that PPV has been at least one of the causal factors. Most importantly, this book has provided a challenge to the hegemonic discourse about violence reduction and managerial police reform that masks the counterproductivity and the cost of these interventions to the marginalised. The empirical and lived experience in the *periferias* is largely disconnected and divergent from the dominant discourse of success depicted by government officials, high-ranking politically connected police and even mainstream academics connected to the government through policymaking.

The voices of people in marginalised communities provide a counter-narrative to the hegemonic top-down discourse about securitisation and PPV's successes. Participants from the two low-income communities studied were deeply dissatisfied with the level of (or lack of) protection on offer from state agents such as the police. Not only were they acutely aware of instances of police misconduct, such as planting drugs to make arrests and demanding money in order to free individuals in their custody, many participants had been the subjects of brutal police practices, particularly during stop-and-searches. These included physical and verbal abuse. While residents demanded more policing, among other demands – such as better vocational training opportunities, more job opportunities and leisure spaces in the community – they did not believe that the current militarised model of policing could resolve crime issues in the community, neither could it foster positive community-police relations. Policing did not, in its current model, offer residents protection – and not least among the reasons for this was the fact that residents in poor communities were themselves seen as "the problem".

Notes

1 I am not implying that "older" democracies are likely to be better on this front, which would potentially dismiss or erase the brutal, racialised practices of policing in "old" democracies. Instead, my intention is to highlight the scale of these issues and problematise their entanglements with the history of undemocratic rule in a post-colonial setting.

2 Interview with a senior member of staff of GACE-PE on 27th January 2016 and discussion with Regina Miki, Brazil's national secretary of public security on 26th February 2016. Miki confirmed that the national level homicide reduction program (*Pacto Nacional de Redução de Homicídios*) based on PPV was ready to be rolled out with some alterations.

According to her, the changes would address gaps in PPV. She explained that the national plan would include some elements of the UPPs program in Rio de Janeiro, insofar as the establishment of permanent and continuous policing would come alongside permanent access to social assistance. She also indicated that the national plan addresses the issue of prison overcrowding, since PPV had not thought of any strategies for this problem.

3 Situational Crime Prevention refers to three main criminological theoretical frameworks: environmental criminology, rational choice and routine activity theory. Some practical examples of this frameworks are: making changes to spaces to make them safer (e.g. lighting, changes in the built environment, using security cameras); police work; using neighbourhood groups to address crime problems; interagency working and sharing responsibility for crime prevention.

4 Homicide rates have been increasing since 2014, coinciding with the period since Brazil entered a new economic downturn.

References

Amorim, A., R. d. A. Melo, and I. d. A. César. 2016. "As unidades socioeducativas na Região Metropolitana do Recife (2011–2012): considerações sobre problemas estruturais, funcionamento e proposta pedagógica." *ARACÊ – Direitos Humanos em Revista* 3 (4): 177–195.

Arias, E. D., and D. M. Goldstein. 2010. "Violent Pluralism: Understanding the New Democracies of Latin America." In *Violent Democracies in Latin America*, edited by E. D. Arias and D. M. Goldstein, 1–34. Durham, NC and London: Duke University Press.

Arnold, M. W., G. H. N. Falbo, and J. N. Figueiroa. 2002. "Years of Potential Life Lost by Children and Adolescent Victims of Homicide, Recife, 1997." *Journal of Tropical Pediatrics* 48 (2): 67–71.

Bratton, W. 2005. "Crime Is Down in New York City: Blame the Police." In *Policing: Key Readings*, edited by T. Newburn, 472–482. Cullompton: Willan.

Brownlee, I. 1998. "New Labour: New Penology? Punitive Rhetoric and the Limits of Managerialism in Criminal Justice Policy." *Journal of Law and Society* 25 (3): 313–335.

Clarke, R. V. G. 1997. *Situational Crime Prevention: Successful Case Studies*. 2nd ed. New York: Harrow and Heston Publishers.

Clarke, R. V. G., and M. Felson. 2004. *Routine Activity and Rational Choice*. New Brunswick, NJ: Transaction Publishers.

Denyer Willis, G. 2015. *The Killing Consensus: Police, Organized Crime, and the Regulation of Life and Death in Urban Brazil*. Oakland: University of California Press.

De Souza, E., and J. Miller. 2012. "Homicide in the Brazilian Favela: Does Opportunity Make the Killer?" *British Journal of Criminology* 52 (4): 786–807. doi:10.1093/bjc/azs011.

Dias, C. C. N. 2011. "Da pulverização ao monopólio da violência: expansão e consolidação do Primeiro Comando da Capital (PCC) no sistema carcerário paulista." PhD thesis. Universidade de São Paulo, USP,São Paulo.

Drybread, K. 2014. "Murder and the Making of Man-Subjects in a Brazilian Juvenile Prison." *American Anthropologist* 116 (4): 752–764. doi:10.1111/aman.12147.

Falbo, G. H., R. Buzzetti, and A. Cattaneo. 2001. "Homicide in Children and Adolescents: A Case–Control Study in Recife, Brazil." *Bulletin of the World Health Organization* 79 (1): 2–7.

Feltran, G. D. S. 2008. "O legítimo em disputa: As fronteiras do "mundo do crime" nas periferias de São Paulo." *Dilemas* 1 (1): 93–126.

Feltran, G. d. S. 2011. *Fronteiras de Tensão: Política e Violência nas Periferias de São Paulo*. São Paulo: Unesp.

Goertzel, T., and T. Kahn. 2009. "The Great São Paulo Homicide Drop." *Homicide Studies* 13 (4): 398–410.

Goldstein, D. M. 2003. *Laughter Out of Place: Race, Class, Violence, and Sexuality in a Rio Shantytown*. Berkeley and London: University of California Press.

Hirschi, T., and M. Gottfredson. 1988. "Towards a General Theory of Crime." In *Explaining Criminal Behaviour: Interdisciplinary Approaches*, edited by W. Buikhuisen and S. A. Mednick, vi, 260 p. Leiden and New York: E.J. Brill.

Huggins, M. K., and M. Mesquita. 2000. "Civic Invisibility, Marginality, and Moral Exclusion: The Murders of Street Youth in Brazil." In *Children on the Streets of the Americas: Globalization, Homelessness and Education in the United States, Brazil, and Cuba*, edited by R. A. Mickelson, 257–268. London: Routledge.

Kahn, T. 2011. *Exploring the Relationship between Crime and Economic Performance in Brazil after 1994 Using Time Series Econometric Technique*. Workshop, Pathfinder PBR5 Network Project.

Leeds, E. 1996. "Cocaine and Parallel Polities on the Brazilian Urban Periphery: Constraints on Local Level Democratization." *Latin American Research Review* 31 (3): 47–84.

Loader, I. 1996. *Youth, Policing, and Democracy*. London: MacMillan.

Macedo, A. d. O. 2012. ""Policia, quando quer, faz!" Analise da Estrutura de Governanca do "Pacto pela Vida" de Pernambuco." Masters, Universidade de Brasilia.

Magaloni, B. 2015. *Police Violence and Crime in Rio de Janeiro: Evaluating the Pacifying Police Units*. Cambridge, MA: Ash Center.

Maguire, M. 2000. "Policing by Risks and Targets: Some Dimensions and Implications of Intelligence-Led Crime Control." *Policing and Society* 9 (4): 315–336.

Manso, B. P., and C. C. N. Dias. 2018. *A guerra: A ascensão do PCC e o mundo do crime no Brasil*. São Paulo: Todavia.

Mesquita, M. 1993. "Assassinatos de Crianças e Adolescentes." *Revista Crítica de Ciências Sociais* 36: 81–102.

MNMMR, IBASE, and USP-NEV. 1991. *Vidas em risco: Assassinatos de crianças e adolescentes no Brasil*. Rio de Janeiro and São Paulo: MNMMR, IBASE, and USP-NEV.

Moore, H. 2015. "'Do You Have My Son?' Criminalization and the Production of (Un) Relatedness in Brazil." In *Criminalized Mothers, Criminalizing Mothering*, edited by J. Minaker and B. Hogeveen, 264–291. Bradford, ON: Demeter Press.

Nolasco, A. G. P. 2010. "Adolescentes em cárceres contemporâneos invisíveis, quem se interessa? Um estudo da FUNASE – Unidade Jaboatão dos Guararapes-PE." Mestrado Profissional em Gestão Pública para o Desenvolvimento do Nordeste (MA in Public Management to the Development of the Northeast), Universidade Federal de Pernambuco (UFPE), Recife-PE.

Pereira, A. 2005. *Political (In)justice: Authoritarianism and the Rule of Law in Brazil, Chile, and Argentina*. Pittsburgh, PA: University of Pittsburgh Press.

Ratton, J. L. 2012. "Apresentação Seminário Políticas Locais de Prevenção da Violência." In *A Segurança Cidadã em debate. Cadernos sobre Segurança e Prevenção da Violência na América Latina*, edited by J. L. Ratton, G. Costa, C. Romero, and L. E. Soares, Vol. URB-Al III, 10–23. Recife: Provisual.

Ratton, J. L., C. Galvão, and M. Fernandez. 2014. "Pact for Life and the Reduction of Homicides in the State of Pernambuco." *Stability: International Journal of Security & Development* 3 (1): 1–15.

Schuler, F. R. 2015. "Entre of proposto e o executado: Uma análise da execução do plano de reordenamento do sistema socioeducativo do estado de Pernambuco nas unidades de intervenção da FUNASE/PE nos anos de 2012 a 2014." Masters in Human Rights, Universidade Federal de Pernambuco (UFPE), Recife-PE.

Silvestre, G. 2008a. "O impacto socioeconômico das unidades prisionais no interior paulista: o caso de Itirapina." Anais do XIX Encontro Regional de História da ANPUH – Seção Poder, Violência e Exclusão, ANPUH/SP-USP, São Paulo, 8–12 September 2008, 1–14.

Silvestre, G. 2008b. "O rastro da indústria penal: A interiorização penitenciária e novo paradigma dos municípios paulistas." *LEVS, Revista do Laboratório de Estudos da Violência e Segurança* 1: 94–99.

Silvestre, G. 2016. "Local Consequences of the Prison Policies in State of São Paulo, Brazil: A Case Study of the Town of Itirapina." *Crime, Law and Social Change* 65 (3): 269–285. doi:10.1007/s10611-015-9583-5.

Soares, L. E. 2008. "Pausa para reflexão como um convite à ação." In *É Possível: Gestão sa Segurança Pública e Redução da Violência*, edited by F. Veloso and S. G. Ferreira, 9–15. Rio de Janeiro: Contra Capa/Instituto de Estudos de Política Econômica (IEPE).

Taylor, I. R., P. Walton, and J. Young. 2013. *The New Criminology: For a Social Theory of Deviance*. Abingdon and Oxon: Routledge.

Veloso, F., and S. G. Ferreira. 2008. "Mecanismos de Gestão na Segurança Pública." In *É Possível: Gestão sa Segurança Pública e Redução da Violência*, edited by F. Veloso and S. G. Ferreira, 25–77. Rio de Janeiro: Contra Capa/Instituto de Estudos de política Econômica (IEPE).

Ward, H. H. 2006. "Police Reform in Latin America: Brazil, Argentina, and Chile." In *Toward a Society under Law: Citizens and Their Police in Latin America*, edited by J. S. Tulchin and M. Ruthenburg, 171–205. Washington, DC: Woodrow Wilson Center Press.

Wilson, J. Q., and G. L. Kelling. 2013. "Broken Windows: The Police and Neighbourhood Safety." In *Thinking about Crime*, edited by J. Q. Wilson, Revised ed., xxviii, 281 p. New York: Basic Books, A Member of the Perseus Books Group.

Wolff, M. J. 2014. "Criminal Authorities and the State: Gangs, Organized Crime, and Police in Brazil." PhD, University of New Mexico, USA.

Zaluar, A. 2004. *Integração Perversa: Pobreza e Tráfico de drogas*. Rio de Janeiro: FGV.

Index

For Product Safety Concerns and Information please contact our EU representative GPSR@taylorandfrancis.com
Taylor & Francis Verlag GmbH, Kaufingerstraße 24, 80331 München, Germany

www.ingramcontent.com/pod-product-compliance
Ingram Content Group UK Ltd.
Pitfield, Milton Keynes, MK11 3LW, UK
UKHW011016180926
475701UK00004B/781
* 9 7 8 1 0 3 2 2 6 4 5 8 5 *